The Winding Stair

The Winding Stair

Francis Bacon, His Rise and Fall

Daphne du Maurier

Doubleday & Company, Inc.   Garden City, New York   1977

Library of Congress Cataloging in Publication Data

Du Maurier, Daphne, Dame, 1907–
    The winding stair.

Bibliography: p. 210
Includes index.
1. Bacon, Francis, Viscount St. Albans, 1561–1626.
2. Statesmen—Great Britain—Biography.   I. Title.
    DA358.B3D84   942.06′1′0924 [B]
        ISBN: 0-385-12383-3
Library of Congress Catalog Card Number 76–41557

"All Rising to Great Place is by a winding Staire."
Francis Bacon, *Essay* No. XI, 1625

Contents

Illustrations

Robert Cecil, Earl of Salisbury, attributed to J. de Critz the Elder, 1602 (*photo National Portrait Gallery, London*)

Prospect of Gray's Inn (*from the Greater London Council Print Collection*)

Execution of Gunpowder Plot conspirators in St Paul's Churchyard, 1606 (*reproduced by courtesy of the Trustees of the British Museum*)

Two engravings of Arundel House, once Bath House, c. 1640, by Wenceslaus Hollar (*photo Radio Times Hulton Picture Library*)

Following page 106

Sir Edward Coke, Lord Chief Justice of the King's Bench, attributed to the British School (*reproduced by permission of the Earl of Leicester, photo Courtauld Institute*)

Robert Carr, Earl of Somerset, after J. Hoskins (*photo National Portrait Gallery, London*)

York House, c. 1623 from a nineteenth-century print based on a drawing by Hollar, now in the Pepysian Library at Magdalene College, Cambridge (*photo Greater London Council Print Collection*)

Sir Tobie Matthew in late middle age. Frontispiece from the Collection of his Letters, 1660

George Villiers, Duke of Buckingham, in 1626 (*photo Mansell Collection*)

Following page 154

The Strand in 1700 (*photo National Monuments Record*)

Coat of Arms of Francis Bacon, Baron Verulam, Viscount St Alban (*photo H. Graeme, Fowey*)

Verulam House, after a drawing by John Aubrey (*reproduced by courtesy of Basil King*)

Charles, Prince of Wales, by Mytens, 1623 (*copyright reserved*)

Tomb of Francis Bacon, Baron Verulam, Viscount St Alban, in St Michael's Church, St Albans (*photo Christian Browning*)

Title-page of the first edition of the *Novum Organum*, 1620

Title-page of *Valerius Terminus*. The list of contents and the word "Philosophy" are in Bacon's handwriting.

My grateful thanks to Joan St George Saunders of Writer's and Speaker's Research for her help in collecting these illustrations.

To the Reader

Golden Lads was a study of Anthony Bacon, his brother Francis and their friends. When Anthony died in May 1601 Francis was forty years old. He was to live for a further twenty-five years, becoming successively Solicitor-General, Attorney-General, a member of the Privy Council and Lord Chancellor. At first simply Sir Francis Bacon, later he was Baron Verulam, and finally Viscount St Alban. He would also marry. His career has been described many times by eminent historians and biographers, and his literary, philosophical, scientific and other works have been studied in depth by scholars throughout the world.

I felt, when I had completed *Golden Lads,* that the ordinary reader (in which category I place myself) has never been sufficiently interested in, or understood, the extraordinary complexity of Francis Bacon's character and the many facets of his personality. The endeavour to explain him would be a challenge.

The result is *The Winding Stair.*

DAPHNE DU MAURIER
1975

Francis Bacon

Born, second son of Sir Nicholas Bacon (Lord Keeper) and Ann (sister-in-law of William Cecil, Lord Burghley)	22 Jan. 1561
Matriculated at Trinity College, Cambridge	10 June 1573
Admitted at Gray's Inn	21 Nov. 1576
First sat in the House of Commons as Member for Melcombe	1584
Knighted by James I	23 July 1603
Confirmed as Learned Counsel	25 Aug. 1604
Solicitor-General	25 June 1607
Attorney-General	26 Oct. 1613
Privy Councillor	9 June 1616
Lord Keeper	3 March 1617
Lord High Chancellor	4 Jan. 1618
Baron Verulam of Verulam	July 1618
Viscount St Alban	27 Jan. 1621
Sentenced by the House of Lords	3 May 1621
Died	9 April 1626

Chapter I

Francis Bacon was forty years old when his elder brother Anthony was buried at St Olave's, Hart Street, in the city of London, on May 17th 1601. Whether Francis was present at the funeral is unknown. Amongst his correspondence there is no letter reporting his loss, and the event seems to have passed without comment, except for a chance remark from the gossip John Chamberlain to Dudley Carleton. Writing on May 27th Chamberlain said, "Anthony Bacon died not long since, but so far in debt that I think his brother is little the better by him."

So much for the casual opinion of one who was well known to statesmen, diplomats, courtiers, and all who moved in such circles at that time. No word of regret for the man who had died, broken in health, in his forty-fourth year, the will to live spent after the trial and execution of the friend and master whom he had served so faithfully, the ill-fated Robert Devereux, Earl of Essex. Possibly the brevity of the announcement was deliberate; it did not do to show sympathy for any of those connected with Essex's rebellion of a few months past. Apart from his closest friends and his immediate family only the common people sighed for the beheaded earl, their hero.

For Francis, the reasons for silence were more profound. When the earl stood trial for treason in Westminster Hall, Francis Bacon spoke for the Crown at the express command of Her Majesty the Queen, a summons he could not disobey. If his words, spoken without malice and with great sincerity—for he believed rebellion to have been a genuine attempt to seize the reins of government—had helped to send the misguided earl to the block, then such had been his distressing, painful duty. The earl had been his patron and friend, and had rendered him many a service, which he had repaid in kind. But his loyalty to the monarch came before friendship or gratitude. He had learnt that loyalty at his father's knee. Sir Nicholas Bacon, Lord Keeper of the Great Seal, held the Crown paramount after God. Francis had

1

a double motive for demonstrating loyalty. He knew that if he used all the powers of oratory at his command—and it was for this skill that he, a junior counsel, had been chosen to speak on such a grave occasion—the fact that his brother Anthony was a close friend and confidant of the accused earl, and could well have been privy to the rebellion even from his sick bed, would not be mentioned at Westminster Hall. Francis might be instrumental in helping to send the Earl of Essex to the block, but in doing so he would save his brother Anthony from the gallows.

Her Majesty, however, demanded even more than this. The younger son of her old servant the Lord Keeper not only spoke with ease and facility; he could also write. It was to him, therefore, that she gave the task of drawing up a *Declaration of the Practices and Treasons attempted and committed by Robert Late Earl of Essex and his Complices, Against Her Majesty and Her Kingdoms*. A thankless undertaking, which, when Francis had completed it, was closely examined by the Queen herself, who erased any words of compassion. The revised document was sent to the press on April 14th, some seven weeks after the earl's execution in the Tower. A little over a month later Francis's brother Anthony died, broken in mind and body.

So the gesture had been largely in vain. Francis had saved his brother's honour and good name, but in doing so had hastened his end. Doubtless Anthony would rather have died shamefully by the hangman's rope within a few days of his beloved earl than have lingered on for those remaining weeks.

"So far in debt," John Chamberlain had told Dudley Carleton, "that I think his brother is little the better by him." Anthony's creditors had not known where to find him. They did not even know where he was buried. But they could crowd upon his brother Francis at his lodging in Gray's Inn, and follow him down to his estate of Gorhambury in Hertfordshire, if need be. Here his mother Lady Bacon, now seventy-three, lived in retirement, worn with distress by the events of the past few months, indeed, of the last few years, from the time of Essex's disgrace on returning from Ireland—where, as commander of the Queen's forces sent to put down the rebellion led by the Earl of Tyrone, he had met with ignominious failure—to his rebellion and execution. So often she had warned Anthony against his devotion to Essex, but to no avail; and now her first-born was dead, deserted by all, alone, perhaps without even a prayer at the last.

Her wits began to go, and she would wander through the rooms and the long gallery at Gorhambury, talking to herself, searching for familiar faces, enquiring for old servants who had served her faithfully in former days, but who were now departed or dead. When Francis, her younger boy, came to ask her about farm rents, deeds, and debts, she could not understand that it was now his business, he was his brother's heir and money must be produced to pay Anthony's creditors. What creditors? Did Francis mean that crowd of hangers-on of whom she had always disapproved? That French page? That seducing Catholic Lawson? She would hear none of it. Such cattle should never move into the manors or the farms. She knew what it would come to. She would be driven from her home in her old age, to wander the countryside, alone and servantless, forsaken by even her one remaining son.

Argument was useless. Francis was unable to pacify his mother, tortured by grief. Yet the debts must be paid, and Gorhambury must be safe in his own hands so that he could settle the estate. Back then to London and Gray's Inn, to consult with his close friends—of whom his mother disapproved as much as she had done of his brother's. One of the chief creditors was no hanger-on, but a genuine friend to him and Anthony—Mr Nicholas Trott, from whom they had both borrowed through the years. Something like £2,600 had been lent in the past, and although part of this had been repaid the interest had mounted, and Francis had been obliged to mortgage his own house, Twickenham Park. Nicholas Trott, who had been patient for so long, had the right of entry if the debt was not paid by November of this year, 1601. Moreover, he was contemplating marriage, which made him all the more anxious for his money.

It was ironical, and hurtful to Francis's pride, that the one hope of repaying this debt was the Queen's promise of £1,200 for his recent services to the Crown—his performance at the trial in Westminster Hall, with the writing of the *Declaration* doubtless thrown in for good measure. This sum had to come from the fines imposed upon those accomplices of the late earl who had not been executed, but had bought their pardon, and the settlement of all these monies was in the hands of the Treasury. Francis would be fortunate if he received the sum before a twelvemonth, and the granting of probate for Anthony's estate would take as long.

During the long vacation, as he walked about the grounds at Gorhambury, his mother closeted with her servants within the house, Francis was able to take stock of his position, to look back over the past two-and-twenty years since his father died; and what he saw was cause for little satisfaction. The hopes his father the Lord Keeper had held for him had not been fulfilled. The precocious youth of eighteen who had travelled to France in the suite of her Majesty's ambassador,

3

intending to dazzle the diplomatic corps of two nations and so win for himself an honoured name in both literary and political circles, had returned home at his father's death to find that no provision had been made for him in the will. He was therefore dependent upon his mother and his elder brother Anthony, except for what he could earn by his own wits, which heaven knew were plentiful enough. The question was, how to employ them?

His father had foretold a brilliant future. Had the Lord Keeper lived, his influence would have set his younger son on the right path either in politics or the law. That influence had died with him. Francis's uncle by marriage, William Cecil, Lord Burghley, who was the Queen's Lord Treasurer and closest adviser, had had his own son, Robert Cecil, to advance on the road to power, and had little desire to see competition in that field. Literature? The grandiose scheme to found some sort of galaxy of poets and writers that would in time rival the French Pleiades found little favour either with his uncle or with her Majesty, upon whose patronage it would depend. The inference appeared to be that the young man whom she had patted upon the head as a child, calling him her "little Lord Keeper," had grown too big for his boots.

There remained the law. A bencher at the Inns of Court, with a seat in Parliament. And hopes of advancement stifled here when, having been a member of the faithful Commons for seven years, he had the hardihood to rise upon his feet and speak against the Triple Subsidy Bill, a special measure necessitated by the grave political situation, providing for a levy from the Queen's subjects which would be raised in three years instead of the customary six. His action so annoyed her Majesty that she forbade him her presence, and promotion of any sort appeared impossible.

Nevertheless, he remained undaunted. If his letter of apology to the Queen failed to move her, then his ally and patron the Earl of Essex would speak for him. But though the earl spoke warmly, even passionately, on his behalf, her Majesty was not interested.

Promotion in the legal field continued to elude him. His rival Edward Coke became Attorney-General, Serjeant Fleming Solicitor-General. As for literature, so far he had written only masques and devices performed at Gray's Inn, with other anonymous trifles that served as exercises for leisure hours. The only published work as yet had been that handful of essays, ten in number, dedicated to his brother because of Anthony's admiration for Montaigne. To fill out the slim volume he had included a fragment called *The Colours of Good and Evil* and a series of religious meditations in Latin, *Meditationes*

Sacrae. These last at least had the merit of pleasing his mother, although the doctrine that absolute truth and freedom from all delusion are necessary for the state of the soul was utterly beyond her.

His personal life had been even less successful. The one young woman he had ever sought in marriage, Elizabeth Hatton, granddaughter of Lord Burghley and widow of Sir Philip Sidney's friend Sir William Hatton, suffered his gallant attentions for several months, and then married his rival in law, Attorney-General Edward Coke, secretly, one November night in 1598. Her motive for doing so went unexplained. Family pressure, possibly, for Edward Coke was a widower, approaching fifty, and could offer his bride wealth and position; whereas Francis had not only been arrested for debt by a Jewish goldsmith a few months previously, narrowly escaping the Fleet prison, but had no sort of status to confer upon a beautiful and high-spirited young lady of the Court who had been born a Cecil. So be it —though if rumour was correct, bride and groom had fought ceaselessly since their wedding night three years ago.

Nevertheless, it was galling to Francis's sensibilities, and his pride, this August of 1601, to know that the Attorney-General and Elizabeth Hatton—she continued to style herself Lady Hatton, thumbing her nose at convention as always—were at this very moment, while Francis walked alone at Gorhambury, entertaining no less a person than the Queen herself, and her vast retinue, at Stoke, Edward Coke's country seat. It might have been otherwise, with Elizabeth, wife of Francis Bacon, receiving her Majesty at Gorhambury, just as his mother and father had done some thirty years ago.

Useless to dwell upon the past. The present had prior claim, above all the necessity to pay his brother's debts and those he had incurred himself. Instead of caging himself from the world as poor Anthony had done, or withdrawing to a cave like the Athenian Timon, he would use all the gifts of intelligence and wit that the good God had bestowed upon him to rise to some place of authority, in Parliament or the law. Not to gratify vanity or pride, not to awaken envy in his fellows or admiration in his friends, but so that the dream he had held from boyhood might be realised, the longing to advance knowledge throughout the world and bring the benefit of this knowledge to all mankind.

"Believing that I was born for the service of mankind," he was to write a few years later, "and regarding the care of the commonwealth as a kind of common property which like the air and the water belongs to everybody, I set myself to consider in what way mankind might be best served, and what service I was myself best fitted by

5

nature to perform." Francis never stated when this belief of his purpose in life first dawned in the complex labyrinth of his mind. Perhaps as a precocious child when the monarch smiled at him. Perhaps at Cambridge, when he found his fellow-students frowning over problems which he could solve without a moment's thought. It was not that he felt himself superior to them: he *knew* he was, and accepted it as a part of the process of nature. This gift of God was not one to be used for personal ends. Much of his mother's early teaching was ingrained in him, though he was possibly unconscious of the fact. "I was not without hope," he continued, "that if I came to hold office in the state, I might get something done too for the good of men's souls. When I found however that my zeal was mistaken for ambition, and my life had already reached the turning-point, and my breaking health reminded me how ill I could afford to be so slow, and I reflected moreover that in leaving undone the good I could do by myself alone, and applying myself to that which could not be done without the help and consent of others, I was by no means discharging the duty that lay upon me—I put all those thoughts aside, and (in pursuance of my old determination), betook myself wholly to this work."

These words, written in Latin on a sheet of paper and thrust aside, were not found until after his death.

Now, in 1601, he still had to make his way in the world. When the Queen summoned Parliament on October 27th, Francis, as the member for Ipswich, was determined to speak, and this time, if it were possible with truth and honesty intact, to do so without giving her Majesty offence. That it was to be the last parliament of her long and glorious reign—and he had known no other in his forty years—he could not foresee; had he done so, part of the Latin eulogy to her memory which he was to write some years later might have fallen from his lips. As it was, the business that came before the Commons was of no great import. There was a bill against Abuses in Weights and Measures and a motion to Repeal Superfluous Laws, both preferred by the Hon. Member for Ipswich, Mr Francis Bacon. "I'll tell you, Mr Speaker, that this fault of using false weights and measures is grown so intolerable and common that, if you would build churches, you shall not need for battlements and bells other things than false weights of lead and brass." The bill was read a second time, and thrown out. As for Francis's second motion—"Laws be like pills all gilt over, which if they be easily and well swallowed down are neither bitter in digestion nor hurtful to the body. . . . The more laws we make the more snares we lay to entrap ourselves"—it caused no comment or

6

discussion: the Hon. Member for Ipswich made little impact on either November 4th or 6th.

On the 20th and 21st the House became more lively. A bill was introduced to declare certain monopoly-patents illegal, and the Queen's own prerogative to grant these monopolies came into question. Francis spoke against the bill, declaring, "I say, and I say again, that we ought not to deal or judge or meddle with her Majesty's Prerogative." The debate that followed, lasting several days, had the final effect of moving the Queen herself to receive her faithful Commons. It was her last meeting with them. They assembled before her at her palace of Whitehall. No monarch could have been more gracious, more condescending, or more kind. She carried a draft of her speech in her hands, but barely glanced at it.

"There is no jewel, be it of never so rich a prize, which I set before this jewel: I mean your love. . . . And though God hath raised me high, yet this I count the glory of my crown, that I have reigned with your loves." The members were on their knees before her, but she bade them rise, and if Francis Bacon had any lingering misgiving over the part she had ordered him to play at the trial of the Earl of Essex it vanished forthwith. She was his Queen and she would command him until death. "There will never Queen sit in my seat with more zeal to my country, care for my subjects, and that will sooner with willingness venture her life for your good and safety, than myself. For it is my desire to live nor reign no longer than my life and reign shall be for your good. And though you have had, and may have, many princes more mighty and wise sitting in this seat, yet you never had, nor shall have, any that will be more careful and loving."

The fact that her astute political sense had prompted her two days earlier to decree that a number of those patents which had made her Commons restive should be revoked, and all of them suspended until they had been examined and any abuses put right, was not lost upon the forty-year-old member she had once called her "little Lord Keeper." It only served to make his admiration for her statesmanship the greater.

Parliament was dissolved a month later, on the same date, it so happened, as the sum long promised by the Treasury to Francis from the fines imposed upon Robert Catesby, a conspirator in the Essex rebellion, was thankfully received and paid into the account of Mr Nicholas Trott. On his forty-first birthday, January 21st 1602, Francis could escape to his retreat at Twickenham Park secure in the knowledge that his late creditor would not now cross the threshold.

Probate of his brother Anthony's goods, rights and credits was finally granted on June 23rd, a fact that apparently escaped the eye of the gossip John Chamberlain, although Mr Nicholas Trott's marriage to a Miss Perins, "a tall lusty wench that would make two of him," was duly recorded. The following autumn, on November 20th, Lady Bacon signed a deed in favour of her "sonn Fraunceys Bacon, for and in consideration of the naturall love and affection which she beareth unto the said Fraunceys Bacon," by which she surrendered to him her life interest in the manors and estates of Gorhambury. Her wits might be failing her, but she had not forgotten her Greek, signing her name A. Bacon χήεα (i.e. widow) as she had always done.

Francis, now in possession of his inheritance but still without promotion, and virtually unemployed politically since Parliament had been dissolved, looked ahead to the future and all he hoped to accomplish—if not this year, then the next: the winning of men's minds to a new understanding, a new freedom, a new knowledge of why they acted as they did, of what God intended them to become, and how the very earth they trod upon, the things they touched, and the air they breathed could help to show them the way ahead.

But first things first. The eight-year-old rebellion in Ireland had at last been crushed, and the Spanish forces which had been aiding the rebels routed. A letter to cousin Robert Cecil, the Queen's secretary, would set forth the means, Francis thought, by which that war-torn country could be ruled in peacetime. Francis covered sheet after sheet of paper with fierce intensity, even though he knew in his heart that his cousin would but skim them and brush them aside. As for her Majesty, she would never read them. Looking out from his window at Twickenham Park late in February 1603, across the river to the towers of Richmond Palace opposite, where the Queen held Court, a sense of impending doom warned Francis that the world about him, which he and his contemporaries had known since birth, would shortly change. The very air was sombre, cold. The clammy, ceaseless rain had turned to a black frost. It was from sitting by an open window in a draught that his father had died.

Francis shivered and turned away, as one of his servants came into the room and told him that rumour had it that her Majesty's health was failing. She had refused an audience to the French ambassador, she was seeing no one, her physicians were anxious.

Francis knew then that intuition had not been at fault. The pall that, as a young man, he had seen in a dream shrouding his father's home, York House, would soon be covering Richmond Palace too.

Chapter II

When it became known that her Majesty Queen Elizabeth had at most, perhaps, a week to live, Francis felt the time was opportune to consider his immediate future. The succession was not in doubt: King James VI of Scotland would be proclaimed King James I of England the moment the Queen breathed her last. It was essential that all men desirous of finding favour with the new monarch, and establishing a foothold on the winding stair to place and position, should make themselves known to those who would have authority in the new Court and the Council.

The most powerful man in England was his own cousin Sir Robert Cecil, who had held the post of Secretary of State to her Majesty for many years. The cousins had never been intimate. Boyish rivalry long past, the friendship that the Earl of Essex had shown to Anthony and Francis had proved an insurmountable barrier, Robert Cecil being the Earl's implacable enemy, and a cool courtesy had developed between them. Even the *volte face* at the trial, when Francis had been commanded to speak for the Crown against his former patron, had not softened the relationship.

Nevertheless, an effort must now be made to heal the breach and affirm his loyalty. Francis did not write direct to his cousin, but to Robert Cecil's personal secretary, Michael Hicks, who had invariably proved a helpful friend and ally, more especially during the financial dealings with Nicholas Trott. His letter, written on March 19th, began, "the apprehension of this threatened judgement of God, if it work in other as it worketh in me, knitteth every man's heart more unto his true and approved friend. . . . Though we card-holders have nothing to do but to keep our cards and to do as we are bidden, yet as I ever used your mean to cherish the truth of my inclination towards Mr Secretary, so now again I pray as you find time let him know that he is the personage in this state which I love most: which containeth all that I can do, and expresseth all which I will say at this time."

A little warm, perhaps? Somewhat overdone? But Michael Hicks would take his meaning. Who next? The Earl of Northumberland, who had shown great friendship to brother Anthony in the past and was married to Dorothy, sister of the late Earl of Essex, was one of those known to have been in correspondence with the King of Scotland, and likely to be early on the scene when the future King of England was proclaimed. Therefore, his letter to Michael Hicks sealed and directed to the address in the Strand, Francis composed another to the earl, but in rather a different vein. He made no allusion to her Majesty's expected demise but said that he had intended writing to his lordship for some time, since "there hath been covered in my mind, a long time, a seed of affection and zeal towards your Lordship, sown by the estimation of your virtues, and your particular honours and favours to my brother deceased, and to myself; which seed still springing, now bursteth forth into this profession." The point being that the Earl of Northumberland's interest in scientific matters was as great as his own, and if anyone in high place was likely to advance research in all these aspects of learning during a new reign Francis could hope for no one better. "To be plain with your Lordship . . . your great capacity and love towards studies and contemplations of an higher and worthier nature than popular . . . is to me a great and chief motive to draw my affection and admiration towards you. And therefore, good my Lord, if I may be of any use to your Lordship, by my head, tongue, pen, means, or friends, I humbly pray you to hold me your own."

If the form of such a letter appears obsequious to the modern eye, it must be remembered that this mode of approach from a commoner to a nobleman was not only natural but obligatory in those days; anything savouring of familiarity, even between close friends, would have been totally out of place.

Then there was David Foulis, ex-ambassador of Scotland, who had been on close terms with brother Anthony when he was resident in London. Indeed, he had served as go-between for much correspondence from the Earl of Essex to King James VI. And there was Edward Bruce, Abbot of Kinloss. It would be premature to forward the letters before the Queen had died, but drafts could be made in good time, and both letters forwarded when the moment was ripe.

Her Majesty Queen Elizabeth died on March 24th, and James was proclaimed King James I of England that same night. A few days later the coffin was taken by barge from Richmond to Whitehall, and thence to Westminster, where it lay in state until the new monarch should make his best wishes known as to the time and date of the funeral.

Francis's letter to David Foulis was on its way north by the 27th, carried by a member of the Council. Three other letters—to the Abbot of Kinloss, and to a couple of Anthony's friends at the Scottish Court (one of them was Doctor Morison, who had supplied the Earl of Essex with much information, and whose frequent visits to London Anthony had paid for from his own purse)—were entrusted to the son of the Bishop of Durham, young Tobie Matthew. Ever since he had performed the part of the squire in a *Device* by Essex at Gray's Inn in 1595, and had won general acclaim for his charm and handsome appearance, Tobie had been one of Francis Bacon's most particular friends.

Nor were these the only letters Tobie took with him. The most important was addressed to the King himself, and in it Francis offered his particular services to the new Sovereign. The Latin phrases with which it opened—and these, as his Scottish Majesty was known to be a scholar of some degree, would surely please—led the writer to a modest reference to the liberty of access which he had "enjoyed with my late dear Sovereign Mistress; a Prince happy in all things, but most happy in such a successor." He continued, "I was not a little encouraged, not only upon a supposal that unto Your Majesty's sacred ears . . . there might perhaps have come some small knowledge of the good memory of my father, so long a principal counsellor in this your kingdom; but also by the particular knowledge of the infinite devotion and incessant endeavours, beyond the strength of his body and the nature of the times, which appeared in my good brother towards your Majesty's service; and were on your Majesty's part, through your singular benignity, by many most gracious and lively significations and favours accepted and acknowledged, beyond the merit of anything he could effect . . . I think there is no subject of your Majesty's, who loveth this island, and is not hollow and unworthy, whose heart is not set on fire, not only to bring you peace-offerings to make you propitious, but to sacrifice himself a burnt-offering to your Majesty's service: amongst which number no man's fire shall be more pure and fervent than mine. But how far forth it shall blaze out, that resteth in your Majesty's employment."

Whether King James, who left Edinburgh on his way south on April 5th, actually received and read the letter, assuredly one of hundreds from his loyal and aspiring subjects, is not recorded. Its existence was common gossip in London, however, for John Chamberlain wrote to

11

Dudley Carleton, "Tobie Matthew has been sent with a letter to the King from Master Bacon, but I doubt neither the message nor the messenger were greatly welcome." Young Matthew, known to have Catholic sympathies despite his father's bishopric, might not, after all, have been the wisest emissary to approach the new King, who had been bred in the Scottish kirk, but Francis, susceptible himself to the charms of his close friend, and aware that his sovereign—if rumour was correct—liked a handsome face and a shapely leg, may have thought this was a risk worth taking.

He had one other ally who had gone north to meet the King, and this was the poet John Davies, later to be Attorney-General in Ireland. The letter Francis addressed to him is chiefly remarkable for its concluding sentence, when, having desired Mr Davies to "impress a good conceit and opinion of me, chiefly in the King," he ended, "So desiring you to be good to concealed poets, I continue, your very assured, Fr. Bacon." So it was not only his closest associates, like Tobie Matthew, who knew how he sometimes spent his leisure hours. . . .

Meanwhile, he had a weightier composition in hand, which was a draft of a proclamation to be read to the King on his arrival in England. It would be anonymous, of course, but might be considered by the Council and subsequently used with no reference to himself. This he sent to the Earl of Northumberland, meaning to call with it in person; but having "taken some little physic" he announced his intention of waiting upon the noble lord the following morning. If the physic was the purge which Francis recommended for opening the liver— "Take rhubarb two drams, steep them in claret wine burnt with mace, and wormwood one dram, steep it with the rest, and make a mass of pills with syrup acetos simplex"—it was as well he decided to postpone his visit a further twenty-four hours. In the event, the proclamation was never used.

The King's progress through England to his capital was a leisurely one. He was entertained at many of the great houses on his way south. The Earl of Shrewsbury welcomed him at Worksop, the Earl of Rutland at Belvoir Castle, and so to Burghley, residence of the second Lord Burghley (father to Lady Elizabeth Hatton), on to Huntingdon and Hertfordshire, and finally to Sir Robert Cecil's estate Theobalds, before going to the Tower of London to await his coronation. His Queen, Anne of Denmark, did not accompany him, nor did any of the royal family; they were to follow later. Somewhere along the route Francis went to greet him, bearing a letter from the Earl of Northumberland, but where is not known. It was most likely at Theobalds, no great distance from Gorhambury.

He recorded his first impression of the new monarch to the Earl. "I would not have lost this journey," he wrote,

"and yet I have not that for which I went. For I have had no private conference to any purpose with the King, and no more hath almost any other English. For the speech his Majesty admitteth with some noblemen is rather matter of grace than of business . . . After I had received his Majesty's first welcome, I was promised private access; but yet, not knowing what manner of service your Lordship's letter might carry, for I saw it not, and well knowing that primeness in advertisement is much, I chose rather to deliver it to Sir Thomas Erskins, than to cool it in my hands, upon expectation of access. Your Lordship shall find a prince the farthest from the appearance of vainglory that may be, and rather like a prince of the ancient form than of the latter time. His speech is swift and cursory, and in the full dialect of his country; and in point of business, short; in point of discourse, large. He affecteth popularity by gracing such as he hath heard to be popular, and not by any fashions of his own. He is thought somewhat general in his favours, and his virtue of access is rather because he is much abroad and in press, than that he giveth easy audience about serious things. He hasteneth to a mixture of both kingdoms and nations, faster perhaps than policy will conveniently bear. I told your Lordship once before, that (methought) his Majesty rather asked counsel of the time past than of the time to come. But it is early yet to ground any settled opinion."

A cautious appraisal, fully justified during the next months as far as Francis himself was concerned, for he remained in the same position that he had held under the late Queen, one of the Learned Counsel, which in fact meant no particular duty in the legal field. Indeed, King James made few innovations on succeeding, preferring to let those who had served his predecessor and held authority under her advise him, though, reasonably enough, he kept a number of his own Scottish friends about him at Court.

Had Anthony Bacon lived he would doubtless have received some greater mark of favour than his brother, because of his secret correspondence with the King through the years, for one of the first acts of condescension on the part of the monarch was to free the Earl of Southampton from the Tower, where he had been imprisoned since the execution of the Earl of Essex, and to welcome to Court Lady Rich, the late earl's sister, and others of his family. Young Robert Devereux, the earl's son, now Earl of Essex in his turn, was to complete his education beside Prince Henry, the King's eldest son. It was unlikely, in the circumstances, that any of these would have kind words to say of Francis Bacon about the Court. Nor did the Earl of Northumberland appear to make much attempt to speak on his behalf.

The only sign of favour came in July, at the time of the coronation
—which was held in pouring rain on the 23rd—when Mr Francis
Bacon, along with three hundred others, was knighted at Whitehall,
presumably for services to the Crown during the previous reign. What
the new knight thought of the coronation itself he did not record.
Plague had broken out in the city, and the ride from the Tower of
London to Westminster could not take place. King James and his
consort Queen Anne went by river to the Palace of Westminster,
where the crowd could not see them, and then on foot to the abbey. In
the abbey itself it seems that the King, whether from nerves or from a
natural disinclination for ceremony, shocked the assembly by permitting Philip Herbert, later Earl of Montgomery, when paying homage,
to kiss him on the cheek, and instead of rebuking the young courtier
laughed and gave him a playful tap. Times had changed indeed.

The coronation over, the King and Queen retired to Woodstock, for
fear of the plague, and Sir Francis Bacon, knowing that months of un-
employment in the political and legal field lay before him, withdrew
to Gorhambury. What now? What lay ahead? Work, yes, some of his
ideas for the future of mankind put down on paper at last. He would
have ample time for it, and time to write a paper on the union of England and Scotland; a paper, addressed to the King, on the subject of
how to reconcile the dissensions at present threatening to tear apart
the Church; and a work in Latin, *Temporis Partus Masculus* (*The
Masculine Birth of Time*), of which he completed only two chapters,
but which was a forerunner of his later thought. Here he wrote as an
older man would if addressing a younger, criticising Plato, Aristotle,
scholasticism, and the philosophies of the Renaissance. None of them
was spared. Of Aristotle he wrote that he "composed an art of
madness and made us slaves of words," of Plato that he produced
"scraps of borrowed information polished and strung together," and of
Galen, the Greek physician, that he had cut short the patient's hopes
and the physician's labours. "Take your Arabian confederates with
you, those compounders of drugs, hoaxing the public with their bogus
remedies." Did he, one wonders, blame his brother Anthony's death on
the taking of too much physic of the wrong sort? "But I hear you ask,"
he continued, "can everything taught by all these men be vain and
false? My son, it is not a question of ignorance, but ill-luck. Everyone
stumbles on some truth sooner or later. . . . A pig might print the letter A with its snout in the mud, but you would not on that account expect it to go on and compose a tragedy. . . . On waxen tablets you
cannot write anything new until you rub out the old. With the mind it

is not so: you cannot rub out the old until you have written in the new."

Looking about him at Gorhambury, with much still to settle there and his mother now confined mostly to her own rooms and unable to give any sort of direction to the household, Francis reminded himself that next year he would be forty-three and still a bachelor. Elizabeth Hatton, wife to the Attorney-General, was now one of the circle of ladies surrounding Queen Anne. No other woman had ever attracted him as she had done. As for seeking a bride amongst the unmarried daughters of other noblemen about the Court, this was out of the question. Of modest fortune with debts still unpaid, despite his estate of Gorhambury, and without promotion in his profession of the law, he was no great catch. Nor, for that matter, had his fastidious eye ever lighted upon one who might be said to suit his particular taste.

No, if he must—and it well might be politic to do so, in order to have a hostess to grace his table at Gorhambury and appear with him in London—then he would choose one who would not only bring him a dowry but whom, if tender enough in years, he could mould to his own will and fancy. She must have looks, a good presence, a quick mind, and an ability to adapt to any suggestion he might put to her. She must be agreeable to his younger friends, such as Tobie Matthew, and to certain of his servants and devoted adherents who flocked about him at Gray's Inn and Gorhambury, scribbling at his dictation, and must accept his manner of life as perfectly natural. Approaching middle age, he was not going to change for any bride whom he chose to honour as Lady Bacon. He would be generous to such a one, and show her great kindness and affection. He had always liked the young, preferring them to his contemporaries; indeed, imagination was ready to take wing at the thought of such an innovation to his household— an untutored maid, eager to learn. There would be little jealousies at first, perhaps, among his willing scribes which he could smooth away, all adding to the flavour of novelty, and as time went on there would be new depth, new harmony.

Earlier that year, when dining at his old home York House with Thomas Egerton, Lord Ellesmere, Lord Keeper of the Great Seal for the past seven years, he renewed acquaintance with the widow of Alderman Benedict Barnham, who had been Member of Parliament for Yarmouth and had died in 1597. His widow Dorothy had made haste the following year to marry Sir John Packington of Hampton Lovett in Worcestershire, well known as a great character about the Court in the preceding reign, and nicknamed "Lusty" Packington. The Queen, amused at his antics, had made him a Knight of the Bath. Lusty Packington found on his marriage that he had four young stepdaughters to take on as well as a bride. Besides a manor in Suffolk which belonged to his wife, and the estate in Worcestershire, Sir John had a lodging in the Strand, hence his and his wife's presence that evening at York House.

Visits between the Packingtons and Francis Bacon were exchanged. Francis was introduced to Lusty's four stepdaughters, a lively quartet, and was told they would each inherit £6,000 and an annual £300 in land from the late Alderman Barnham, which sums would come to their husbands when they married. The second daughter, Alice, was the most striking of the sisters, with a quick tongue suggesting a certain intelligence that would ripen with years. Francis was so impressed with what he saw, after a few encounters, that in a letter to his cousin, now Lord Cecil, in July, before the coronation, he declared that it was his intention "to marry with some convenient advancement." He continued with some words about his prospective knighthood, which he said he would be content to have, and then told his cousin, "I have found out an alderman's daughter, an handsome maiden, to my liking."

What Lord Cecil thought of the prospective match is unrecorded. Preoccupied with affairs of state and arrangements for the coronation, he was doubtless relieved that cousin Bacon had lowered his sights and was not aiming at some scion of the nobility. Let him marry his alderman's daughter if he desired, and fortune so favoured him. Francis omitted to tell Lord Cecil that Alice Barnham, in July of 1603, was just eleven years old.

Chapter III

It was fortunate for Francis that his services as Learned Counsel were
not required during the summer and autumn of 1603, or he might
have found himself once more speaking for the Crown against such
persons as Lord Cobham, Sir Walter Ralegh and others, who had been
arrested on charges of desiring to overthrow the government, and
even dispossess King James and place his cousin Lady Arabella Stuart
upon the throne. How much truth there was in the allegations it is
difficult to judge. Several Jesuits and Catholic priests were hanged,
but Ralegh, despite the venomous attack upon him by Attorney-
General Edward Coke, did not suffer the supreme penalty. Nor did
Lord Cobham; both were imprisoned in the Tower.

Ralegh had never been a favourite with the citizens of London, but
now he became a popular hero, as the ill-fated Earl of Essex had once
been. It is a curious trait in the English character that a man has only
to be imprisoned, no matter what the offence, for a wave of sympathy
to go to him, and his accusers to feel the backlash of dislike or even
hatred. Francis had known the force of this in 1601 when Essex was
condemned to death. Now he may have experienced some grim satisfaction in the realisation that his rival Edward Coke bore the full burden of public animosity, even though the victim had escaped the
block.

Comparisons with the earlier trial in 1601 were bound to be made,
and the moment was opportune to finish his *Apologia* concerning the
late Earl of Essex, which he had begun the previous summer, in an attempt to seek a reconciliation with the earl's family and close friends.
A letter to the Earl of Southampton on his release from the Tower had
brought no result, so, Francis decided, his only recourse was to write a
full account of all that had taken place between himself and Essex,
and between himself and Queen Elizabeth (with the exception of certain reservations concerning his brother Anthony). When it was
finished he dedicated it to Lord Mountjoy—lover of several years'

17

standing of Penelope Rich, Essex's sister—who since the coronation had been Duke of Devonshire. Mountjoy's neck had been in considerable danger at the time of the late earl's disgrace, but his success in the campaign against the Irish rebels had spared him from the suspicion of complicity.

Printed early in 1604, the *Apologia* is believed to have been widely circulated. Unfortunately no record exists of what Francis's contemporaries thought of it, more especially the members of the Essex family, though Penelope Rich, so greatly revered by Anthony Bacon, who was to marry the Duke of Devonshire the following year, must surely have read it.

The ladies of the Court were fully occupied by the new year festivities at Hampton Court, and doubtless had no time to read political pamphlets, Queen Anne being a devotee of masques and extravaganzas. The masque which was performed, by Samuel Daniel, was entitled the "Vision of the Twelve Goddesses." Her Majesty herself appeared as Pallas Athene, and Lady Rich, black-eyed, golden-haired, was Venus. Lady Bedford—whom Anthony Bacon's French page Jacques Petit had once attended—played the part of Vesta. Another of the sparkling goddesses was Elizabeth Hatton, always in demand on these occasions. If Francis was a spectator, as seems probable, perhaps he thought of eleven-year-old Alice Barnham, as the goddesses danced and turned upon the floor, with ten-year-old Prince Henry, already a favourite with the ladies, being tossed from one to the other amid applause.

But it seems that the older courtiers were not amused. There were too many Scots gentlemen in his Majesty's entourage, with their uncouth accent, their laughter over-loud, their jests ribald, none of which did the monarch appear to think out of place. King James himself was doubtless glad to have a certain amount of relaxation before the more solemn business of a week later, when on January 14th, in an effort to reconcile the various religious factions, the lords of the Council and the bishops were summoned to appear before him at Hampton Court to discuss the future of the church in England and Ireland, and the Book of Common Prayer. The conference lasted three days, and it appears that the King made a very admirable opening speech; indeed, one of the ministers of religion, Dr Montague, later wrote of "the King alone disputing with the bishops, so wisely, wittily and learnedly, with that pretty patience, as I think never man living heard the like." It seems very probable that Francis's paper on the *Pacification and Justification of the Church of England*, dedicated to his Most Excellent Majesty, had been read with more than usual care by the King.

However, it was impossible to please everyone, and the upshot of the conference was that the King supported his High Church bishops, and the Puritans amongst the clergy found their demands dismissed, which boded ill for future pacification.

This discontent found vent in the first Parliament of the new reign, which King James opened on March 19th. Many questions came to the forefront, the expenses of the royal household being one of them, and the privileges and prerogatives of the monarch. Those members of Parliament who held low-church or Puritan views tended to be the most adamant in favour of reform. The King believed himself supreme, ruling by divine right. His predecessor Queen Elizabeth may have had the same belief, but more than forty years of dealing with an English Parliament had taught her when to be firm and when to relent; and whatever her own feelings she knew that the monarch must appear to acquiesce to the demands of the faithful Commons. King James lacked this experience, and consequently found himself in some difficulty, instinctively supporting the Lords when discretion should have given a more gracious hearing to the Lower House.

Francis was elected spokesman for the Commons on various committees, one of the most important issues of this first session being the question of the union between England and Scotland, how such a union should be styled, and whether the ancient name of England should lapse and the two kingdoms become Great Brittany. This last suggestion was ill-received by both the English and the Scots, and Francis needed all the tact and discretion at his command to keep tempers cool. The argument continued through April and May, reports being drafted from the Commons to the Lords, and back again from the Lords to the Commons. Finally, on June 2nd, a bill was passed appointing a commission to look into the whole question of the proposed union, and to report its findings at the end of October.

It had been an exhausting session, especially for Francis, but when Parliament was prorogued on July 7th he could turn once more to his own concerns, the concluding of his extremely obscure work entitled *Valerius Terminus of the Interpretation of Nature*. This in fact he left unfinished, and it was not published for another hundred and thirty years. It was *Valerius Terminus*, written in English and begun the preceding year, which had for preface the Latin paper already referred to, with its opening words, "Believing that I was born for the service of mankind. . . ." The work is a collection of fragments, written in the hand of one of Francis's many scribes, with annotations and corrections in his own.

It is an interesting fact, observed by the great scholar and biographer of Francis Bacon, James Spedding, that it was about this period of his life that Francis's handwriting underwent a remarkable change, "from the hurried Saxon hand full of large sweeping curves and with letters imperfectly formed and connected, which he wrote in Elizabeth's time, to a small, neat, light and compact one, formed more upon the Italian model which was then coming into fashion." This would seem to suggest that not only the thought and intellectual powers but also the character and personality of Francis the man were continually in process of transformation, of development and change. Indeed, in an age when there was no specialised learning as there is today, but when all educated men were expected to have some understanding of every branch of knowledge, Francis's infinitely complex mind far surpassed those of his contemporaries: the politician, the scholar, the philosopher, the scientist, the lawyer, the essayist, the deviser of masques and entertainments—a man with so many facets to his character must have bewildered his contemporaries, who would recognise one aspect and not another, believing the one they saw to be the whole man. Hence, perhaps, the dislike, even the fear, of those in his own day who did not understand him, and the incredulity of succeeding generations; while to counter this we have the admiration, even the adulation, of his close friends, echoed in our own time by the more extravagant claims that have been made about him.

It is fascinating to speculate what a mid-twentieth-century psychiatrist might have unravelled from a recumbent Francis on a couch: what childhood dreams of glory were kindled when he stood in the shadow of his father the Lord Keeper as he bowed before the Queen; what fires of rebellion smothered in the presence of his mother; and, despite his real love and affection for his elder brother, what unacknowledged jealousy lingered through the years for Anthony's friendship with Montaigne, and for his especial place in the intimate Essex-Southampton circle. Francis Bacon was an enigma then, as he is now, and perhaps most especially when he penned those words which open his *Valerius Terminus*.

This work was found in the eighteenth century amongst the papers of the Earl of Oxford, and is today in the British Museum. In his later works, Francis was to expand and develop the ideas put forward in these fragments, but his argument, then as always, was that God has given man the gift of thought, the ability to explore all knowledge providing he uses it "for the benefit and relief of the state and society of man; for otherwise all manner of knowledge becometh malign and serpentine, and therefore as carrying the quality of the serpent's sting and malice it maketh the mind of man to swell; as the Scripture saith excellently: knowledge bloweth up, but charity buildeth up." Further on, in the same opening chapter, he writes, "And therefore knowledge that tendeth but to satisfaction is but as a courtesan, which is for pleasure but not for fruit or generation. And knowledge that tendeth to profit or profession or glory is but as the golden ball thrown before Atalanta, which while she goeth aside and stoopeth to pick up she hindereth the race."

In mid-August, King James was well satisfied to conclude a treaty with Spain, and the Spanish envoys were entertained to a banquet at Whitehall. The war between the two countries, which had continued intermittently for so many years, was over at last. Toasts were drunk, gifts were exchanged, and no one was better pleased at the outcome of the negotiations than Queen Anne, who had long hoped for peace. She even helped to furnish rooms at her own private residence of Somerset House for Juan de Velasco, Constable of Castile, the spokesman of the mission.

Once again there was merriment and dancing, with young Prince Henry performing in fine style. There were whispers amongst the spectators that a marriage was to be arranged between the Prince and the Infanta Anna, daughter of King Philip III of Spain. Fortunately for the blood-pressure of the Puritan members of the Court, these rumours were unfounded. The revels continued, with bears fighting greyhounds and mastiffs attacking a bull. This last was evidently designed to please the Spanish guests, and delighted all but Prince Henry, who was fond of animals; indeed, it was said that on a previous occasion, at the Tower of London, when three dogs were put in a lion's cage and only one survived the mauling, the Prince sent for the dog to St James's Palace where he could see to its care himself. Such solicitude for the helpless was one of the finest things in his endearing character. He would surely have been horrified if he had ever been told of the celebrations in Oslo when his Scottish father and Danish mother were married, and King James ordered four young Negroes to dance naked in the snow before the royal carriage to amuse the crowd. The Negroes died later of pneumonia.

Possibly, when Francis Bacon was composing his *Masculine Birth of Time,* addressed to a young student, and his *Valerius Terminus,* he had in mind the immense importance of forming the ideas and nurturing the understanding of the future Prince of Wales, the heir to the two kingdoms.

It was during the visit of the Spanish envoys in August 1604 that King James was pleased at last to grant Sir Francis, by letters patent, the office of Learned Counsel, which until then had only been a verbal agreement. At the same time he gave him a pension of £60 a year. A small sum, and not one that was likely to increase the Gorhambury coffers, but a favour nevertheless, and an encouragement to continue yet another manuscript, this time a lengthy examination of *Certain Articles or Considerations Touching the Union of the Kingdoms of England and Scotland.* The commissioners who had been appointed before Parliament was prorogued in July to look into this question consisted of forty-eight Englishmen and thirty-one Scots. They met at the end of October, and although the final proceedings were not concluded until early December, it was largely owing to Francis Bacon that they came to unanimous agreement in all particulars. There were no disputes, no wrangling, every deliberation was handled with tact and delicacy, and the matter of the King's style or title, which hitherto had been a large bone of contention, was decided upon as King of Great Brittany, France and Ireland.

Here the business ended for the moment. The commissioners' report would have to pass through Parliament eventually, but this was deferred until the following year. With the threat of a return of the plague, Parliament was prorogued for ten months on December 24th, and the member for Ipswich, his work on the union concluded, could forget political affairs.

Once again there were festivities at Court. Queen Anne's brother Ulric, Bishop of Schwerin and Schleswig, was a visitor to England and must be entertained, and young Philip Herbert, whom the King had tapped so playfully on the cheek at the coronation, was married to Lady Susan Vere, a granddaughter of the first Lord Burghley. The King himself gave the bride away in Whitehall chapel, and inevitably celebrations followed. There was a masque which lasted for three hours, the fun waxing so fast and furious that some of the ladies not only lost their jewels but had their skirts torn for good measure. A more attractive spectacle was seen on Twelfth Night, when little Prince Charles, just five years old, was invested as Knight of the Bath, but because he walked with such difficulty—he suffered from some weakness in his joints—he was obliged to watch from the arms of the Lord Admiral while another nobleman took the oath for him.

Francis, knowing that the House of Commons would not claim his attendance until October, that his mother was safely cared for at Gorhambury, and that Alice Barnham, not yet thirteen, was playing with her sisters under the care of her mother and Lusty Packington either in Suffolk or in Worcestershire, could relax from domestic matters, and, surrounded by his books and papers and his willing pens in the comfortable lodgings in Gray's Inn, turn once more to composition —this time a major work that he would finish, *The Advancement of Learning.*

Chapter IV

"I have taken all knowledge to be my province," Francis, aged thirty-one, had written to his uncle, the Lord Treasurer; and now, twelve years later, he desired to give some proof of it, not only to men of understanding but to his sovereign. The work was to consist of two parts, or books, and each would bear a dedication to the King.

Francis felt with deep conviction that learning was not a matter for scholars only, but for all men; and his purpose was to show what wealth of interest awaited the reader whose mind was not dulled by past tradition of scholarship but was ready and alive to explore a whole new world of thought, just as his contemporaries were inspired to cross the oceans and discover the new lands that lay beyond. "It would be a disgrace for mankind if the expanse of the material globe, the land, the seas, the stars, were opened up and brought to light, while, in contrast to this enormous expansion, the bounds of the intellectual globe should be restricted to what was known to the ancients."

It was part of his thesis to show that true learning had, from the very dawn of history, been the natural part of all heroic men, of soldiers, statesmen, rulers. God, in the beginning, had created light, and this light, as Francis saw it, was not just the brightness of the sun above the earth, but the light of understanding which turned man from a brute beast into a being who could comprehend, whose garden, the world about him, comprised all things for his need. Because of the divine spark within him all that he saw, all that he touched—water lapping the shores, plants and trees that bore fruit—served to enlighten him. "Nothing," Francis believed, "was denied to man's enquiry and invention," and in the first book, certainly begun and possibly finished by the end of 1604, he cited numerous examples, from the scriptures and history, of those men who not only led exacting and extremely active lives but had used the light with which God had graced them to further knowledge: Moses the lawgiver, "God's first pen," Solomon the king, Xenophon the Athenian, Julius Caesar, Alex-

24

ander the Great. Soldiers and orators—Francis returns to them again and again, with Julius Caesar cited the most frequently. Earlier in the first book, when discussing leisure and how it should be spent, he quoted the Greek orator Demosthenes to his adversary Aeschines. "That was a man given to pleasure, and had told him that his orations did smell of the lamp. Indeed, said Demosthenes, there is a great difference between the things that you and I do by lamp-light." A sly dig from Francis himself, surely, at some of his own friends.

He was at great pains to distinguish between the proven facts of history, on the one hand, and tradition, which was so often at fault; and in the first book he showed how these misconceptions had come about—mostly from learned men "who have withdrawn themselves too much from the contemplation of nature and the observations of experience, and have tumbled up and down in their own reasons and conceits." The genuine seeker after truth must be all-embracing in his thirst for knowledge, and must not hesitate, when he looks about him, to probe the depths of his own being, recognise the defects and then remedy them, so that what good qualities he may possess develop to the full. "It were too long to go over the particular remedies which learning doth minister to all the diseases of the mind," Francis observes, and a chord is struck in the memory of the ordinary reader, the phrase is somehow familiar. "Canst thou not minister to a mind diseas'd, Pluck from the memory a rooted sorrow . . . ?" Yes, *Macbeth*, said to have been acted at Court the following year, though, like *Julius Caesar*, it was not published until seven years after William Shakespeare's death. "It were too long to go over the particular remedies which learning doth minister to all the diseases of the mind; sometimes purging the ill humours, sometimes opening the obstructions, sometimes helping digestion, sometimes increasing the appetite, sometimes healing the wounds."

His final paragraph is a supreme example of his wit and style, and one has an impression of him seated in his chamber at Gray's Inn, a group of chosen law-students grouped about him, and one or two of his closer friends besides—Tobie Matthew almost certainly. As his Majesty's Learned Counsel read aloud from the manuscript between his hands, he would now and again throw a quizzical glance from his "lively, hazel eye" at his avid listeners.

"I do not pretend, and I know it will be impossible for me by any pleading of mine, to reverse the judgement, either of Aesop's cock, that preferred the barleycorn before the gem; or of Midas, that being chosen judge between Apollo president of the Muses, and Pan god of the flocks, judged for plenty; or of Paris, that judged for beauty and love against wisdom and power; or of Agrippina (let him kill his mother that he be emperor) that preferred empire with condition never so detestable; or of Ulysses (that preferred an old woman to an immortality) being a figure of those which prefer custom and habit before all excellence; or of a number of the like popular judgements. For these things continue as they have been: but so will that also continue whereupon learning hath ever relied, and which faileth not: *Justificata est sapientia a filiis suis*—Wisdom is justified of her children."

Then the folding of the manuscript with a smile, and the opening of a discussion upon it, for according to his first biographer, the chaplain Dr Rawley, who would later enter his service, he was "not one that would appropriate the speech wholly to himself, or delight to outvie others, but leave the liberty to the co-assessors to take their turns. Whereupon he would draw a man on and allure him to speak upon such a subject, as wherein he was peculiarly skilful, and would delight to speak. And for himself, he condemned no man's observations, but would light his torch at every man's candle."

Whether Francis at this period of his life dined in the great hall at Gray's Inn or with chosen companions in his own lodgings we do not know, but like his brother Anthony before him, he seems to have enjoyed good fare.

"In his younger years," wrote Dr Rawley, "he was much given to the finer and lighter sorts of meats, as of fowls, and such like; but afterwards, when he grew more judicious, he preferred the stronger meats, such as the shambles afforded, as those meats which bred the more firm and substantial juices of the body, and less dissipable; upon which he would often make his meal though he had other meats upon the table."

"Stronger meats from the shambles" suggests a slaughterhouse running with blood, and the carcass of a great pig hanging from its hook to be cut and roasted later for Learned Counsel's table. Small wonder that "once in six or seven days he took a maceration of rhubarb infused into a draught of white wine and beer mingled together for the space of half-an-hour immediately before his meal (whether dinner or supper) that it might dry the body less, which, as he said, did carry away the grosser humours of the body and did not diminish or carry away any of the spirits, as sweating doth." It was probably the unfortunate effects of rhubarb that had prevented Francis from calling upon the Duke of Northumberland two years previously, and the habit seems to have been continued. As to exercise, Dr Rawley informs the reader "that he would ever interlace a moderate relaxation of his mind with his studies, as walking, or taking the air in his coach, or gentle exercise on horseback, and playing at bowls," but since Rawley's own observation was of his master's later years, possibly in 1605 relaxation was of another kind. Certainly it must not be forgotten that Ely Place, or Hatton Hall, the residence of Elizabeth Hatton, was only a short distance from Gray's Inn, and despite her marriage to the Attorney-General Edward Coke there had never been an open rupture in the relationship between that spirited lady and her former suitor.

So, after dining on "the lighter sorts of meats" with his companions and scribes, or taking a gentle walk, Francis would return to composition, and the continuation of the second book of his *Advancement of Learning*, which was to be at least three times the length of the first. Even his dedication to the King was more detailed. Of especial interest to the modern reader is his suggestion that professors and lecturers at universities and other places of learning should be better paid. Also that the governors of such institutions should consult with one another more, and have more frequent visits from "princes or superior persons." Both in the dedication and in the second book itself he uses his favourite analogy of comparing the work necessary in a garden to that of the cultivation of the mind, proof of his own tremendous interest in horticulture, which was to increase with the years. He observes to the King, "For if you will have a tree bear more fruit than it hath used to do, it is not anything you can do to the boughs, but it is the stirring of the earth and putting new mould about the roots that must work it," which leads him on to explain, "And because founders of colleges do plant, and founders of lectures do water, it followeth well to speak of the defect which is in public lectures; namely, in the smallness and meanness of the salary or reward which in most places is assigned to them; whether they be lectures of arts, or of professions." He also advised that there should be "more intelligence mutual between the universities of Europe than now there is."

The second book covers every aspect of learning; natural history, civil history, divinity, philosophy, natural philosophy, physics and metaphysics, medicine, etc. Despite the formidable list of subjects discussed, it is not a difficult book to read, and perhaps one of the reasons it is neglected in our own time is because so much of what Francis persuasively advocated, which was revolutionary at the beginning of the seventeenth century, has since been adopted and accepted as natural. Above all *The Advancement of Learning* is important because for the first time it defined the steps of scientific method, and stressed the importance of seeking truth through reason rather than through revelation: it may, in fact, truly be described as marking the birth of scientific philosophy.

The reader intent on discovering clues to Francis the man behind the thoughts to which he gave utterance will find a rich reward in certain sentences and paragraphs scattered here and there amongst the whole, as when, for instance, he says that certain men of learning esteem it a "kind of dishonour unto learning to descend to enquiry or meditation upon matters mechanical," and proceeds to tell the tale of the philosopher who "while he gazed upwards to the stars fell into the water; for if he had looked down he might have seen the stars in the water, but looking aloft he could not see the water in the stars."

He is particularly discerning in his discussion on the art of medicine. "The lawyer is judged by the virtue of his pleading, and not by the issue of his cause. The master in the ship is judged by the directing his course aright, and not by the fortune of the voyage. But the physician, and perhaps the politique, hath no particular acts demonstrative of his ability, but is judged most by the event; which is ever but as it is taken: for who can tell, if a patient die or recover, or if a state be preserved or ruined, whether it be by art or accident? And therefore many times the imposter is prized, and the man of virtue taxed. Nay, we see the weakness and credulity of men is such, as they will often prefer a mountebank or witch before a learned physician." Evidently a hit at the quacks of his own time, who were legion, as they are now.

A few pages further on he has something to say on another subject that is frequently argued in medical circles today. "Nay further, I esteem it the office of a physician not only to restore health, but to mitigate pains and dolors; and not only when such mitigation may conduce to recovery, but when it may serve to make a fair and easy passage. So it is written of Epicurus, that after his disease was judged desperate, he drowned his stomach and senses with a large draught and inguration of wine; whereupon the epigram was made, he was not sober enough to taste any bitterness of the Stygian water. But the physicians contrariwise do make a kind of scruple and religion to stay with the patient after the disease is deplored; whereras in my judgement they ought both to inquire the skill, and to give the attendances, for the facilitating and assuaging of the pains and agonies of death." Small wonder that Francis had marked his passage thus, "Of euthanasia at the end." Was he thinking once again of his brother Anthony?

The temptation to continue quoting from this fascinating work must be quelled . . . but then suddenly, later in the second book, we find him once more reverting to the diseases of the body, and saying, "So in medicining of the mind, which are not other than the perturbations and distempers of the affections . . ." and two pages later, "Is not the opinion of Aristotle worthy to be regarded, werein he saith that young

men are not fit auditors of moral philosophy, because they are not settled from the boiling heat of their affections, nor attempered with time
and experience?" And the probing reader asks, yes, but who said the
same in verse? It was Hector, in *Troilus and Cressida,* published four
years later.

> Not much
> Unlike young men, whom Aristotle thought
> Unfit to heare Moral Philosophie.
> The Reasons you alledge, so more conduce
> To the hot passion of distemp'red blood,
> Then to make up a free determination
> 'Twixt right and wrong.

Francis has a chapter on poetry in his *Advancement of Learning,*
and curiously enough it is one of the shortest, for, he writes, "In this
third part of learning, which is poesy, I can report no deficience. For
being as a plant that cometh of the lust of the earth, without a formal
seed, it hath sprung up and spread abroad more than any other kind."
He concludes with the line, "But it is not good to stay too long in the
theatre." What does he mean? Not good for whom? For a writer who
must not let himself be seduced by his imagination when more important work needs to be done? So the chapter ends abruptly, and he
passes on to the "palace of the mind." Finally, in the conclusion to the
whole book, he says, "I have been content to tune the instruments of
the Muses, that they may play that have better hands."

The Advancement of Learning was ready for publication in the autumn of October 1605, and was printed by Henry Tomes and sold at
his shop at Gray's Inn Gate, in Holborn. Francis had sent advance
copies to the Earl of Northampton (one time Lord Harry Howard,
friend of the Earl of Essex and brother Anthony), with a request that
he should present the book to his Majesty. He also sent copies to the
Lord Chancellor Lord Ellesmere, who had introduced him to Sir John
and Lady Packington, to the Lord Treasurer Lord Buckhurst, to
cousin Robert Cecil, now Earl of Salisbury and Chancellor of Cambridge University, to Sir Thomas Bodley at Oxford University, and of
course to Tobie Matthew, who was in Italy at the time—indeed, he
had been travelling abroad since the preceding April. His letters were
in his customary formal style when addressing his superiors, but he
was on easier terms with young Tobie. "I have now at last taught that
child to go, at the swaddling whereof you were. My work touching the
Proficiency and *Advancement of Learning* I have put into two books;
whereof the former, which you saw, I count but as a page to the lat-

ter. I have now published them both; whereof I thought it a small adventure to send you a copy, who have more right to it than any man, except Bishop Andrews, who was my inquisitor." (This was Dr Launcelot Andrews, an old friend and Dean of Westminster, who was about to become Bishop of Chichester, and to whom Bacon had more than once sent manuscripts for scrutiny and criticism.)

Francis had, so he thought, timed the moment of publication well, just before Parliament assembled for the new session; but unfortunately for him—a fate common to writers throughout the centuries when their books are overtaken by public events—the impact that his two volumes might have made was entirely overshadowed by the discovery of a plot to blow up the Houses of Parliament when the Lords and Commons should be assembled before his Majesty on the opening day, November 5th. *The Advancement of Learning,* save for a casual mention by Chamberlain that "Sir Francis Bacon hath set forth a new work," appears to have awakened no other comment. The great Powder Treason, known to the world since as the Gunpowder Plot, took precedence not only over all other business in both Houses of Parliament but in the minds and hearts of all subjects loyal to the Crown.

Francis, thankful that his Majesty's life had been spared, as well as his own and that of other members of the Commons and the Lords, shed no tears over the fact that his own ten months and more of composition had misfired. The two books must be translated into Latin, the universal language of scholars at that time, and distributed in the continent of Europe, where their argument would be more readily appreciated and understood. When opportunity served, during the years that lay ahead, he would find time to incorporate all the ideas he had expressed in his *Advancement of Learning* in yet a further major work, written wholly in Latin.

Chapter V

The perpetrators of the great Powder Treason were all arrested, imprisoned, tried and condemned to death, the executions taking place on the last two days of January 1606. No mercy killing for them. They were hanged, drawn and quartered, amongst them Sir Everard Digby, who in his defence spoke warmly for the Catholic cause. Guy Fawkes, alias Johnson, alias Guido Fawkes, who had actually been found with the thirty barrels of powder under Parliament House, declared that the desperate state of the nation demanded a desperate remedy, and confessed that he had desired to blow all the Scots back to Scotland. This admission, in the presence of King James, whose own father, Lord Darnley, had been similarly murdered at Kirk o' Field in 1567, when James was only one year old, was hardly one to induce clemency in the monarch, who had lived in the fear of assassination ever since.

November 5th was declared to be a public holiday in perpetuity in thankfulness for his Majesty's escape, and detestation for all papists throughout the country began to grow amongst the people. Further arrests were made, houses owned by those with Catholic sympathies were searched, and a bill was introduced in Parliament on January 21st to establish laws against recusants, the name given to all those who refused to attend the services of the Church of England.

Francis had taken no part at all in the treason trials, but in the House of Commons he was selected as a member of the committee appointed to look into the question of the laws against recusants, and indeed he was active throughout the whole of February, March and April, serving on various committees.

The tricky question of a subsidy for the throne came up again, and it was perhaps fortunate for King James that while this was being discussed there was an alarming report on March 22nd that his Majesty had been found stabbed in his bed! A totally unfounded rumour, immediately contradicted by a proclamation, but it had the effect of

mellowing those members of Parliament who might otherwise have
been ill-disposed to grant an additional levy. How the report came
about is unknown, but Robert Cecil, Earl of Salisbury, was a subtle
man, well versed in political moves, and he may have considered that
a shock to the faithful Commons would not come amiss at this moment, as an additional jolt four months after the Powder Treason.
Some historians of our day have declared that the Powder Treason itself was an ingenious "plant" on the part of Salisbury to frighten the
King, but such an idea has no documentary proof, and seems an unfair
indictment of a statesman whose loyalty and service to the monarch
had never been in doubt. In any event the March scare was short-
lived, bells rang in the churches, the people ran out into the streets,
and everyone rejoiced that King James was safe, while Francis Bacon
rose to his feet in the House to urge that the bill for the subsidy
should be passed, giving thanks at the same time that the sovereign
was alive and well.

During the present session and before, when he was still working on
his *Advancement of Learning*, his intimacy with Sir "Lusty" Packington and Lady Packington had grown. Although his object was undoubtedly to win their consent to a marriage with Lady Packington's
daughter Alice, one wonders what possible rapport he could have had
with the parents, so dissimilar to himself in character and pursuits.
There could have been one bond—a mutual interest in building and in
gardening. "Lusty" had built his own house, Westwood Park, at
Hampton Lovett, and had dug a great lake in the grounds, which was
a source of annoyance to his neighbours, who declared that by doing
so he had interfered with the King's highway. Who better to advise
him about this lake, and his rights, than Learned Counsel Francis
Bacon, friend of Lord Keeper and Lord Chancellor Ellesmere? And
who better, in addition, to advise him about another quarrel, this time
with Lord Zouche, who was claiming jurisdiction over Worcestershire,
while Lusty himself was sheriff for the town of Worcester?

The grounds and the offending lake would certainly make a point of
contact between hot-tempered Lusty Packington and Francis, who
was forever thinking out his own improvements to Gorhambury. It is
pleasant to speculate upon the two men pacing the grounds, Lusty
blustering away about his rights, and Francis nodding agreement but
making diplomatic suggestions, and at the same time noting the improvements in looks and carriage of his host's stepdaughter Alice.
Hampton Lovett was about twenty-five miles from Stratford-on-Avon,
through which Francis would pass on his journeys to and from London, and where, in the year 1605, William Shakespeare purchased for

£440 a thirty-one-year lease of tithes around Stratford and the neighbouring villages.

Some time during 1605, or early in 1606, Francis Bacon and Sir John and Lady Packington came to an agreement concerning the future of Miss Alice Barnham, with her £6,000 inheritance and her £300 a year from land. The articles of marriage, dated May 10th 1606, settled the Manors of Gorhambury, Westwick and Praye, including the advowsons of St Michaels and Redbourne, upon trustees, so that the same should be for Alice for life, and of the clear value of £300 per annum. If Francis should die first he would leave to her "goods and money worth £1,000 with her apparel, linen and personal ornaments, and such jewels as she should possess during covertures, but no jewel over £100 in value. If he should survive her, the Manors to be for him and his issue by her, and in default for his Trustees."

Benedict Barnham, Alice's father, had left a will shortly before he died. At this time Alice was five years, ten months and thirteen days old. When she was married to Francis Bacon—who was forty-five—Alice, according to the reckoning of the Rev. C. Moor, writing in the *Genealogist's Magazine* in 1937, was "twelve days under fourteen years of age." Perhaps there is a slight error here, and May 10th was in fact her fourteenth birthday. The extreme youth of the bride does not seem to have been noticed by the gossips or by any of Francis Bacon's later biographers, including James Spedding and W. Hepworth Dixon. The only contemporary allusion to the wedding, indeed, is contained in the letter from Dudley Carleton to John Chamberlain on the following day, May fifth. "Sir Francis Bacon was married yesterday to his young wench in Marylebone Chapel. He was clad from top to toe in purple, and hath made himself and his wife such store of fine raiments of cloth of silver and gold that it draws deep into her portion. The dinner was kept at his father-in-law Sir John Packington's lodging over against the Savoy, where his chief guests were the three knights Cope, Hicks and Beeston [Sir Michael Hicks, Sir Walter Cope and Sir Hugh Beeston, all three members of Parliament]; and upon this conceit, as he said himself, that since he could not have my L. of Salisbury in person, he would have him at least in his representative body."

Francis's choice of purple as a wedding-garment is intriguing. Roman emperors and Persian kings wore purple. Perhaps, in fantasy, he saw himself as Julius Caesar or Darius. There is no record listing the other guests who attended the wedding, or where the honeymoon —if one took place—was spent. Twickenham Lodge would seem more suitable than Gorhambury, in view of the fact that on May 13th he was obliged to read a Petition of Grievances to his Majesty—those of the faithful Commons, not his own. Moreover, the towers of Richmond Palace on the opposite bank of the Thames, as seen from Twickenham Lodge, might have greater appeal for a bride of just fourteen than the imposing rooms and gallery at Gorhambury, especially if a visit to Hertfordshire entailed a meeting with her mother-in-law, the dowager Lady Bacon, confined to her own quarters and likely to be totally bewildered at the sudden appearance of a "wench" in silver and gold.

So the wedding night came and went with what success or failure we shall never know. It would be cynical to assume that his remarks in a later essay, "Of Marriage and Single Life," referred to Alice when he said, "Wives are young men's mistresses, companions for middle age, and old men's nurses. So as a man may have a quarrel to marry, when he will; but yet he was reputed one of the wise men that made answer to the question when a man should marry, 'A young man not yet, an elder man not at all.'"

However, it must be confessed that the Latin work he was to write the year after his marriage, *Cogitata et Visa de Interpretatione Naturae* (*Thoughts and Conclusions on the Interpretation of Nature*), has an interesting passage describing the legend of Scylla: "That lady had the face and countenance of a maiden, but her loins were girt about with yelping hounds. So these doctrines present at first view a charming face, but the rash wooer who should essay the generative parts in hope of offspring, is blessed only with shrill disputes and arguments." The marriage of Francis Bacon and Alice Barnham was childless. . . .

Parliament was prorogued from May 27th until November 16th, so the groom had nearly six months in which to woo his bride, and win her esteem if not her passion. Perhaps a visit to Court would bring stimulation. King Christian of Denmark, Queen Anne's brother, arrived for a state visit early in July, alighting from his flagship at Gravesend, where he was met by his brother-in-law King James and his nephew young Prince Henry, who conducted him in the royal barge to Greenwich. The poor Queen had only lately recovered from the birth of a baby daughter who had died after a few hours, and it was hoped that the King of Denmark's visit would help to soften her bereavement. There was a state ride through London, after which every sort of entertainment was provided for the royal visitor—excursions to St Paul's, to Westminster Abbey, and to the Tower to watch the inevitable bear-baiting by mastiffs, followed by hawking and hunting in the country.

The Earl of Salisbury gave a magnificent party at Theobalds where

34

he was host to both King James and King Christian and their retinues, though Queen Anne herself was not present. It is likely that Francis and his lady were invited, being relatives of the earl, and if they were indeed present Francis may have felt obliged to escort his young bride from the scene. The banquet was all very well, but it was followed by a masque intended to represent the Queen of Sheba visiting Solomon. Unfortunately, the Court lady acting the part of the Queen of Sheba had indulged herself too freely at the banquet, with the result that she tripped up the steps when presenting gifts to the Danish king, and spilt a mass of wine, cream and jellies on his lap.

The King of Denmark, who had also "drink taken," cleaned himself up and invited the lady to dance, but fell flat on his face and had to be carried to an inner room to recover. The Masque proceeded, each performer more tipsy than the last; some staggered and went to sleep, others were speechless and retired, as the Danish king had done, only to be violently sick in an outer hall, and the final mummer, representing peace, was so bellicose that she demanded battle of everyone in her path and struck them over the head with her olive branch. What the unfortunate host thought of it all history does not record, but the proverbial saying "turned in his grave" would certainly have applied to his father, the great statesman Lord Treasurer Burghley.

As to Francis himself, he had hopes of a rise in status this month of July, the post of Solicitor-General being likely to fall vacant. His old rival Edward Coke had been promoted to the post of Chief Justice of the Common Pleas, and the new Attorney-General was Sir Henry Hobart. However, Serjeant Doderidge continued to hold the place of Solicitor-General for the time being, thus bringing the usual disappointment to Learned Counsel Sir Francis Bacon. Nevertheless he was aware that changes might take place in the not too distant future, and had written letters to his Majesty, to Lord Salisbury and to the Lord Chancellor expressing his hopes.

In his letter to Lord Chancellor Ellesmere, who had first introduced him to the Packingtons, he makes the first reference to his marriage that occurs amongst his correspondence at this time. "And herewithal, my good Lord, I humbly pray your Lordship to consider that time groweth precious with me, and that a married man is seven years elder in his thoughts the first day. And therefore what a discomfortable thing is it for me to be unsettled still?" He has a further allusion at the end of the letter. "But to conclude, as my honourable Lady your wife was some mean to make me change the name of another, so if it please you to help me, as you said, to change my own name, I can be but more and more bounden to you: and I am much deceived, if your Lordship find not the King well inclined, and my Lord of Salisbury forward and affectionate."

There is no record of the answers Francis received, but there was certainly no change in his status at this time.

The second reference to his marital state comes in a letter to his cousin Sir Thomas Hoby, dated August 4th 1606, concerning the death of a mutual friend. Condolences over, Francis says, "Your loving congratulations for my doubled life, as you call it, I thank you for. No man may better conceive the joys of a good wife than yourself, with whom I dare not compare. But I thank God I have not taken a thorn out of my foot to put it into my side. For as my state is somewhat amended, so I have no other circumstance of complaint. But herein we will dilate when we meet; which meeting will be much more joyfully if my Lady bear a part to mend the music: to whom I pray let me in all kindness be commended."

Thomas Posthumus Hoby, younger son of Francis's aunt Elizabeth Russell, had married a rich widow with estates in the north of England, and was therefore well content with his lot. He too was childless, and his north-country neighbours seemed to have laughed at him, calling him "the busiest saucy little Jack in all the country, and would have an oar in anybody's boat." It is to be hoped the two cousins met, and dined, and introduced their wives, and music was made; perhaps Alice performed upon the virginal.

Where Francis and Alice lived when Parliament was in session is something of a mystery. Francis undoubtedly would continue to make use of his chambers in Gray's Inn, but he could hardly take his lady there, and he was to be very active indeed when the House met in the February of 1607 after the Christmas recess. Twickenham Lodge was no longer in his possession; it became the property of Lucy, Countess of Bedford, during that year. It is possible that Lusty Packington, who quarrelled violently with his wife, Alice's mother, just about this time, and according to the gossips had "parted with her on foul terms," made his lodgings in the Strand available to his daughter and son-in-law. A countryman by taste and inclination, Lusty would prefer his estate at Hampton Lovett to the hurly-burly of the Strand, and Lady Packington, likewise possessed of a difficult temper, and with a brood of young Packingtons to bring up (fruits of her marriage with Lusty), besides her own Barnham daughters, may well have retired to her own estate in Suffolk. Francis had experience now of the trials that in-laws could bring, and he had little time to spare, with the question of the naturalisation of the Scots coming up for heated debate in the House of Commons.

Feeling on this matter ran very high indeed. Certainly there had been a great influx of citizens from north of the border since his Majesty's accession, and many sections of society felt that they were taking over land, institutions and privileges that belonged by right to the English. Guido Fawkes had not been alone in wanting to blow every Scot back into Scotland.

It was, in a curious way, like the situation in our own time when persons from the Commonwealth can, by law, claim British citizenship and take up their residence in this country, and it roused the same heated passions. Those members of Parliament who were against the union of Scotland and England were also against the naturalisation of Scottish subjects of both realms who had been born prior to the death of Queen Elizabeth, and had since shared equal rights with the English. Francis, who was a fervent supporter of the union and of naturalisation, made one of the longest speeches of his political career in reply to the member for Bucks, who had launched a tirade, lasting a whole day, against all things Scottish. Would anyone, he said, mingle two swarms of bees? Why, then, two hostile swarms of men? And if Queen Mary had borne a son to King Philip of Spain, would Parliament have naturalised the people of Sicily and Spain?

Francis rose to his feet on Tuesday, February 17th, and from the length of his reported speech he must have spoken for several hours, with apparently no interruptions. He soon dismissed the implication that the Scottish settlers since the accession were in danger of swamping the native English population. "I would fain understand," he said, "in these four years' space . . . how many families of the Scottishmen are planted in the cities, boroughs and towns of this kingdom. For I do assure myself, that, more than some persons of quality about his Majesty's person here at the Court, and in London, and some other inferior persons that have a dependency upon them, the return and certificate, if such a survey should be made, would be of a number extremely small."

He informed Mr Speaker and the House "that this realm of England is not yet peopled to the full . . . [and] if we were, it were not possible that we should relinquish and resign such an infinite benefit of fishing to the Flemings, as is well known we do." (A stab here at the fishermen on the continent, who were over-fishing the Channel to the detriment of our own fishing fleet. A bone of contention still!)

One great objection to naturalisation was that the laws of the two kingdoms differed. "It is true for mine own part, Mr Speaker," Francis declared, "that I wish the Scottish nation governed by our laws; for I hold our laws, with some reducement, worthy to govern, if it were the

37

world. But this is that which I say . . . that according to true reason of estate, naturalisation is in order first and precedent to union of laws. . . . For naturalisation doth but take out the marks of a foreigner, but union of laws makes them entirely as ourselves."

Possibly one of his strongest and most eloquent arguments in favour of naturalisation was that, if two kingdoms were united without this additional bond, then history had proved that the union in time dissolved, and the people separated or rebelled. He gave examples from ancient Rome, from Sparta, and in more recent times from Aragon in Spain, from Florence and Pisa and from the Turkish empire. "I do believe," he continued, "and I would be sorry to be found a prophet in it, that except we proceed with this naturalisation, though perhaps not in his Majesty's time, who hath such interest in both nations, yet in the time of his descendants, these realms will be in continual danger to divide and break again."

Even more vital was the safety of the realm. "Touching surety, it was well said by Titus Quintius the Roman touching the state of Peloponnesus, that the tortoise is safe within her shell. But if there be any parts that lie open, they endanger all the rest."

Francis's concluding words were, "So my duty is performed. The judgement is yours. God direct it for the best."

Perhaps his friend and contemporary, the dramatist Ben Jonson, was thinking of this speech and of others that were to come later, when he wrote of Francis Bacon in after years, "No man ever spake more neatly, more pressly, more weightily, or suffered less emptiness, less idleness, in what he uttered. No member of his speech but consisted of his own graces. His hearers could not cough, or look aside from him, without loss. He commanded where he spoke, and had us angry and pleased at his devotion. No man had their affections more in his power. The fear of every man that heard him was, lest he should make an end."

The proceedings continued through February and March and the matter was referred to the judges in the Upper House and back to the Commons, the whole question of naturalisation becoming "bogged down," as we should say in modern slang, as to where the law stood, and whether those Scots born since the King was crowned should have equal rights in England, or if there should be a distinction made between those born before and those since.

Just before the Easter recess his Majesty himself addressed the House, hoping, very naturally, that his faithful Commons would pass an act of general naturalisation, and that the union of the two kingdoms would follow in due course. He was to be disappointed. Both questions were postponed indefinitely. The only allied bill that secured further readings and was passed was one for abolishing hostile laws between the two kingdoms, and this did not come about until June 30th. As to the act of union, neither his Majesty King James I, nor Francis Bacon his Learned Counsel, who had spoken so eloquently in its favour, would see such an act passed in their lifetime. Nor any member of the faithful Commons. More than a century would pass before England and Scotland became legally one kingdom.

Francis may have failed in his objective, but his fervour, at long last, had impressed his sovereign. On June 25th, just before the end of the session, he became Solicitor-General, a position for which he had waited for thirteen years. It was promotion at long last—and the office was also worth £1,000 a year. His foot was set on the first step of the winding stair.

Chapter VI

The improvement in status brought little personal satisfaction to Francis. He showed evidence of this in his private memoranda, written during July the following year and never intended to be seen by any eye but his own—the memoranda were not discovered until 1848—where a brief note refers to his mood after becoming Solicitor-General. "I have now twice, upon amendment of my fortune, disposition to melancholy and distaste, specially the same happening against the long vacation when company failed and business both, for upon my Solicitor's place I grew indisposed and inclined to superstition."

He mentions "old symptoms as I was wont to have it many years ago, as after sleeps; strife at meats, strangeness, clouds, etc." A tendency to hypochondria, which had been so strong in his brother Anthony, was now growing upon him too, and the memoranda have many jottings of remedies for indigestion, bowel troubles and "vicious humours"—indeed, for almost every ailment likely to attack the inner man.

One of the habits he found it almost impossible to break was the tendency to fall asleep in the afternoon, or immediately after dinner, which induced "languishing and distaste and feverish disposition" more than any other. He would awake with pains in his side or in the belly under the navel, pains which could only be relieved with castor oil, or a change of position. Evidently the presence of his young wife at such times did nothing to improve matters, but must have increased his nervous irritation. Fortunately Alice's sister Dorothy, a year or so younger than herself, had also found herself a husband, one Sir John Constable, a young barrister of Gray's Inn and therefore known personally to Francis. They were married some time during 1607, and his Majesty, apparently at the request of his new Solicitor-General, knighted the bridegroom in October. What John Constable had done to deserve the honour is unrecorded, but the sisters and brothers-in-law being friends eased the conscience of Francis where his own wife was concerned. When he himself was out of sorts, and Alice asked for entertainment, the Constables would oblige.

He had an added anxiety in that his young friend Tobie Matthew, who had turned Catholic while in Italy—a closely guarded confidence until now—returned to England in August 1607. As he was the son of the present Archbishop of York, his Catholicism was something that could not be kept secret for long; and it became the Solicitor-General's painful duty to inform the Archbishop of Canterbury, Dr Bancroft, that the young man was not only in London but determined to hold firmly to the Catholic faith. Tobie, handsome, witty, something of a dilettante until the present, had been wandering about the continent against his parents' wishes, visiting Florence, Siena, Rome; and he spoke fluent Italian. His travels, and possibly the influence of the Jesuits, had matured him, and although Francis could not condone his Catholicism here was just the intellect he needed to probe him out of his own seasonable melancholy into discussing *Cogitata et Visa de Interpretatione Naturae*, the Latin treatise he had been writing, and to inspire him further to plan in outline the great work which lay ahead, and which at this stage he liked to call his *Instauratio Magna*.

Unfortunately, all attempts by the learned divines, including the Archbishop of Canterbury himself, to persuade Tobie to abjure his new faith failed, and he found himself in the Fleet prison. Francis was able to see him, however, as the gossips discovered. "Tobie Matthew hath leave to go as often as he will with his keeper to Sir Francis Bacon, and is put in good hope of further liberty." Thus Dudley Carleton to his correspondent John Chamberlain. Tobie was thirty years old on October 3rd 1607, and, with the anniversary of the Powder Plot coming up in a month's time, Francis was well aware how the association of ideas might harm his young friend in the eyes of authority. A letter to Tobie, undated, must have been written about this time, in which Francis says, "Do not think me forgetful or altered towards you. But if I should say I could do you any good, I should make my power more than it is. I do hear that which I am right sorry for; that you grow more impatient and busy than at first; which maketh me exceedingly fear the issue of that which seemeth not to stand at a stay. I myself am out of doubt, that you have been miserably abused, when you were first seduced; but that which I take in compassion, others may take in severity. . . . And I entreat you much, sometimes to meditate upon the extreme superstition in this last Powder Treason; fit to be tabled and pictured in the chambers of meditation, as another hell above the ground: and well justifying the censure of the heathen, that superstition is far worse than atheism; by

41

how much it is less evil to have no opinion of God at all, than such as is impious towards his divine majesty and goodness. Good Mr Matthew, receive yourself back from these courses of perdition."

By these "courses of perdition" Francis meant Tobie's refusal to take the oath of allegiance to the King, a most dangerous course, which might have cost him his life.

Tobie was still in the Fleet at the new year, which came in bitterly cold, with the Thames frozen over, and the Archbishop of Canterbury travelled to Court across the ice from Lambeth Palace, which was hardly likely to improve his temper. The usual festivities were held, with a Masque of Beauty devised by Ben Jonson on January 10th, Queen Anne performing with her ladies, as was her custom, Lady Elizabeth Hatton amongst them. Everything went smoothly, and this time there was no break in decorum, no stumbling upon the floor. It is to be hoped that Francis allowed his lady to be present, in the company of her sister, Lady Constable, for once again he found himself involved in her family affairs. This time it was Lady Packington who was putting them all to trial. There was apparently some difficulty over Dorothy Constable's marriage settlement, and Francis, who seems to have been a trustee, became exasperated.

"Madam, you shall with right good will be made acquainted with anything which concerneth your daughters, if you bear a mind of love and concord; otherwise you must be content to be a stranger unto us. For I may not be so unwise as to suffer you to be an author or occasion of dissension between your daughters and their husbands, having seen so much misery of that kind in yourself. And above all things I will turn back your kindness, in which you say you will receive my wife if she be cast off. For it is much more likely we have occasion to receive you being cast off, if you remember what is passed. But it is time to make an end of these follies. And you shall at this time pardon me this one fault of writing to you. For I mean to do it no more till you use me and respect me as you ought."

And please God, he might have added, that she does not take it into her head to come and live with us, whether at Gorhambury or elsewhere. It is evident from his private memoranda later that year that the Bacons were living at some period during 1608 at a house called Fullwoods, which does not suggest an address in town, but by July they were installed at Bath House off the Strand. It is likely that their London quarters were shared with the Constables, giving Francis opportunity to escape to Gray's Inn whenever possible. This would have been particularly convenient in early February, as owing to an outbreak of plague Tobie Matthew was allowed out on parole. On Febru-

42

ary 7th he was called before the Council, and told by the Earl of Salisbury that he could go free but under the surveillance of "some friend of good account" for a period of six weeks, after which he "must depart the realm." Tobie chose a Mr Jones to watch over him, who may have been the Mr Edward Jones known well to Francis Bacon—one-time secretary to the late Earl of Essex, an acquaintance of both Francis and his brother Anthony, and "a great translator of books." Certainly it must have been possible for Solicitor-General Sir Francis and his protégé Tobie Matthew to meet at Gray's Inn without further obstacle or embarrassment. Tobie's actual date of departure is uncertain, but it seems to have been within the next two months. He was to remain abroad for ten years, during which time letters passed continually between the two friends.

The year 1608 was to be one of intense literary activity for Francis. Despite his position as Solicitor-General there was little official business for him to do, and Parliament itself was not called for the whole of the year, the excuse in January having been fear of "the sickness," or plague. King James could spend plenty of time at his favourite sport, hunting. He had persuaded his Secretary of State, Lord Salisbury, to give him his estate Theobalds as a hunting lodge, in exchange for his own palace at Hatfield.

Robert Cecil, Earl of Salisbury, had one taste in common with his cousin Francis Bacon, a passion for building. The old palace, where Princess Elizabeth had learnt of her accession to the throne in 1558, would not do; it must be rebuilt. He engaged the best designers and architects, and the project, which took over five years to complete, is said to have cost more than £38,000. Just as their fathers had engaged in friendly competition in the building of Theobalds and Gorhambury some forty years previously, now Francis and Robert Cecil, on equable terms—for ill-feeling between them seems to have mellowed during recent months—exchanged advice about design.

"To give directions of a plot to be made to turn the pond-yard into a place of pleasure, and to speak of them to my L. of Salisbury," says a note in the private memoranda. And Francis writes of his plans for the grounds round about Gorhambury, "to be enclosed square with a brick wall, and fruit-trees plashed upon it," but then continues with far more grandiose ideas, of walks on various levels, and "all the ground within this walk to be cast into a lake, with a fair rail with images gilt round about it and some low flowers specially violets and strawberries. In the middle of the lake where the house now stands to make an island of 100 broad; and in the middle thereof to build a house for freshness with an upper gallery open upon the water, a terrace about that, and a supping room open under that; a dining-room, a bed-chamber, a cabinet, and a room for music, a garden; in this ground to make one walk between trees; the galleries to cast northwards; nothing to be planted here but of choice."

Some of these plans were to be put into operation during the coming years, and may well have been begun during the summer of 1608 —discussions about it would keep Alice and the Constables employed —but Francis had so many projects in mind at this time, which he jotted down in his memoranda, that it is a wonder he kept pace with half of them. His *Advancement of Learning* having made little impact in 1605, he wondered whether his arguments for the spread of knowledge would have more success if he could become head of some school or college. A note on July 26th says, "Laying for a place to command wits and pens. Westminster, Eton, Winchester, Trinity College, Cambridge, St John's in Camb, Maudlin in Oxford." Later there is a suggestion for founding a college for inventors, with libraries and laboratories, and allowances for students to make experiments.

His interest in things scientific was increasing all the time, and he made a list of persons who might be of use, "my Lord of Northumberland (in the Tower of London for suspected if doubtful complicity in the Powder Treason), Ralegh, and therefore Harriot," the latter a great mathematician intimate with Ralegh, whom he instructed in mathematics. "Making much of Russell that depends upon Sir David Murray (Thomas Russell was experimenting in separating silver from lead ore, and Sir David Murray was Keeper of the Privy Purse), and by that means drawing Sir Dav. and by him and Sir Th. Chal. in time the prince."

Sir Thomas Challoner, old friend of brother Anthony, was now Governor to the Household of Prince Henry, whose investiture would take place in two years' time, and it was to the future Prince of Wales that Francis looked for real encouragement in the spread of learning. His Majesty was all very well, but he mistrusted scientific experiment, especially after the Powder Treason, and these days spent much of his leisure time in hunting rather than in reading, with his new young Scottish favourite Robert Carr, who had replaced the Earl of Montgomery in his affections.

The future Prince of Wales had a respect for tradition as well as for future experiment, and would be one of those to read another Latin work Francis was engaged upon that summer of 1608, *In felicem memoriam Elizabethae*, a treatise in praise of his former Sovereign. *Cogitata et Visa* had meanwhile been laid aside for *Redargutio Philosophiarum* (*A Refutation of Philosophies*), both of which would have been discussed with Tobie Matthew before his friend went overseas. It was in *Cogitata et Visa* that Francis retold the legend of Scylla, the maiden "whose loins were girt about with yelping hounds" (no disrespect intended towards his young wife). The work, written in the third person—"Francis Bacon thought thus, etc., etc."—was a further development of his ideas and arguments.

For instance, in the opening section: "The human discoveries we now enjoy should rank as quite imperfect and undeveloped. In the present state of the sciences new discoveries can be expected only after the lapse of centuries. The discoveries men have up to now achieved cannot be credited to philosophy."

He has one of his familiar digs at academies of learning. "Far the greater number of persons there are concerned primarily with lecturing and in the next place with making a living; and the lectures and other exercises are so managed that the last thing anyone would be likely to entertain is an unfamiliar thought. Anyone who allows himself freedom of enquiry or independence of judgement finds himself isolated. In the arts and sciences, as in mining for minerals, there ought everywhere to be the bustle of new works and further progress."

(How Francis would have been welcomed by the students in universities some three and a half centuries later!)

He also tilted at his former target in *The Masculine Birth of Time*, the Greek philosophers. "The opinions and theories of the Greeks are like the arguments of so many stage plays, devised to give an illusion of reality, with greater or less elegance, carelessness or frigidity. They have what is proper to a stage-play, a neat roundness foreign to a narration of fact."

In chapter 14 something of his own personality can be glimpsed between the lines. "Speaking generally, the human mind is so uneven a mirror as to distort the rays which fall upon it by its angularities. It is not a smooth flat surface. Furthermore, every individual, in consequence of his education, interests, and constitution is attended by a delusive power, his own familiar demon, which mocks his mind and troubles it with unsubstantial spectres." Was Francis's own "familiar demon" one that led him into "melancholy and distaste," and "inclined [him] to superstition, strangeness, clouds" as described in his memoranda? Later in the same chapter we have another revelation. "Bacon [always the third person] found himself in disagreement with both the ancients and moderns. A wine-drinker and a water-drinker, says the familiar jest, cannot hold the same opinion; and while they drink an intellectual beverage . . . Bacon prefers a draught prepared from innumerable grapes, grapes matured and plucked in due season

45

from selected clusters, crushed in the press, purged and clarified in the vat: a draught moreover which has been so treated as to qualify its powers of inebriating, since he is resolved to owe nothing to the heady fumes of vain imaginings." Surely here is an echo from the second book of his *Advancement of Learning*, where, in the brief chapter on poetry, he concluded, "But it is not good to stay too long in the theatre."

The remaining chapters of *Cogitata et Visa* concentrate on improving Man's lot, and the benefits that inventions confer on the whole human race.

"It is this glory of discovery that is the true ornament of mankind," he wrote, and gave illustrations in three inventions unknown to antiquity, "To wit, printing, gunpowder, and the nautical needle. These have changed the face and status of the world of men. . . . The human mind and its management is ours to improve. There are no insuperable objects in the way; simply it lies in a direction untrodden by the feet of men. It may frighten us a little by its loneliness; it offers no threat. A new world beckons. The trial should be made. Not to try is a greater hazard than to fail."

Inspiring words to all creative men in his own day and in succeeding ages, whether scientists, inventors, explorers or writers.

Francis showed *Cogitata et Visa* to certain friends apart from Tobie Matthew, one being Sir Thomas Bodley at Oxford, who he hoped would show warm appreciation, but the reception was guarded, the great scholar seeming to have found the ideas expressed too advanced for academic approval.

So the work remained unpublished, as did its successor *Redargutio Philosophiarum, The Refutation of Philosophies*, until after the writer's death. In this latter book, as might be expected from the title, Francis repeated and developed much of what he had already said in *The Masculine Birth of Time* and *Cogitata et Visa*. This time, however, he wrote as if he were a philosopher addressing a gathering of learned men of mature age. Perhaps in fantasy he already saw himself chancellor of a university speaking before a gathering of dons.

The opening words are in forthright style. "We are agreed, my sons, that you are men. This means, as I think, that you are not animals on their hind legs, but mortal gods. God, the creator of the universe and of you, gave you souls capable of understanding the world but not to be satisfied with it alone. He reserved for himself your faith, but gave the world over to your senses. . . . He did not give you reliable and trustworthy senses in order that you might study the writings of a few

46

men. . . . Nay, from the moment you learn to speak you are under the necessity of drinking in and assimilating what I may be allowed to call a hotch-potch of errors. Errors sanctioned by the institutions of academies, colleges, orders, and even states themselves. . . . I do not ask you to renounce them in a moment. I do not wish to hurry you into isolation. Use your philosophy. Adorn your conversation with its jewels. Use it when convenient. Keep one to deal with nature and the other to deal with the populace. Every man of superior understanding in contact with inferiors wears a mask. . . ."

Here is a revealing line from Francis Bacon in the summer of 1608, forty-seven years old, his curling brown hair greying, as were his moustache and beard, his face more lined, his frame fuller, more set, but the hazel eyes as lively as ever, the smile—when it came—something between compassion for those who heard him, and contempt. "Every man of superior understanding in contact with inferiors wears a mask." Here is the essence of the man at last, the boy who believed himself, as brother Anthony might have told him, *capable de tout.* Who might have founded an English Pleiades, groomed a successful leader, had the attentive ear of two monarchs, helped to frame new laws and a union of kingdoms, composed anything from the lightest of trifles to the most profound of discourses, and who now, in middle age, married to a girl just turned sixteen who was more like a daughter than a wife, had the attention of few save his closest friends; and even with these, as with his superiors in rank and status, and with his servants too, he wore a mask.

Concealment, like the "worm in the bud" in a different context, affected the many facets of his personality, and never more, perhaps, than at this period when sovereign and state made small demand upon him, and he had all the time in the world at his disposal; time to explore the many motives that drove man—including himself—to triumph or despair, which, by examining them closely, he came to recognise and understand better, and himself as well.

"My time is running out, sons, and I am tempted by my love of you and of the business in hand, to take up one topic after another. I yearn for some secret of initiation which, like the coming of April or of spring, might avail to thaw and loosen your fixed and frozen minds. . . . Shake off the chains which oppress you and be masters of yourselves. . . . I only give you this advice, that you do not promise yourself such great things from my discoveries as not to expect better from your own. I foresee for myself a destiny like that of Alexander—now pray, do not accuse me of vanity till you have heard me out. While his memory was fresh his exploits were regarded as portents. But when admiration had cooled and men looked more closely into the matter, note the sober judgement passed upon him by the Roman historian: 'All Alexander did was dare to despise shams.' Something like this later generations will say of me."

Chapter VII

None of his contemporaries was prepared to compare Francis Bacon with the great figures of the past; nevertheless he continued to circulate his Latin compositions amongst his friends, both at home and abroad. His memorial to Queen Elizabeth found little favour with the gossips who had sight of it. John Chamberlain, with his customary malice, mentioned it to his friend Dudley Carleton with scant respect.

"I come even now," he wrote on December 16th 1608, "from reading a short discourse of Queen Elizabeth's life, written in Latin by Sir Francis Bacon. If you have not seen nor heard of it, it is worth your enquiry; and yet methinks he doth *languescere* towards the end, and falls from his first pitch: neither dare I warrant that his Latin will abide test or touch."

Francis himself, like many writers who tend to be better pleased with those of their compositions that have not appealed to popular taste, had a regard for the brief treatise on his late sovereign that was to last him throughout his life; indeed, it was one of the few by which he hoped to be remembered. Queen Elizabeth had neither favoured nor promoted him since the day in his childhood when she called him "her little Lord Keeper"; yet he never could forget her, nor the fact that she had been one of the greatest monarchs the kingdom of England had ever known. Posterity would recognize this truth.

Whether King James read the treatise, or the future Prince of Wales, remains conjecture; certainly Francis would have sent it to them. Sir George Cary, ambassador in France, received a copy, as did Tobie Matthew, who, according to the letter from Francis enclosed with it, "would be more willing to hear Julius Caesar commended than Queen Elizabeth."

The new year opened with dull, heavy weather, no frozen Thames as in 1608, and with little news for the gossips to report beyond the fact that Parliament was to be prorogued once more until November, and that the unfortunate Sir Walter Ralegh, still imprisoned in the

49

Tower, was now obliged by the King's order to relinquish all his estates to his Majesty's favourite, Sir Robert Carr, not surprisingly a gentleman of the bedchamber. Ralegh pleaded most eloquently for his son's inheritance, while his wife and children went down on their knees before the sovereign in a last attempt to move the royal heart. It was no use. King James is reported to have said, "I maun ha' the land, I maun ha' it for Robbie," and the favourite, who already possessed rentals of £600 a year and a gold tablet set in diamonds, was further enriched.

Francis Bacon, never a gossip, made no allusion to the rising fortunes of the Scottish favourite when he wrote to Tobie Matthew, as he was to do frequently during the coming year, for with Parliament in what appeared to be an indefinite recess, and the governing of the country secure in the hands of the Council headed by his cousin the Earl of Salisbury, who besides being Secretary of State had now the office of Lord Treasurer, there was no official business for the Solicitor-General.

It is frustrating for later generations that Francis was not more explicit to his friend Tobie when discussing his literary compositions. In one letter about this time he writes, "I have sent you some copies of the *Advancement,* which you desired; and a little work of my recreation, which you desired not. My Instauration I reserve for our conference; it sleeps not." He also refers to "works of the *Alphabet* . . . in my opinion of less use to you where you are now, than at Paris." This last must have referred to his personal cipher, which seems to have aroused much controversy in later centuries. "The little work of his recreation" was not the memorial to Queen Elizabeth, which Tobie had already received, nor the Latin treatise *De Sapientia Veterum* (*The Wisdom of the Ancients*) which, although it may have been started in the spring of 1609, was certainly not finished until the end of the year.

Once again, therefore, as in 1608, Francis had almost a twelvemonth in which to devote himself to literary composition, and although he reported progress to Tobie throughout the year of his *Instauratio Magna,* and even sent him extracts from it, this immense work was so erudite that it could hardly be described as recreation. Nor would the result of this vast labour in Latin be given to the world for another eleven years.

So we are left to speculate upon how he employed his time, and speculation can be a hazardous game. The private memoranda are no help. The only manuscript of this extant—doubtless there were others that were destroyed or lost—belongs to the preceding summer of 1608, and according to his biographer Spedding it was the work of seven consecutive days, from July 25th until July 31st. There are certainly jottings upon work in hand, and a tantalising note to the effect that he had a book which "receiveth all remembrances touching my private of whatsoever nature and hath 2 parts, *Diariu* and *Schedulæ*. The one being a journal of whatsoever occurreth; the other kalenders or titles of things of the same nature, for better help of memory or judgement, herein I make choice of things of most present use." He then refers to several books, all to be sorted under different headings. That he had already begun to enlarge his original book of essays, of which there had been ten in number, dedicated to his brother Anthony, is evident from the note in the memoranda *Scripta in Politicis et Moralibus;* a manuscript with this title is in the British Museum. It seems likely that had he been sending any of these essays to Tobie Matthew, Francis would have mentioned them by name.

The only entries in the memoranda referring to his personal life in that July of 1608 are estimates of his assets, property and otherwise, rents at Gorhambury, and so on. It seems certain that he was a tenant at Bath House, at this period, for the furniture there is valued at £60, with the furniture at Gray's Inn, including his "books and other implements," at £100. A somewhat touching entry comes under the heading of "jewels of my wife."

An upright feather	£100
A crooked feather	£100
A fleur de lys feather	£100
The pendants my tokens	£50
The necklace of pearl	£50
My fair diamond ring	£45

The items would hardly have qualified Alice Bacon to make a dazzling appearance at Court, with all eyes turned upon her in admiration. It is not difficult to imagine what Lady Hatton would have said, had her former suitor Francis bestowed them upon her. . . . Finally, following upon these and other items, he gives a list of debts "absolutely cleared," the names of one or two former creditors familiar to the reader, such as Nicholas Trott, and Alderman Spenser who had been Lord Mayor of London when brother Anthony lived in Bishopsgate. It was Alderman Spenser who used to entertain at Crosby Hall, and whose daughter eloped from a window in a laundry basket and ran off with Lord Compton.

The private memoranda, however, had been laid aside by 1609, and apart from the letters to Tobie Matthew we hear nothing about

51

Francis Bacon, not even from the gossips Chamberlain and Carleton. Indeed, their own letters that year report little of interest to the reader of today, and the one publication, on May 20th, calculated to excite later generations to a frenzy of controversy passed without any comment whatsoever.

This was the appearance in quarto of "Shake-Speares Sonnets. Never before Imprinted. George Stevens at London. By G. Eld. for T.T. and are to be solde by John Wright, dwelling at Christ Church gate 1609." The spelling of the author's name is intriguing, with the Christian name William omitted. There was only one printing, and the poems were not to appear again until 1640. Scholars and historians have argued the question of the dedication for over a hundred and fifty years.

To the only begetter of
these ensuing sonnets
Mr. W. H. all happiness
and that eternity
promised
by
our ever-living poet
wisheth
the well-wishing
adventurer in
setting
forth
T.T.

Does "begetter" mean procurer—i.e., he who sold the sonnets to T.T. (Thomas Thorpe the publisher)—or their inspirer, the "lovely boy" to whom most of the sonnets are addressed? If the former, as A. L. Rowse asserts, then the leading favourite for the identity of Mr W.H. is William Harvey, third husband of the dowager Countess of Southampton and stepfather of the young Earl of Southampton, Henry Wriothesley, whom the majority of scholars believe to be the "lovely boy." Others, however, claim that the word "begetter" means inspirer, and here a string of claimants run the race, the main rival to Henry Wriothesley—his initials reversed—being William Herbert, the 3rd Earl of Pembroke. Hard upon their heels gallops Leslie Hotson's William Hatcliffe, a student at Gray's Inn, who was Prince of Purpoole in the annual revels of 1588–89. This ingenious theory has a certain appeal for those who, like the present writer, can fancy a young barrister of Gray's Inn as author of many of the sonnets; nevertheless, that same young barrister, when moving with his brother Anthony in higher circles, where the Earls of Essex and Southampton held sway, would have found even greater inspiration in that lively group of friends than in the confines of the Inns of Court.

Essex and Southampton both wrote poems, as did Robert Sidney, brother of the famous Philip, and Fulke Greville, a close friend to Francis Bacon. Whether all the sonnets—some of them among the best-loved poems in the English language, others not so often read—were penned by the same author, without contributions from a separate source, has been discussed by scholars the world over, along with the interpretation of the more baffling lines—does this one relate to some contemporary event, does that allude to an inner struggle within the poet himself? Even the date of composition has not been finally proved, though 1592–94 is generally assumed to be correct. Many belonging to that glittering circle surrounding the Earls of Essex and Southampton may have contributed a poem that eventually found its way into Thomas Thorpe's collection of sonnets.

By the time the sonnets appeared in 1609 the author or authors could no longer have been young. Some, possibly, were dead, despite that dedication which speaks of "our ever-living poet." Even T.T. the publisher may have been as confused as we are about their true identity.

It must not be forgotten that Anthony Bacon, brother of Francis, was sending sonnets back to England from France as early as the mid-1580's; and as a close confidante of the Essex circle, devoted to Robert Devereux, he cannot be entirely dismissed, should the authorship have been shared. In the not-so-often quoted sonnets 37, 66 and 89, where the poet writes of his lameness—though with quite another connotation, according to A. L. Rowse—the meaning may have been quite simply that he who wrote was lame. Perhaps William Shakespeare also walked with a limp.

Dark ladies come and go. In 1609 the favourite Moll Fitton, claimed as the original by those who fancy William Herbert, Earl of Pembroke, as Mr W.H., was widowed and had retired into the country. Emilia Lanier, the latest to join the course, had vanished into obscurity; though possibly it was a relative of hers, Bassano, who was "server" or waiter to Francis Bacon some years later, the only Italian amongst some seventy of his servants.

Elizabeth Hatton, wife of Chief Justice Coke, was forgotten by no one. In the March of 1610 she gave a supper-party, according to the gossips, and there was some trouble about the seating of her table, whether the Earl of Airlie should take precedence over the Earl of Pembroke. Prominent in the circle about Queen Anne, and well to the

53

fore when masques were produced at Court, she would be a favourite
topic of the gossips seven years later. But when the sonnets were first
penned, possibly in the 1590's, she was the widow of William Hatton
(a contender for Mr W.H.?), who had fought beside Philip Sidney in
the Netherlands, and was a stepbrother to William Underhill, the
owner of New Place, Stratford-on-Avon. In 1597, when William Underhill sold New Place to William Shakespeare, Francis Bacon courted
Elizabeth Hatton, and—so the gossips said—had Fulke Greville as
one of his rivals. Was she dark or fair? Alas, no portrait exists to tell us.
The mystery remains. Dark ladies, lovely boys and ever-living poets
continue to baffle many of us in the present century, despite the cer-
tainty of scholars and historians.

Meanwhile, at long last, Parliament met on February 9th 1610.
Among the most pressing matters to be discussed were his Majesty's
finances. It was a delicate business, and Francis was given the unen-
viable task of producing a balance sheet.

King James had now been on the throne for seven years, and the
Crown's expenditure had increased enormously. The monarch's own
generosity, and his extravagance at Court, were not solely to blame for
this. Those who served him were also at fault, members of the Council
and the Earl of Salisbury in particular. Where they led, others followed, hoping for a share in the pickings which went with patronage.
Something in the nature of £75,000 had been spent by the Office of
Works on new buildings in less than four years, but the Crown debt
was over £400,000. How this was to be paid, whether by cutting expenditure, and at the same time getting Parliament to agree to an increased subsidy, was to be the main business of this session of Parliament, which, apart from the short recess at Easter, lasted until late
July. Francis, as Solicitor-General, was active throughout, since it was
his duty to present the King's case, being careful to ensure that his
Majesty was given no offence, but equally that the faithful Commons
should have no diminution of their rights but be consulted on every
aspect of the matter at issue.

Once again the thorny question of prerogative and privilege came
up for debate, and whether the monarch had the power to levy duties
on imports without the sanction of Parliament, or whether Parliament,
by withholding subsidies, should have control over the monarch. King
James, who believed in his divine right to govern, found himself involved in a confrontation which touched on the whole relation between the sovereignty of the Crown and the liberty of the subject.

The mood of the Commons had been softened in 1606, when the

question of subsidies had also come up, by the sudden unfounded rumour of the King's assassination. On May 14th 1610 assassination actually took place in France. King Henry IV was stabbed to death by a fanatic who jumped on the running-board of his coach. He died instantly. The news was broken to both Houses of Parliament by the Earl of Salisbury. Whether the tragic end of this truly great king had a conciliatory effect upon the British monarch, and upon his faithful Commons, remains conjecture. Certainly there was some point of meeting between them, the King yielding on some points, the Commons on others. The arguments continued throughout June and July, and by the summer recess a contract had been drawn up by which the monarch agreed to the withdrawal of certain privileges and prerogatives in exchange for an annual grant of £200,000.

The recess, unfortunately, gave both monarch and Commons a chance to re-think their position, and when they assembled again in October opinion had hardened. The King now demanded a grant of £500,000, and if this was not agreed upon then he would be free of the contract. (The reader is reminded of another contract or compact in our own times, between government and trades unions!) The Commons, not surprisingly, would not acquiesce, and negotiations broke down.

An interesting side-line is that one of the members of the Lower House who spoke with great determination to the effect that no subsidy should be granted to the Crown unless the contract was upheld was Nathaniel Bacon, Francis's half-brother, who had also been knighted after the King's accession. A rich landowner in his mid-sixties, living in Norfolk and married to a wealthy widow, he doubtless resented the increased drain upon his resources. Francis himself took a more moderate line, speaking in favour of supplies being granted to the King and weighing his words with his usual caution.

In the event no conclusion was reached, and the contract came to nothing. The Crown was in heavy debt, and the emptiness of the Exchequer was by now known not only to the Commons but to people everywhere. Ambassadors were unpaid, and those on pension forced to borrow. The House adjourned on November 24th, and was dissolved in February, 1611. Nothing of any consequence had been resolved.

The Court does not seem to have suffered the financial straits that might have been expected. The usual festivities took place. Henry Prince of Wales, who had been invested the preceding June, produced his first masque on New Year's Day. It was called *Oberon, The Fairy Prince*. He had hoped to have his performers mounted, being a keen

55

horseman, but King James demurred, on the grounds that it would hardly be seemly with all this talk of extravagance. Queen Anne, however, indulged her ladies and herself as usual. Ben Jonson and Inigo Jones produced a lavish show for them, *Love Freed from Ignorance and Folly*, in which her Majesty appeared as Queen of the Orient.

We have no means of knowing whether Francis Bacon and his lady applauded as spectators. It seems more likely that henceforth, with Parliament dissolved, he would spend more time at Gorhambury, which, after so many years, he could look upon as his entirely. Alice, now eighteen, was sole mistress of her household, for Lady Ann Bacon had died in August of 1610. We would have no knowledge of the fact but for a letter which Francis wrote on August 27th to his old friend Sir Michael Hicks.

"It is but a wish and not in any ways to desire it to your trouble. But I heartily wish I had your company here at my mother's funeral which I purpose on Thursday next in the forenoon. I dare promise you a good sermon to be made by Mr Fenton the preacher of Gray's Inn, for he never maketh other. Feast I make none. But if I might have your company for two or three days at my house I should pass over this mournful occasion with more comfort. If your son had continued at St Julian's it might have been an adamant to have drawn you: but now if you come I must say it is only for my sake."

We have no record of the sermon, but it certainly would have contained tributes to the great piety of the deceased, and to her learning. Those sermons she had translated from Italian and Latin long ago had not been forgotten, nor perhaps the reformer Theodore Beza's dedication to her in his meditations. Her learned sisters, too, may have had a mention: Mildred, wife of Lord Treasurer Lord Burghley, who had died as long ago as 1589, and Elizabeth, Lady Russell, only the year before, in 1609.

Ann Bacon was eighty-two when she died, and the only record of those last years at Gorhambury is the word of Bishop Goodman, who wrote "she was little better than frantic in her age." She was buried at St Michael's Church, St Albans. The well-worn phrase "a merciful release" was true for her. Those penalties of extreme age, an inability to move, to feed unaided, incontinence, all would have been hers, and one can only hope that the widows or the daughters of her former trusted servants, "Goodman" Fynch, Tom Gotherham, and others, cared for her until the end. As for her daughter-in-law Alice, of whom, alas, we know so little, it would be pleasant to think that she showed kindness and compassion to the old lady who had so much wanted "childer's childer" from her two sons Anthony and Francis, and was destined to have none.

Francis's letter to Sir Michael Hicks is at least proof of his own regard; and the fact that in his own will he desired to be buried at St Michael's, for "there was my mother buried," shows that despite the anxiety and concern she had caused him during those years of senility he hoped, when his own end came, to share her grave.

As for his literary achievements of the past year, he had published nothing since his Latin treatise *De Sapientia Veterum,* which had appeared in 1609 and had enjoyed some popular success. This was the book which he had sent to Tobie Matthew in February of 1610, and of which he had written, "I send you a little work of mine that hath begun to pass the world. They tell me my Latin is turned into silver, and become current. Had you been here, you should have been my inquisitor before it came forth."

In *De Sapientia Veterum* Francis re-tells the story of some thirty-one fables and myths of ancient Greece, giving his own interpretation; how they came into being, and how they influenced the thought and actions of man throughout the ages. It is not surprising that the work was popular in his own day, and indeed for anyone fascinated today by the old classical fables they make compulsive reading. It is particularly interesting that Francis, who condemned the Greek philosophers, should have a different attitude to myth and fable, looking upon them in the nature of parables, intended from the earliest times to show man to himself. His reading of the classics had always been profound, and quotations from them sprinkle his political speeches and his philosophical works; but now it was as though his mind was reaching back before the dawn of history, enquiring whether there had been a time when beings of superior knowledge had peopled the earth, leaving behind them this legacy of myth or parable to instruct those who came after them. The thirty-one fables show him at a most perceptive stage of his life, when, temporarily free from political activity, he could turn fantasy to concrete thought.

The legend of Orpheus perhaps concerned him most, that master of harmony who drew even the wild beasts of the woods unto him, to be ultimately destroyed by Bacchus and the Thracian women, and he drew from this a parallel of what might ultimately be the fate of our own country if wars and seditions came to ravish it. "And if such troubles last, it is not long before letters also and philosophy are so torn in pieces that no traces of them can be found but a few fragments, scattered here and there like planks from a shipwreck; and then a season

57

of barbarism sets in, the waters of Helicon being sunk under the ground, until, according to the appointed vicissitude of things, they break out and issue forth again, perhaps among other nations, and not in the places where they were before."

The influence upon man of Bacchus seems to have been one that Francis found most insidious and deplorable, inflaming passion, celebrating a conquest over reason. "And again that part of the allegory is especially noble which represents Bacchus as lavishing his love upon one whom another man had cast off. For most certain it is that passion ever seeks and aspires after that which experience has rejected. And let all men who in the heat of pursuit and indulgence are ready to give any price for the fruition of their passion, know this—that whatever be the object of their pursuit, be it honour or fortune or love or glory or knowledge, or what it will, they are paying court to things cast off—things which many men in all times have tried, and upon trial rejected with disgust."

Strangely bitter words, suggesting, when Francis penned them, one of those passing moods of melancholy that seized him from time to time, a mood redeemed when he came to interpret the fable of Prometheus, who, as a punishment for stealing fire—which he gave to man—was condemned by Zeus to eternal torture, until Hercules set him free. Francis concluded this fable by comparing it to the mysteries of the Christian faith. "The voyage of Hercules especially," he says, "sailing in a pitcher to set Prometheus free, seems to present an image of God the Word hastening in the frail vessel of the flesh to redeem the human race."

De Sapientia Veterum bore a dedication to his "Nursing Mother," the university of Cambridge, and to his cousin the Earl of Salisbury, Lord High Treasurer of England and Chancellor of the university.

The year 1611 opened without prospect of employment. Parliament was not summoned, and a history of the present reign, which he proposed to the King, met with no encouragement. His Majesty was not interested: Robert Carr, his own Endymion, about to become a Knight of the Garter and Viscount Rochester, claimed his full attention. So be it. The idea was abandoned. Francis would turn his inventive mind to other projects, other plans. To buildings, to gardens, to the completion of his essays; and, since King James himself had no leisure these days for recreation other than hunting and dalliance with his gentleman of the bedchamber, this time the essays would bear a dedication to his successor, God willing—the Prince of Wales.

1. The Right Honourable Sir Francis Bacon, Lord High Chancellor of England (*engraving by Francis Holl, after Simon Pass, photo H. Graeme, Fowey*)

2. Head of Queen Elizabeth, from her tomb in Westminster Abbey *(reproduced by courtesy of the Dean and Chapter of Westminster)*

3. Robert Cecil, Earl of Salisbury, attributed to J. de Critz the Elder, 1602 *(photo National Portrait Gallery, London)*

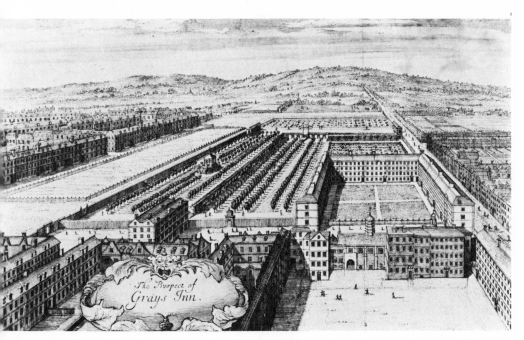

4. Prospect of Gray's Inn *(from the Greater London Council Print Collection)*

5. Execution of Gunpowder Plot conspirators in St. Paul's Churchyard, 1606 *(reproduced by courtesy of the Trustees of the British Museum)*

6. Two engravings of Arundel House, once Bath House, c. 1640, by Wenceslaus Hollar *(photo Radio Times Hulton Picture Library)*

Chapter VIII

The completion of twenty-four essays may have occupied Francis Bacon for a couple of months, but they could scarcely have been stimulation enough for his pen during the whole year of 1611. His biographer James Spedding suggests that he employed himself revising speeches and other business, which seems dull work for the most brilliant intellect of the day.

His contemporary, Mr William Shakespeare of London and Stratford, actor-dramatist, was able to see three of his own plays produced that year. *Cymbeline* and *The Winter's Tale* were performed at the Globe Theatre on bankside in the month of May, and the *Court Revels* inform us that *The Tempest* was given before the King at Whitehall on Halloween, October 31st. The dramatist's mood had mellowed, the scholars say; dark ladies belong to the past, and the heroines of these three plays are young, artless women, Perdita, Imogen, Miranda, inspired, so some suggest, by the actor-dramatist's daughters Susanna and Judith. Susanna would have been twenty-eight in 1611, and Judith twenty-six. Susanna was already married, with a child of three. Perhaps the inspiration may have come from quite another young woman just turned nineteen?

Masques were all the rage in 1611, delighting the Queen, and the appearance of Juno, Ceres, and attendant nymphs in the fourth act of *The Tempest* has a flavour of *De Sapientia Veterum* about it. The shipwrecked fleet, "safely in harbour . . . in the deepe Nooke, where once thou calldst me up at midnight to fetch dewe from the still-vext Bermoothes," so Ariel reports to Prospero, was a topical allusion to the lately wrecked ship *Admiral*, belonging to the Virginia Company. Possibly William Shakespeare had shares in this as well as Francis Bacon and his patron the Earl of Southampton. In any event, shipwrecks were in vogue. Gonzalo, "an honest old counsellor" in the play, has a speech in Act II that scholars tell us Shakespeare must have based on

59

a reading of the English translation of the essays of Montaigne, a copy of which, with his name upon it, is in the British Museum.

William Shakespeare, like Francis, was obviously a botanist, his plays being full of the fragrance of wild flowers, as the avid reader knows very well. How the gardens at New Place, Stratford, which he bought in 1597 from William Underhill (stepbrother to Lady Hatton's first husband) compared with those at Gorhambury we cannot tell, for unfortunately the property was pulled down in 1759; but being in the centre of town it could hardly have given great scope to his imagination. A modest lay-out, perhaps, and pleasant in spring, so that he could sing, like Autolycus in *The Winter's Tale*,

> When Daffadils begin to peere,
> With heigh the Doxy over the dale . . .

A visit to Gorhambury would have helped William Shakespeare with his third play of 1611, *Cymbeline, King of Britain*, for here in Hertfordshire lived the original of his protagonist, Cunobelinus, king of the Catuvellauni, whose tribal area covered the whole of that county. It seems the play was popular, and like *The Tempest* included a masque, with Jupiter descending "in Thunder and Lightening, sitting upon an Eagle: he throws a Thunder-bolt. The Ghostes fall on their knees."

However, "these things are but toys," as Francis was to write towards the end of his life, in the essay on *Masques and Triumphs*, published in 1625, and are not for "serious observations." It was unwise to dwell amongst them, just as it was not good "to stay too long in the theatre."

Public life was about to claim him once again. His cousin, the Earl of Salisbury, became seriously ill during the autumn of 1611, as did the Attorney-General Sir Henry Hobart. Francis took the opportunity of writing to his Majesty to remind him, as tactfully as possible, of a promise made some months previously: "I do understand by some of my good friends, to my great comfort, that your Majesty hath in mind your Majesty's royal promise, which to me is *anchora spei*, touching the Attorney's place. I hope Mr Attorney shall do well. I thank God I wish no man's death; nor much mine own life, more than to do your Majesty service." The Attorney-General recovered, but the hint might strike a chord, when occasion served. A new year's letter to Salisbury did not touch on his cousin's health, but mentioned that "though I find age and decays grow upon me, yet I may have a flash or two of spirit left to do you service."

The Earl of Salisbury, in fact, was a very sick man, and in February of 1612 was discovered to have an abdominal tumour. He was courageous enough to travel to Bath, hoping that the waters would help him to recover, but the effort was too much for him, and he died on May 24th, at Marlborough, on the journey home. His death was almost as great a loss to the country as his father's had been, fourteen years before; and although in his time he possessed many enemies, had never been popular with the ordinary people, and was certainly not infallible where the Treasury was concerned, yet he had steered the ship of state with a steady hand under two monarchs of very different temperaments, and his loyalty to both had never been questioned.

He was buried early in June at his home in Hatfield, the ceremony a simple one by his own wish, and his cousin Francis Bacon was one of the family mourners. The two men had never been intimate. The unspoken jealousy of boyhood days seems to have clung to them, perhaps unconsciously, throughout their lives, though of late this had not been so apparent. How much this jealousy had been fostered in early youth by their mothers, Mildred and Ann, who, though affectionate sisters, were rivals in scholarship, and who both had husbands in high place, is something the psychologists must decide.

Robert Cecil was very short in stature, and was said to have one shoulder higher than the other. When his cousin Francis wrote his essay *Of Deformity*—one of those to be published later in the year— the gossip John Chamberlain told Dudley Carleton "the world takes notice that he paints out his little cousin to the life." Perhaps. The essay is astute rather than unkind. "Whosoever hath anything fixed in his person that doth enduce contempt, hath also a perpetual spur in himself to rescue and deliver himself from scorn; therefore, all deformed persons are extreme bold; first, as in their own defence, as being exposed to scorn, but in process of time by a general habit. Also it stirreth in them industry, and especially of this kind, to watch and observe the weakness of others. . . . Still the ground is, they will, if they be of spirit, seek to free themselves from scorn: which must be either by virtue or malice; and, therefore, let it not be marvelled, if sometimes they prove excellent persons. . . ."

Francis wrote to the King on May 31st, as soon as he heard of his cousin's death, though we have no means of knowing whether the letter was actually sent, and, if it was, whether a reply was ever received. "Your Majesty hath lost a great subject and a great servant. But if I should praise him in propriety, I should say that he was a fit man to keep things from growing worse but no very fit man to reduce things to be much better." (Something that could be said about holders of

61

high office in later centuries.) "For," Francis continued, "he loved to have the eyes of all Israel a little too much upon himself, and to have all business still under the hammer and like clay in the hands of the potter, to mould it as he thought good. . . ."

Francis, in this letter, was not seeking the position of Secretary of State, which his cousin's death had laid vacant, but rather to have the private ear of the King and advise him how to deal with the Commons. "My offering," he concludes, "is care and observance; and as my good old mistress was wont to call me her watch-candle, because it pleased her to say I did continually burn—and yet she suffered me to waste almost to nothing—so I must much more owe the like duty to your Majesty, by whom my fortunes have been settled and raised."

A later letter is more specific. In this Francis would seem to be applying to become a member of the Council. "If your Majesty find any aptness in me, or if you find any scarcity in others, whereby you may think it fit for your service to remove to business of state . . . I will be ready as a chessman to be wherever your Majesty's royal hand shall set me."

As it turned out, the appointing of a new Secretary of State and Lord Treasurer was postponed. Nor was Parliament called. The Earl of Northampton, the one-time Lord Harry Howard, friend of the Earl of Essex and Anthony Bacon, was temporarily given the lead in Council affairs, possibly because he had influence with the King's favourite, Sir Robert Carr, recently given the title of Earl of Rochester. However, Francis himself was not ignored by his Majesty, who seemed ready to listen to his advice even if he did not necessarily act upon it.

There was, naturally, much jockeying for the position of Secretary, the two names most frequently mentioned being Sir Henry Wotton and Sir Ralph Winwood, along with Sir Henry Neville; but, John Chamberlain told Carleton in August, as for the position of Lord Treasurer, "point encore, parce qu'il n'y a point de trésor."

Francis himself was busy with legal cases during the summer, but one of his most important duties as Solicitor-General was to arrange the levy—and this dated from long custom—to be raised for the marriage of the Princess Elizabeth, who was now sixteen, to Prince Frederick, Elector Palatine. The contract of marriage had been signed in May, and the Elector was expected to arrive in England in the autumn. Fortunately the princess was as popular as her brother the Prince of Wales, and as the Elector was a Protestant the people looked forward to the wedding and the festivities.

The levy brought some £22,000 into the Exchequer, but as even more than this was spent on the wedding arrangements the national debt remained as it was—*"point de trésor."* Francis took the opportunity of writing a private letter to the King "upon the subject of the repair and improvement of your Majesty's means. . . . For it will not be wrought by any one fine extract or strong water, but by a skilful compound of a number of ingredients. . . . And as your Majesty's growing behind-hand hath been the work of time; so must likewise be your Majesty's coming forth and making even."

A commission was appointed, with Francis, the Chancellor of the Exchequer, Sir Julius Caesar, and the Attorney-General, Sir Henry Hobart, among its members, to look into the vexed question of the King's finances, and Francis appears to have framed the final report. This was submitted in mid-October, by which time the Elector Palatine had arrived to greet his bride. Prince Frederick, who had landed at Gravesend, was housed at Essex House with some hundred and seventy of his attendants, a "train of very sober and well-fashioned gentlemen," according to the gossips. The prospective bridegroom was most dutiful in paying immediate court to the princess, and was liked by everyone. All seemed set fair for a joyous conclusion to the betrothal when, suddenly, tragedy struck the royal family and the whole nation.

The Prince of Wales, who had not spared himself in entertaining the guests from the Palatinate, swimming in the Thames at midnight and riding ceaselessly, fell ill of what the royal physicians diagnosed as "a tertian fever," but what seems in fact to have been typhoid. He was obliged to cancel his appearance at the Lord Mayor's show at Guildhall, and the Elector Palatine went without him. Even now, in early November, no one appeared to grasp the gravity of the disease, although the Prince of Wales grew rapidly weaker, and the inevitable "bloodletting" and shaving of his head, where much of the pain lay, proved no remedy. Realisation that he was not likely to recover began to spread through the capital when it was learnt that their Majesties had not attended divine service on November 5th, the anniversary of the Powder Treason, and a day of thanksgiving, and that the Bishop of Ely had said special prayers for the heir to the throne.

The Queen and her daughter had small faith in the royal physicians, and the princess, who with her brother had a longstanding friendship with Sir Walter Ralegh, implored the prisoner to send a cordial that he had once recommended in her own case, which had proved effective. This Ralegh did—he had his own laboratory in the Tower—but alas, it was no use. Late on Wednesday, November 4th, the Prince of

Wales fell into a coma, his last words being "Where is my dear sister?", after which he neither stirred nor spoke again, but died between eight and nine o'clock on Friday evening.

When the eldest son of the monarch dies speculation inevitably follows as to whether the course of history might have been otherwise had he lived. The nearest analogy to Henry, eldest son of James I, must be Arthur, eldest son of Henry VII. Both were well-loved young men of blameless character. Whether a King Arthur, wedded to Katharine of Aragon, would have kept his kingdom Catholic must be a matter for historians to argue. The same could be said about a King Henry IX, who might, perhaps, have listened to his faithful Commons and spared his country civil war. However that may be, the death of Henry Prince of Wales was a very great loss indeed, to the dynasty and to the two kingdoms.

Francis Bacon, whose new collection of essays had been entered at the Stationers' Hall on October 12th, with a dedicatory letter to the Prince, had presumably not yet had it distributed for sale. The essays made their appearance in December, with the original dedication exchanged for one to his brother-in-law Sir John Constable. It must have been now, also, that he wrote a tribute in Latin to the Prince of Wales, which, as it was not discovered until 1753, may have been for private circulation only. Some extracts from the tribute shed light on the young man's character, as Francis judged it.

"He died to the great grief and regret of the whole kingdom, as being a youth who had neither offended men's minds nor satiated them. The goodness of his disposition had awakened manifold hopes amongst numbers of all ranks, nor had he lived long enough to disappoint them. Moreover, as among the people generally he had the reputation of being firm in the cause of religion; so the wiser sort were deeply impressed with the feeling that he had been to his father as a guard and shield against the machinations of conspirators—a mischief for which our age has hardly found a remedy. . . .

"In body, he was strong and erect, of middle height, his limbs gracefully put together, his gait kinglike, his face long and somewhat lean, his habit rather full, his countenance composed, and the motion of his eyes rather sedate than powerful. His forehead bore marks of severity, his mouth had a touch of pride. And yet when one penetrated beyond those outworks, and soothed him with due attention and seasonable discourse, one found him gentle and easy to deal with; so that he seemed quite another man in conversation than his aspect promised; and altogether he was one who might easily get himself a reputation at variance with his manners.

"He was fond of antiquity and arts; and a favourer of learning, though rather in the honour he paid it than the time he spent upon it. In his morals there was nothing more to be praised than that in every kind of duty he seemed to be well trained and comformable. He was a wonderfully obedient son to the King his father, very attentive also to the Queen, kind to his brother; but his sister he especially loved; whom he also resembled in countenance, as far as a man's face can be compared to that of a very beautiful girl.

"The masters and tutors of his youth also, which rarely happens, continued in great favour with him. . . . His passions were not over vehement, and rather equable than great. For of love matters there was wonderfully little talk, considering his age; insomuch that he passed that extremely slippery time of his early manhood, in so great a fortune and in very good health, without being particularly noted for any affairs of that kind. . . .

"In understanding he was certainly strong, and did not want either curiosity or capacity. But in speech he was somewhat slow, and as it were embarrassed; and yet if you observed diligently the things he said, whether in asking questions or expressing opinions, they were ever to the point, and argued no ordinary capacity; so that his slow and seldom speaking seemed to come rather from suspense and solicitude than weakness or dullness of judgement. In the meantime he was a wonderfully patient listener. . . . He seldom let his thoughts wander or his mind lose its power of attention . . . a habit which promised great wisdom in him if he had lived. Many points there were indeed in this prince's nature which were obscure, and could not be discovered by any man's judgement, but only by time, which was not allowed him. Those however which appeared were excellent; which is enough for fame. . . ."

If the Prince of Wales had lived, he would have been nineteen the following February. The state funeral took place on December 7th, and neither the King nor the Queen attended. The King was said to be unable to bear such a tragic ceremony, the Queen herself was ill, and the Princess Elizabeth was heartbroken. Princes Charles, Duke of York, was the chief mourner, with the Elector Palatine. Henry Prince of Wales was buried beside his grandmother Mary Queen of Scots in King Henry VII's chapel in Westminster Abbey.

Court and national mourning was necessarily brief, not only because of the state of the Exchequer and the enforced delay of the royal wedding, but possibly also to put a stop to the inevitable rumour that the loved prince had been poisoned. Jesuits under the bed escaped the usual blame, and the more malicious whispers were that the King, jealous of his heir and to please his favourite Rochester, had given orders that a fatal dose should be administered to the patient. Fortunately few believed this.

Preparations were made for the marriage to take place on St Valentine's Day, 1613, in the Chapel Royal at Whitehall, and the magnificence of the occasion succeeded in eclipsing the unhappy event of the preceding year. John Chamberlain, describing the scene, wrote that, "The bridegroom and bride were both in a suit of cloth of silver . . . and the bride was married in her hair, that hung down long, with an exceeding rich coronet on her head, which the king valued the next day at a million crowns." He also observed that "this extreme cost and riches makes us all poor."

Masques were staged by the gentlemen of the Middle Temple and Lincoln's Inn, and another the following evening by those of the Inner Temple and Gray's Inn, "whereof," said John Chamberlain, "Sir Francis Bacon was the chief contriver. . . . They made choice to come by water from Winchester Place, in Southwark, which suited well with their device, which was the marriage of the river Thames to the Rhine; and their show by water was very gallant, by reason of infinite store of lights, very curiously set and placed, and many boats and barges, with devices of lights and lamps . . . which passage by water cost them better than three hundred pounds." Unfortunately, when the masquers landed at the Privy Stairs, there seems to have been standing room only for the spectators, and the ladies of the Court could see nothing at all. As for his Majesty, he fell asleep! The whole performance, at the earnest entreaty of Sir Francis Bacon, had to be enacted once again upon the Saturday. It was much applauded, and the masquers were all invited by the King to a supper in the marriage-room the following night.

The festivities continued throughout the month, and by March a sum of £50,000 had been spent. His Majesty began to lose heart, and ordered some of his son-in-law's retinue back to the Palatinate. Bride and bridegroom were due to sail in March, but the journey was postponed, there not being seamen enough to man his Majesty's ships. Finally, on April 14th, two months after the wedding, the Elector Palatine and his bride the Princess Elizabeth sailed from Rochester.

His Majesty's Solicitor-General could now turn his attention once more to legal business, to the Crown finances, and, more important still, to the necessity of recalling Parliament to deal with the matter. First, though, something must be said about his collection of essays that had appeared in December of the year before, with its dedication to his brother-in-law, which runs thus,

"My last essays I dedicated to my dear brother Master Anthony Bacon, who is with God. Looking amongst my papers this vacation, I found others of the same nature; which if I myself shall not suffer to be lost, it seemeth the world will not, by the often printing of the former. Missing my brother, I found you next; in respect of bond of near alliance, and of straight friendship and society, and particularly of communication in studies. Wherein I must acknowledge myself beholding to you. For as my business found rest in my contemplations; so my contemplations ever found rest in your loving conference and judgement. So wishing you all good, I remain,

"Your loving brother and friend,
"Fra. Bacon."

Of the original ten essays—now increased to thirty-eight—one was omitted, that on *Honour and Reputation*. Many of them show Francis in astute and perceptive mood, though possibly they do not have the all-embracing wisdom and compassion of the last edition, published in 1625 and with the number of essays increased to fifty-eight, which contains phrases quoted and requoted through the centuries down to our own time. We have already seen something of *Of Marriage and Single Life*, which may have had a bearing on his own experience, its opening sentence—"He that hath wife and children hath given hostages to fortune; for they are impediments to great enterprises, either of virtue or mischief. Certainly, the best works, and of greatest merit for the public, have proceeded from the unmarried or childless men" —suggesting that a lack of sons and daughters did not greatly concern him. Indeed, in *Of Parents and Children* one is inclined to suspect that fatherhood had never been one of his ambitions, or had been put aside from his thoughts after his marriage to Alice Barnham. "The joys of parents are secret, and so are their griefs and fears; they cannot utter the one, nor they will not utter the other. Children sweeten labours, but they make misfortunes more bitter. . . . The perpetuity by generation is common to beasts; but memory, merit and noble works are proper to men."

Perhaps some of the most astute sayings are to be found in the essay *Of Wisdom for a Man's Self*: "Wisdom for a man's self is, in many branches thereof, a depraved thing: it is the wisdom of rats, that will be sure to leave a house, somewhat before it fall: it is the wisdom of the fox, that thrusts out the badger who digged and made room for him; it is the wisdom of crocodiles, that shed tears when they would devour. . . . And whereas they have all their time sacrificed to themselves, they become in the end themselves sacrifices to the inconstancy of fortune, whose wings they thought by their self-wisdom to have pinioned."

Chapter IX

It was now midsummer, and the commissioners who had been appointed over twelve months earlier to consider the Crown revenue presented their findings to the Chancellor of the Exchequer, Sir Julius Caesar, who drafted a full report. The Crown was in debt to the tune of £500,000 and there was an annual deficiency of £160,000. Somehow the money must be raised, but there was still no attempt by his Majesty to recall Parliament. There was still no Secretary of State at the head of affairs, and no Lord Treasurer; the Council carried on as best it could.

Francis, who had never been a strong supporter of the great contract between King and Parliament that had come under so much discussion during the last session, made lengthy notes about this time on what he believed to be the reasons why Parliament should be recalled; he was anxious that when the Commons did eventually meet they should not go over the same old ground as they had done before, which was apt to divide members into factions, the King's supporters versus the others. This he felt to be dangerous, both for the monarchy and for Parliament. It was not safe, he thought, to combine and make parties in the House, but that men "must be left to their consciences and free votes."

When he had completed his notes, he wrote a private letter to his Majesty, giving his opinion that many of the old grievances brought up in the last Parliament were now "dead and flat, and that there had been no new matter either to rub up or revive the old or to give other cause of discontent"; he thought "the case much amended to your Majesty's advantage." The opposition to the King's business was weaker, and he advised the monarch to take a rather different line with Members in future. "That your Majesty do for this [next] Parliament put off the person of a merchant and contractor, and rest upon the person of a King. . . . Until your Majesty have tuned your instrument you will have no harmony. I, for my part, think it a thing inestimable to your Majesty's safety and service, that you once part with your Parliament with love and reverence. . . ."

He suggested "that this Parliament may be a little reduced to the more ancient form, which was to voice the Parliament to be for some other business of state, and not merely for money . . . that the people may have somewhat else to talk of and not wholly of the King's estate . . . And therefore I could wish it were given out that there are means found in his Majesty's estate to help himself, which I partly think is true."

Once again, however, the question of the Crown finances and the recalling of Parliament was postponed, and we have no record of whether his Majesty did or did not reply to the letter from his Solicitor-General. King James was preoccupied with the future of his favourite Robert Carr, Earl of Rochester, who had fallen in love with the young Countess of Essex. The King, hoping to please Rochester, now a member of the Privy Council and possessing more power with his royal master than anyone else, was anxious that a divorce should be arranged as soon as possible between the countess and her husband the Earl of Essex, so that she could marry the favourite.

Robert, 3rd Earl of Essex, had been a boy of fourteen when he married Frances Howard, aged thirteen, daughter of the Earl of Suffolk, in January of 1606, the same year that Francis Bacon had married Alice Barnham. The marriage seemed doomed to failure from the start. The earl went abroad to finish his education and did not return for three years, during which time his bride amused herself at Court—not distinguished for its moral tone under the reigning monarch. Being a scheming young woman, encouraged also by her powerful Howard kinsmen, she had caught the eye of the reigning favourite with considerable success. She based her desire for a dissolution of her marriage on the plea that it had never been consummated, owing to inability on the part of her husband.

One of her strongest supporters was her great-uncle Lord Harry Howard, Earl of Northampton, who foresaw power for himself and the family once the divorce was arranged and his great-niece married to Rochester. An opponent of the divorce was the favourite's own close friend and adviser Sir Thomas Overbury, who feared that if the marriage took place the country would be virtually governed by the Howards, who would become the most powerful faction in the kingdom, Rochester himself having a very limited knowledge or understanding of state affairs. The upshot was that Overbury fell out with the favourite and was clapped into the Tower in April 1613, fell sick rather mysteriously during the summer, and died on September 14th.

A few weeks later the marriage between the Earl of Essex and his countess was dissolved and "pronounced a nullity by the Bishop of Winchester." All was apparently set fair for the countess to wed Rochester. The sequel was to prove disastrous, as we shall see.

Francis Bacon had, fortunately for him, not become involved in the divorce proceedings. He was concerned in matters more important for his own future. The Chief Justice of the King's Bench, Sir Thomas Fleming, had died in August, which meant a re-shuffle for position amongst the judges, and the possibility that the Attorney-General, Sir Henry Hobart—recovered from his illness of the year before—would be promoted and would thus leave his position vacant.

This time a letter to the King bore fruit. "I have served your Majesty above a prenticehood, full seven years and more, as your solicitor, which is, I think, one of the painfullest places in your kingdom, specially as my employments have been; and God hath brought mine own years to fifty-two, which I think is older than ever any solicitor continued unpreferred. . . . He also suggested that his old rival, Sir Edward Coke, should be made Chief Justice of England, and Sir Henry Hobart step into Coke's shoes as Chief Justice of the Common Pleas. Coke, it seems, was furious when the re-shuffle duly took place.

"This is all your doing," he said to Francis, after the event; "it is you that have made this great stir."

"Your Lordship," replied Francis, "all this while hath grown in breadth; you must needs now grow in height, or you will be a monster." The quip was hardly likely to improve their continued bitter relations.

The promotions took place on October 27th, and Francis Bacon became Attorney-General the same day. Fifty-two years of age, as he had told his Majesty, and exactly nineteen and a half years ago, at thirty-three, he had seen that post he so much coveted go to Edward Coke, now Chief Justice of England. A somewhat wry satisfaction, on reflection, that he had suggested his rival's promotion, yet gratifying, nevertheless; as for himself, he had turned the second corner of the winding stair to great place. "A full heart is like a full pen," he wrote to the sovereign; "it can hardly make any distinguished work. . . . This is my hope, that God who hath moved your heart to favour me will write your service in my heart."

But, just as in 1607 on becoming Solicitor-General he had noted in his private memoranda "upon amendment of my fortune disposition to melancholy and distaste . . . strangeness, clouds, etc," so now, early in November 1613, on rising to the place of Attorney-General, he succumbed to a fit of the stone that lasted a fortnight. Hardly a propitious start to his new career, but an interesting sidelight to his personality which now, in middle age, showed a greater resemblance to his brother Anthony's than it had done when he was younger; the same tendency to nerves, one might almost say to panic, when brought face to face with reality and his own future. Yet he gave no sign of this in the House of Commons.

It could be that his "fit of the stone" was due to quite another cause, for on November 25th John Chamberlain, writing to his crony Carleton, said, "The last week, a proper young fellow that served Sir Francis Bacon was arraigned at the King's Bench for killing a Scot [in a duel]; and being found guilty of manslaughter, was burnt in the hand. The matter was eagerly pursued and brought out of the country to be tried here, for fear of partiality, and had a very sufficient and extraordinary jury. Yet all are not satisfied that they found so much, the fellow being assaulted by two, the one before and the other behind, and being dangerously hurt at least in four places." No names are given, but such a circumstance could only have been at best embarrassing to the new Attorney-General, and a fit of the stone may have seemed politic. Subsequently Francis, in his new capacity, wrote *A Proposition for the Repressing of Singular Combats or Duels*, which had the full approval of the King.

Christmas, however, was approaching, and the wedding of the favourite Rochester, who had been created Earl of Somerset in honour of the occasion, was fixed for December 26th. It was ironic that the service took place in the private chapel at Whitehall where the bride had become Countess of Essex in 1606, and that it was conducted by the same prelate, the Bishop of Bath and Wells. Sensitivity was oddly lacking, more especially in that the bride wore her hair flowing loose upon her shoulders, the traditional symbol of virginity. The only difference was that she was not this time given away by his Majesty— who, however, paid for the whole ceremony—but by her father the Earl of Suffolk.

The traditional masques and festivities were held on the wedding night and into the new year, while the usual newsvendor, John Chamberlain, had this to say, writing on December 23rd, "Sir Francis Bacon prepares a masque to honour this marriage, which will stand him in above £2,000. And though he have been offered some help by the House, and especially by Mr Solicitor, Sir Henry Yelverton [the new Solicitor-General], who would have sent him £500, yet he would not accept it, but offers them the whole charge with the honour. Marry his obligations are such, as well to his Majesty as to the great lord and to the whole house of Howards, as he can admit no partner.

His house at Gorhambury has gone, some say to the Earl of Somerset, others to the Earl of Suffolk."

Francis had obligations to the sovereign for promoting him to the Attorney-ship, but why he should be equally obliged to the favourite, and to the house of Howard, is not clear. As to the house at Gorhambury going to anyone, this was idle rumour, typical of the gossip of the day.

"But his bounty is no whit abated," Chamberlain continued, "for he feasts the whole university of Cambridge this Christmas, and hath warrants to his friends and acquaintances far and near to furnish him with venison to bestow on the colleges. He carries a great port in his train, as well as in his apparel and otherwise, and lives at a great charge, and yet he pretends he takes no fees, nor intermeddles in mercenary causes, but wholly applies himself to the King's affairs."

The Masque of Flowers, presented by the young gentlemen of Gray's Inn, was performed on Twelfth Night, and later printed with a dedication to Sir Francis Bacon, "the principal and in effect the only person that did both encourage and warrant the gentlemen to show their good affection towards so noble a conjunction in a time of such magnificence."

The fit of the stone had been overcome, and it is to be hoped that a surplus of venison did not play havoc with the digestion, necessitating rhubarb. Chamberlain's gossip, of course, was generally tinged with malice and gross exaggeration, but it is very likely he was telling the truth when he wrote, "He carries a great port in his train, as well as in his apparel and otherwise," for certainly the retinue of servants, secretaries, personal attendants, call them what you will, was rapidly increasing, and would continue to increase from this time onward.

Presumably they were not all housed at Gorhambury, for in his new capacity as Attorney-General he would be spending more time in London, and the lodgings at Gray's Inn would hardly accommodate them either. The elusively named "Bath House," which would appear to be the residence in the Strand that became known as Arundel Palace, must surely have continued to be the headquarters of the Attorney-General at this period. The young Earl of Arundel, now twenty-seven, was a scholar and a great lover of art, frequently abroad in Italy, and being head of the Howard family he was a cousin to the new Countess of Somerset and her father the Earl of Suffolk. While he was abroad the earl left the care of his estates in the hands of his relative, and if Francis Bacon had the tenancy of Bath House or Arundel Palace, herein would be an explanation of why John Chamberlain wrote "that he had obligations to the whole house of Howard." The building was, according to Stow, "one of the finest and most commodious of any in London, from its great number of apartments on the same floor: but the prints lately given of it prove that the buildings, notwithstanding they covered a great extent of ground, were both low and mean: the views from the extensive gardens, up and down the river, were remarkably fine."

Possibly Francis Bacon, his lady, and a number of their attendants were lodged in part of the property, which, from Hollar's engraving dated 1604, certainly seems to have been divided up into separate dwellings, and could perhaps be described as "low and mean," though to the modern eye picturesque.

All the great houses were in the Strand, with grounds descending to the river, and anyone who lived there, whether as tenant or as owner, would feel obliged to keep up a certain standard or he would lose face with his neighbours. Francis himself had been born in York House, closer to Whitehall, and had never forgotten the splendour of his boyhood days when his father was Lord Keeper of the Great Seal. To live in style came naturally to him, especially after the years of borrowing from his brother and his friends as a young lawyer in Gray's Inn. One of these very good friends, Sir Michael Hicks, was no longer available to tender helpful advice; he had died "of a burning ague" four months after the Earl of Salisbury in the summer of 1612.

So, with the Christmas and new year festivities over, combined with the celebration of the birth of their Majesties' first grandchild and the first child of the Elector and Electress Palatine, Sir Francis Bacon, Attorney-General, could sit down and pen a letter to the sovereign jogging the royal memory that "time runneth." He would before long summon Parliament, and Francis humbly prayed his Majesty once again "not to buy and sell this Parliament, but to perform the part of a King, and not of a merchant or contractor. . . . If your Majesty had heard and seen the thunder of the bells and the lightning of the bonfires for your grandchild, you would say there is little cause to doubt the affections of the people of England *in puris naturalibus.* God preserve your Majesty."

Meanwhile, he must make his second speech as Attorney-General before the Star Chamber at the last sitting in Hilary Term, his first having been five days previously, on the suppression of duels. Now, on January 31st, it was not a question of persons being charged with fighting each other. The prisoner was one William Talbot, a member of the Irish Parliament, a Catholic, who had refused to take the oath of allegiance to one whom he termed a "heretical" king. He had been confined in the Tower for several months in consequence, and was now to hear formal sentence pronounced against him. "I brought before you at the last sitting of this term the cause of duels," the Attorney-General told his Lordships, "but now this last sitting I shall bring before you a cause concerning the greatest duel which is in the Christian world, the duel and conflict between the lawful authority of sovereign kings, which is God's ordinance for the comfort of human society, and the swelling pride and usurpation of the See of Rome . . . tending altogether to anarchy and confusion."

He continued with a blistering attack not against the prisoner Talbot, who was not accused of personal disloyalty, but upon Papal power that could cause disruption amongst his Majesty's Catholic subjects so that they grew bewildered as to where their true obedience lay. "The allegiance of his subjects is pinned upon the Pope's acts. And certainly, 'tis time to stop the current of this opinion of acknowledgement of the Pope's power *in temporalibus,* or else it will sap and supplant the King's seat. . . . As for the point of matter of faith . . . is nothing exempted from it? If a man should ask Mr Talbot whether he do condemn murder, or adultery, or rape, or the doctrine of Mahomet . . . must the answer be . . . that therein he will submit himself to what the Church shall determine?"

He concluded with some gracious words towards the prisoner himself. "I know my Lords out of their accustomed favour will admit you not only to your defence concerning that that hath been charged, but to extenuate your fault by any submission that now God shall put into your mind to make."

In the event, William Talbot was released and returned to Ireland, nor does it seem that he paid the fine of £10,000 imposed upon him.

Meanwhile Parliament had at last been summoned for April 5th, and, as Chamberlain wrote on March 3rd, "Here is much jostling for places in Parliament," which for once was without exaggeration, for when the elected members assembled two-thirds had never served in Parliament before. This boded ill for the traditional style of Parliament that Francis had hoped to see restored, for the country and the sovereign's sake. He himself had been returned for three seats, St Albans, Ipswich and Cambridge university—the venison had brought its reward—but he very nearly sat for none of them, as questions were raised as to whether an Attorney-General should hold a seat in the Commons, a state of affairs for which there was no precedent. A committee was formed, the matter was discussed, and finally it was agreed that the Attorney-General should be permitted to attend. He took his place as member for the university, but it was an embarrassing start to the new session, with so many new faces, and the usual air of decorum noticeably absent. A further misfortune, so Francis felt, and some others too, was that his Majesty had at last chosen a new Secretary of State to replace the Earl of Salisbury, in the person of Sir Ralph Winwood, who, although he had been a minister in both France and Holland, had no experience of Parliament or government, and little grace of personality.

However, it was not the fault of the new Secretary of State that the session, known later as the Addled Parliament, was disastrous from start to finish. Dissent was rife amongst the members and no one could agree about anything. A motion for supply—for which the Attorney-General made an excellent but moderate speech, suggesting that the question should be put to a committee of the whole House— was deferred; Sir Henry Neville's faction, called the Undertakers, were accused of desiring to undermine the authority of Parliament by ingratiating themselves with the sovereign; the Upper House refused to confer with the Lower House; the Speaker fell sick, and small wonder; finally his Majesty himself, who had shown considerable patience up to the present, announced his intention of dissolving Parliament unless they proceeded at once to discuss the question of supply.

The faithful Commons, shocked and concerned, still failed to agree, and Parliament was dissolved on June 7th. The Attorney-General, who had advised the monarch the year before in his private letter to "part with his Parliament in love and reverence," saw his worst fears realised. Sovereign and Commons could hardly have been on less agreeable terms.

The Archbishop of Canterbury, all credit to him, then stepped into the breach with a suggestion that every bishop in the country should "send unto the King the best piece of plate he had," and doubtless the humbler sort of clergy would follow suit, as well as judges, aldermen and persons of note throughout the land. Which indeed some of them did, though not to any great extent, and the generosity of these private individuals hardly helped the Exchequer. The money was paid into the Jewel House at the Tower, and whether it then passed into the royal purse we are not told; but the Earl of Northampton, who had been caretaker of the Treasury since Salisbury died, suddenly died himself of a swelling in his thigh which had turned "venomous," and the King at once promoted the Earl of Suffolk in his stead. Suffolk's son-in-law Somerset became Lord Chamberlain, and there was a re-shuffle later amongst two other ministers, Sir Fulke Greville, poet and friend of Francis Bacon, becoming Chancellor of the Exchequer in place of Sir Julius Caesar, who was now Master of the Rolls.

75

Parliament dissolved, there was no immediate business for the Attorney-General, but a quotation from a speech he was preparing on deer-stealing in the forest of Gillingham gives a brief, rather typical indication of how a man in his position felt on such a subject in the year 1614. "Forests, parks, and chases, they are a noble portion of the King's prerogative: they are the verdure of the King, they are the first marks of honour and nobility, and the ornament of a flourishing kingdom. . . . It is a sport proper to the nobility and men of better rank; and it is to keep a difference between the gentry and the common sort; and so I hold this fault [of poaching] not vulgar. [These forests] are an excellent remedy against surcharge of people and too many inhabitants, that the land through it grow not to sluttery, etc. And these green spots of the King are an excellent ornament to the beauty of the realm."

No sluttery, we may safely assume, at Gorhambury, where Francis Bacon could relax in the company of his lady and his closer friends— though Tobie Matthew was still absent in Italy. No persons, either, of the common sort at Apethorpe, Sir Anthony Mildmay's house, where that August his Majesty was entertained, and introduced to an exquisite young man of twenty-two named George Villiers, younger son of Sir George Villiers of Brooksby. He was no horseman, but he fenced and danced well, and his manners were modest and delightful. His Majesty was charmed.

The sun was about to sink below the horizon for Robert Carr, Earl of Somerset.

Chapter X

While the usual masques took place on Twelfth Night 1615, and young George Villiers hovered around at Court, hoping to catch the eye of his Majesty—who soon removed himself to hunt at Royston—Francis Bacon found himself engaged in preparing two cases of prosecution for treason, to be brought against Edmund Peacham, a minister of the church, who held the living of Hinton St George in Somerset, and Oliver St John, a gentleman from Marlborough. Edmund Peacham had not only made certain charges against the Bishop of Bath and Wells, but had written a pamphlet, intended for the press, containing accusations against the patron who had presented him with the living—a grandson of Sir Amias Paulet, the ex-ambassador in whose service Francis had travelled as a young man—and reviling the King and the royal family into the bargain. His papers had been seized, and he had been committed to the Tower.

Oliver St John's fault was equally serious. Furious at the action of those loyal gentlemen the preceding autumn who had sent gifts to bolster up the King's finances, he wrote a public letter to the Mayor of Marlborough soundly denouncing them, and accusing his Majesty of violating his oath to the people. In consequence he too found himself in the Tower.

Sedition and treason were synonymous in his Majesty's eyes. His Attorney-General knew this, and had every sympathy with the sovereign. He was particularly concerned also that his old friends the Paulet family should have been dragged into the Peacham affair. On January 21st the Attorney-General, with the Secretary of State, the Master of the Rolls and other officials of the Council, went to the Tower to question Peacham, and, as was the custom of the day, the unfortunate minister of Hinton St George was "put to the torture." He denied all the allegations, and Francis wrote to the King, "It grieveth me exceedingly that your Majesty should be so much troubled with this matter of Peacham, whose raging devil seemeth to be turned into a dumb

77

devil. But although we are driven to make our way through questions, yet I hope well the end will be good."

The end was some way off, for the case was not straightforward. The Council had, it seemed, acted prematurely in questioning the prisoner without consulting the judges, and the judges were not agreed that the accusation to be brought against the prisoner should be that of treason. Francis, as Attorney-General, was obliged to consult in private with Lord Chief Justice Sir Edward Coke, and report back to the King.

It was inevitable, perhaps, that the mutual dislike and mistrust between the two men should colour every discussion they ever held. The interview could hardly be called a success. The Attorney-General insisted that Peacham should be indicted for treason, while the Lord Chief Justice took copious notes and would not commit himself, saying he would deliver his opinion in writing. When he did, the gist of his opinion was "that no words of scandal or defamation, importing that the King was utterly unworthy to govern, were treason, except they disabled his title."

There were some weeks of delay, and on March 10th Peacham was examined once more. This time he went so far as to deny that the seditious papers had been written by him at all, and maintained that they were by quite another man who bore the same name, had stayed with him some years past, and must have left his papers lying about the house! Francis, reporting to his Majesty, wrote, "This miscreant wretch goeth back from all, and denieth his hand and all . . . but this denial of his hand, being not possible to be counterfeited, and to be sworn by Adams [a witness] and so oft by himself formally confessed and admitted, could not mend his case before any jury in the world; but rather aggravateth to it by his notorious impudency and falsehood, and will make him more odious." The hearing of the case was postponed until the Somerset assizes the following August, in which the Attorney-General had no part. Peacham was condemned for high treason but not hanged, and died in Taunton prison seven months later.

The second case of treason, that of Mr St John of Marlborough who had protested against gifts of money being sent to the King, came up for hearing in the Star Chamber at the end of April. The Attorney-General delivered a speech in forceful style, accusing the prisoner of seditious libel, "a wicked and seditious slander, or (if I shall use the Scripture phrase) a blaspheming of the King himself; setting him forth for a prince perjured in the great and solemn oath of his coronation, which is as it were the knot of the diadem; a prince that should be a violator and infringer of the liberties, laws, and customs of the kingdom; a mark for an Henry the Fourth; a match for a Richard the Second. . . ."

The Star Chamber passed a sentence of life imprisonment and a fine of £5,000. Two months later Oliver St John made a full acknowledgement of his fault, and some time afterwards was released from the Tower.

Yet a third indictment of high treason was heard in the King's Bench on May 17th against one John Owen, a recusant (a Catholic who refused to attend the Church of England or admit the King's sovereignty), at whose trial the Attorney-General also spoke very earnestly, the case being similar to that against William Talbot, indicted for the same reason early in January. Owen was condemned, but like the others never hanged, and released after three years on condition he left the country.

Term ended, and Francis Bacon was able to relax once more at Gorhambury, relieved doubtless that the prosecutions for treason had been disposed of without great difficulty and his Majesty spared much trouble and annoyance. He could not foresee that a case far more serious than any of those tried hitherto, implicating the King to a highly embarrassing extent, would engage the attention of the whole country by the autumn.

The trouble started with a rumour, which, spreading during the late summer, came to the ears of the Secretary of State, Sir Ralph Winwood. This rumour was to the effect that Sir Thomas Overbury, the one-time close friend of the Earl of Somerset who had been imprisoned in the Tower two years previously and had died rather suddenly on September 15th 1613, had not died from natural causes, as had been supposed, but by poison administered to him by persons within the Tower.

Sir Ralph Winwood made immediate enquiries of the Lieutenant of the Tower, Sir Gervase Elwes, who at first hedged, saying there had been some intention of the part of the under-keeper Richard Weston to poison the prisoner, but this he had discovered and prevented. Ordered to write a full account of this, Sir Gervase then admitted that he had since heard that the prisoner Overbury had indeed been poisoned, by an enema impregnated with arsenic supplied by an apothecary's boy, and he, Elwes, had kept the information to himself for fear of impeaching certain "great persons." These great persons were, it seemed the Earl and Countess of Somerset.

The rumour was no longer a rumour, and could not be suppressed.

79

The Secretary of State informed his Majesty, who ordered a full enquiry, and the whole affair was put into the hands of that highest justice in the land, Sir Edward Coke.

Whether indeed the King would have ordered such an enquiry in 1613, when Overbury died, seems extremely doubtful. The Earl of Somerset was then in high favour, and about to marry the Countess of Essex. The relationship between monarch and favourite had changed since the marriage. Somerset had become overbearing and difficult, and the engaging young George Villiers, promoted to be a gentleman of the bedchamber, was greatly liked not only by the King but by Queen Anne as well, who had always been on bad terms with Somerset. Thus what might have been disastrous for King James in 1613, had the truth of the murder become public knowledge, was now, in 1615, more in the nature of an acute embarrassment. He could only hope that Chief Justice Coke would handle the matter with discretion, and that the minor persons involved in the murder would be arrested, tried and punished, and there would be an end of the whole sorry business.

It was not to be. The commission of enquiry, set up by Coke, found that there had been several attempts to poison Sir Thomas Overbury, before the fatal enema of arsenic, and that these had come from the kitchens within the Tower, supplied by a certain Mrs Turner, known personally to the Countess of Somerset.

Mrs Turner was arrested. So were Richard Weston and the Lieutenant of the Tower, Sir Gervase Elwes. At this point the Earl of Somerset lost his nerve and implicated himself by sending a constable to Mrs Turner's house to seize her papers, with the intention of destroying them. On learning of this deliberate defiance of the law, the commission of enquiry committed the earl to custody.

There was small hope of hushing things up now, and Chief Justice Coke was intent upon bringing down the haughty earl and his countess (who, incidentally, was now pregnant), besides the smaller fry who were actually indicted for complicity in the murder.

These minor persons were tried and disposed of first. They had all confessed: Weston, the under-keeper, had administered the poison; Mrs Turner had sent it; the apothecary had supplied it to Mrs Turner; the Lieutenant of the Tower, Sir Gervase Elwes, had connived at the administration. They were all hanged at the beginning of November.

So far his Majesty's Attorney-General, Sir Francis Bacon, had taken no part in the proceedings; Lord Chief Justice Coke had been in charge. Francis first became involved after the execution of the keeper Weston, when two friends of the Earl of Somerset were arrested for unlawfully questioning the wretched man on the scaffold and endeavouring to wring a final confession from him. This was an unprecedented offence, and the two allies, Sir John Wentworth and Sir John Hollis, appeared in the Star Chamber and were charged by the Attorney-General with obstructing justice. "Of the offence of these two gentlemen in general, your lordships must give me leave to say, that it was an offence greater and more dangerous than is conceived. I know well that as we have no Spanish inquisitions, nor justice in a corner, so we have no gagging of men's mouths at their death; but that they may speak freely at the last hour. But then it must come from the free motion of the party, and not by temptations of questions. The questions that are to be asked ought to tend to further revealing of their own or others' guiltiness. But to use a question in the nature of a false interrogatory, to falsify that which is *res judicata* [a case already decided] is intolerable."

Wentworth and Hollis received a sentence from the Star Chamber but were later pardoned, and it was not until after the new year, in January 1616, that Francis had an interview with his Majesty to give him his own frank opinion of the evidence that had so far been brought implicating the Earl of Somerset in the affair of the poisoning. The earl meanwhile had been relieved of his seals of office and committed to the Tower, while his countess had given birth to a daughter on December 9th.

"I said to your Majesty," Francis wrote on January 22nd, "that which I do now repeat, that the evidence upon which my Lord of Somerset standeth indicted is of a good strong thread, considering impoisoning is the darkest of offences; but that the thread must be well spun and woven together. For your Majesty knoweth that it is one thing to deal with a jury of Middlesex and Londoners, and another to deal with the peers; whose objects perhaps will not be so much what is before them in the present case, which I think is as odious to them as to the vulgar, but what may be hereafter. . . .

"Two things . . . I do in all humbleness renew. First, that your Majesty will be careful to choose a steward of judgement, that may be able to moderate the evidence and cut off digressions; for I may interrupt, but I cannot silence. The other, that there may be special care taken for the ordering of the evidence, not only for the knitting, but for the list, and—to use your Majesty's own word—the confining of it. This to do, if your Majesty vouchsafe to direct it yourself, that is the best; if not, I humbly pray you to require my Lord Chancellor, that he together with my Lord Chief Justice will confer with myself, and my fellows, that shall be used, for the marshalling and bounding of the evidence, that we may have the help of his opinion, as well as that of my Lord Chief Justice; whose great travels as I much commend, yet that same *plerophoria*, or over-confidence, doth always subject things to a great deal of chance."

Francis knew very well that Lord Chief Justice Coke's "plerophoria" in the past had led to many extraneous matters being brought up for heated discussion and argument in the trials of great persons—his personal animosity to Sir Walter Ralegh at Winchester had been one, while (dating back to when he had held the post of Attorney-General) his vituperation of the 2nd Earl of Essex had scandalised not only those present in Westminster Hall but the ordinary people. If the Earl of Somerset was indeed guilty of being accessory to the crime of poisoning Sir Thomas Overbury, then the crime must be proved when his case came up for trial; the Attorney-General would do his duty as prosecutor accordingly, but he would not be a party to any vilification of the accused's character or relationship with others which might lead to defamation of his Majesty and indeed the Crown.

The trial, which had been appointed for hearing at the end of January or early February, was suddenly postponed by Lord Chief Justice Coke, who announced that he had received fresh evidence in a confidential dispatch from Spain which must first be sifted, and persons questioned. He hinted, at the same time, that this evidence might involve the Earl of Somerset in the graver charge of treason.

High treason could hardly be termed a "digression." The ambassador to Spain who had sent the dispatch, Sir John Digby, was sent for, and arrived post-haste in London with all particulars. It was the Attorney-General's duty to examine the two people mentioned by the ambassador as being concerned: one, Sir Robert Cotton, had been employed by the Earl of Somerset at the Spanish court; the other, Sir William Monson, was a pensioner of Spain.

Francis kept the King fully informed of the examiniations, and of everything that was taking place relating to the forthcoming trial, but a significant change in his correspondence was that, instead of immediately contacting his Majesty, he would now first get in touch with, or write to, the new favourite who had been knighted the year before, Sir George Villiers.

Francis had never been on close terms with Robert Carr, Earl of Somerset. Nor did he correspond with him; he had approached his Majesty direct. Now all was changed. George Villiers was far easier to deal with than Somerset, and Francis knew, from long observance in such matters, that the one-time favourite, whether found guilty or not

1. King James I by Mytens, 1621
(photo National Portrait Gallery, London)

2. Queen Anne by Isaac Oliver
(photo National Portrait Gallery, London)

3. Henry, Prince of Wales, by Isaac Oliver, c. 1612
(copyright reserved)

4. Princess Elizabeth, later Electress Palatine and Queen of Bohemia,
by Isaac Oliver, c. 1610 *(copyright reserved)*

guilty of the crime imputed to him, would never again possess the power he had once had with the King. Sir George Villiers was the rising star—indeed he had already risen; he not only had the ear of the King, but was encouraged in this by the Queen, who was pleased to call him her "watch-dog," and had even written little notes to him beginning "My kind Dog," and wishing him all happiness. Such a likeable young man, who made himself pleasant to everyone regardless of rank, would prove a useful ally in the months to come.

When the Lord Chancellor fell ill in February, and for a moment it was feared he might not recover, the occasion seemed opportune to thank George Villiers for having mentioned to his Majesty that if the worst should happen perhaps the Attorney-General might fill the breach:

"Sir,
"The message which I received from you by Mr Shute hath bred in me such belief and confidence, as I will now wholly rely upon your excellent and happy self. When persons of greatness and quality begin speech with me of the matter, and offer me their good offices, I can but answer them civilly. But those things are but toys. I am yours surer to you than to my own life. For, as they speak of the turquoise stone in a ring, I will break into twenty pieces, before you have the least fall. God keep you ever.
                              "Your truest servant,
                                   "Fr. Bacon.
"My Lord Chancellor is prettily amended. I was with him yesterday almost half an hour. He used me with wonderful tokens of kindness. We both wept, which I do not often."

"Those things are but toys. . . ." A favourite expression of the Attorney-General's. It was the opening line of his as yet unpublished essay *Of Masques and Triumphs,* which may well have been written at this time and put aside, it being a habit of authors to quote from their own compositions when the ink on the manuscript has barely dried.

By April Francis was in constant communication with George Villiers, reporting on the examination of those held in custody, including the Earl of Somerset, who had been examined on the eighteenth of the month.

"He is full of protestations, and would fain keep that quarter towards Spain clear: using but this for argument, that he head such fortunes from his Majesty, as he could not think of bettering his conditions from Spain, because as he said he was no military man . . . For the conclusion of your letter concerning my own comfort, I can say but the psalm of *Quid retribuam?* God that giveth me favour in his Majesty's eyes will strengthen me in his Majesty's service.

"Your true and devoted servant.

"To requite your postscript of excuse for scribbling, I pray you excuse that the paper is not gilt, I write from Westminster Hall, where we are not so fine."

A certain lightness of touch, almost of banter, perhaps, was creeping into the correspondence between the Attorney-General, now fifty-five, and young Sir George Villiers, twenty-four, who on St George's Day, April 23rd, was made a Knight of the Garter. His Majesty came up from Theobalds to town for the feasting on the evening of this great occasion, though whether the Attorney-General was present to toast the newly dubbed knight we have no means of knowing. The gossips, of course, reported the event, amidst other burning topics of the day, but omitted to mention—either because they had not heard it or because the item was without news value—that the actor-dramatist and property-owner Mr William Shakespeare had died on St George's Day at Stratford-on-Avon, where he had been living in retirement since about 1612.

On April 28th the Attorney-General wrote at some length to the King giving his opinion that it would be best if "Somerset should make a clear confession of his offence, before he be produced to his trial. . . . That confession and penitency are the footstools of mercy. . . . That the great downfall of so great persons carrieth in itself a heavy punishment, and a kind of civil death, although their lives should not be taken. All which may satisfy honour, for sparing their lives."

This was not to suggest that Francis was hoping for an acquittal— far from it; but, as he told his Majesty, it should be his care "so to moderate the manner of charging him, as it make him not odious beyond the extent of mercy." (And it is interesting to note that during his term of office as Attorney-General not one man whom he prosecuted in person lost his life in consequence. Francis Bacon had many failings, but lack of compassion for the fallen was not one of them.)

The Countess of Somerset was tried before her lord, on Friday May 24th. She had already confessed during examination, and now, pleading guilty, awaited judgement. "She won pity," noted the gossip John Chamberlain, "by her sober demeanour, which in my opinion was more curious and confident than was fit for a lady in such distress." The prisoner having pleaded guilty, there remained only for the Attorney-General to ask their lordships for judgement against her. His opening words showed his hope for clemency.

84

"It is, as I may term it, the nobleness of an offender to confess; and therefore those meaner persons, upon whom justice passed before, confessed not; she doth. I know your Lordships cannot behold her without compassion. Many things may move you, her youth, her person, her sex, her noble family; yea, her provocations, and furies about her; but chiefly her penitency and confession. But justice is the work of this day; the mercy-seat was in the inner part of the temples; the throne is public. But since this Lady hath by her confession prevented my evidence, and your verdict, and that this day's labour is eased; there resteth, in the legal proceeding, but for me to pray that her confession be recorded, and judgement thereupon."

Their Lordships gave sentence of death by hanging, but few of those present believed that it would be carried out, basing their impression "on Mr Attorney's speech"; and the countess was taken back to the Tower.

The following day the Earl of Somerset appeared at Westminster Hall on a charge of having poisoned Sir Thomas Overbury, the accusation of treason having been dropped, as no evidence had come to light in the examination of other witnesses. Since his plea was not guilty, the full weight of prosecution was in the hands of the Attorney-General. "Far be it from us," he said, "by any strains of wit, or art, to seek to play prizes, or to blazon our names in blood, or to carry the day otherwise than upon just grounds. We shall carry the lantern of justice, which is the evidence, before your eyes upright, to be able to save it from being put out with any winds of evasions or vain defences, that is our part; and within that we shall contain ourselves; not doubting at all but that this evidence in itself will carry that force as it shall need vantages or aggravations."

The proceedings lasted some eight hours, many of those present avid to hear every sordid detail down to the last night of torment endured by the murdered Sir Thomas Overbury, with some wondering if the rumours of 1612 would circulate once more, that the loved Prince of Wales had also been poisoned thus, and at the instigation of the same earl who was being tried for his life today. Or, more damning still, would the Earl, when he rose to defend himself, implicate the King and perhaps blurt out the nature of their close relationship through the years?

Those who hoped for scandal were disappointed. John Chamberlain reported to his crony Carleton, "When I wrote last I left the Earl of Somerset pleading for his life; but that he said for himself was so little, that he was found guilty by all his peers; which did so little appal him, that when he was asked what he could say why sentence should not be pronounced, he stood still on his innocence, and could hardly be brought to refer himself to the King's mercy." And another scribe, Edward Sherburn (later to join Francis Bacon's "train of attendants"), wrote, "His lordship's answers were so poor and idle as many of the lords his peers shook their heads and blushed to hear such slender excuses come from him, of whom much better was expected. The only thing worth note in him was his constancy and undaunted carriage in all the time of his arraignment, which as it began so did it continue to the end, without any change or alteration."

And at no time during his defence did the Earl of Somerset utter one word against his Majesty. Like his countess, he was condemned to death and returned to the Tower, but to the chagrin of the London crowds, who had hoped to see a scaffold erected on Tower Hill—for the earl had never been popular—his Majesty changed the sentence to life imprisonment, and in July the countess received a full pardon.

"'Tis different for them than what 't would be for us," the crowds must have said, when they heard of the gracious living permitted to the prisoners in the Tower, furniture of crimson velvet, satin-covered chairs. Baulked of the hanging spectacle, the disgruntled Londoners were obliged to wait until one of their own kind was burnt at Smithfield for killing her husband, a joiner, by flinging a chisel into his belly—a slightly cleaner method of disposal than inserting into someone an enema of arsenic.

And the Attorney-General? The part he had taken in the trial pleased his Majesty, who offered him the choice of being immediately sworn a member of the Council, or the assurance that when the position of Lord Chancellor should fall vacant he would receive the nomination. Francis Bacon chose the former, writing to Sir George Villiers on June 3rd, "The King giveth me a noble choice, and you are the man my heart ever told me you were."

Chapter XI

Some twenty years earlier, in October 1596, Francis Bacon had written a letter of advice to the favourite of the day, Robert Devereux, Earl of Essex, a very different character from George Villiers. Highly intelligent, moody, impulsive, Robert Devereux at twenty-nine epitomised the flower of English manhood during the latter part of the reign of that most astute monarch, Queen Elizabeth. Francis Bacon was only seven years his senior, a barrister with a seat in Parliament but no position in government, relying, for the advice he tendered, upon his own acute powers of observation as to how political affairs should be handled, with especial regard for the workings of her Majesty's own mind.

George Villiers, with only a brief experience of Court life and the inevitable intrigues and jealousies that hummed about it, had, at this stage of his career, no political ambition. He desired only to please, to fall out with nobody; and now that Somerset was in disgrace and was never likely to appear on the scene again, young Villiers found himself in the extraordinary position of being courted on all sides by all men, the established favourite of a very different monarch from the one who had boxed Robert Devereux's ears at the first display of temper.

He was, in fact, extremely vulnerable to anyone who might take advantage of his lack of experience, and there was plenty capable of doing just that. Francis Bacon knew that Queen Elizabeth had kept the control of affairs within her hands, and could, besides, rely on the most able of statesmen. It was otherwise with King James. He was the sovereign, yes, and very conscious of it, but he was not interested in the workings of government or the intricate nature of an English parliament, possibly because he did not fully understand the system. It was for this reason that he had allowed the Earl of Somerset and the Howard faction so much latitude in affairs of state; it was simpler to let things slide and go hunting in the country, trusting that somehow matters would be arranged and everything—including his finances—

eventually be solved. Francis Bacon knew that George Villiers possessed a far more equable and malleable temperament than Somerset, and if his Majesty, bored or irritated by some state business, should say to him, as he had said to Somerset, "You arrange it, you do as you think fit," the inexperienced young man would find himself the prey of dangerous, and rival, cabals, whose opposing advice might in time threaten the safety of the realm.

It had never been an idle fantasy, during the first years of the new reign, when Francis—still without employment fitted to his genius—had indulged in dreams of becoming governor of some university, some college of learning, where young men could be moulded and trained to understand all branches of knowledge, the better to equip themselves to serve their country. In Villiers he now saw a youth, willing, indeed eager, to learn, who had risen to high place by chance, by charm; here, Francis believed, was a student whom he could mould and advise, the thirty-two years between them no impediment, rather the reverse. George Villiers would listen, just as men had listened to the speaker in *Redargutio Philosophiarum*. As the students in Gray's Inn had listened, and as Tobie Matthew, still out in Italy, had listened. Tobie, in fact, had actually met and become friendly with George Villiers when the favourite was travelling on the continent. Robert Devereux had not needed instruction in political and world affairs; he knew as much about them as Francis Bacon himself. The warning to him had been to keep out of them, to remain a courtier, close to the Queen, and to avoid above all things popularity and a tendency to martial ardour. George Villiers, on the contrary, seemed likely to have political business thrust upon him by an indulgent monarch; if so, he must learn his trade.

In August 1616 George Villiers was created Viscount Villiers, and the Attorney-General, now a member of the Council, wrote congratulating him from Gorhambury. He also took the opportunity, about this time, to send the young man a long letter of advice concerning the future. What Villiers thought of the advice is unknown. Two versions of the same letter, widely differing, were found amongst Francis Bacon's papers and published after his death. The more concise version would seem to be the original, and one has an impression of Francis sitting in his library at Gorhambury, or perhaps in a corner of the long gallery, seeing himself as master of his old college Trinity at Cambridge, or Magdalen at Oxford, and addressing, not the heir to the throne, but the nearest thing to it, the reigning favourite.

"Remember then what your true condition is. The King himself is above the reach of his people, but cannot be above their censures; and you are his shadow, if either he commit an error and is loath to avow it, but excuses it upon his Ministers, of which you are the first in the eye: or you commit the fault, or have willingly permitted it, and must suffer for it; so perhaps you may be offered as a sacrifice to appease the multitude. . . .

"It is true that the whole kingdom hath cast their eye upon you, as the new rising star, and no man thinks his business can prosper at Court, unless he hath you for his good Angel, or at least that you be not a Malus Genius against him. This you cannot now avoid unless you will adventure a precipice, to fall down faster than you rose. Opinion is a master wheel in these cases." Francis then propounded a number of rules to be observed at those times when the favourite should be importuned by suitors: that the suitor should do so in writing, and await a reply at Villiers's convenience; that Villiers should take an hour or two to sort the petitions, and that he should not rely upon his own judgement, or that of his friends, but should take council of men well versed in their professions who were competent to give an opinion; that, having considered these opinions, he should then set aside certain hours during the week in which to frame his own reply.

Francis next considered, under various headings, the subjects that were likely to emerge for consultation in the future, about which Villiers should acquaint himself and so be able to discuss them with some assurance. Religion, negotiation with foreign princes, war by sea or land, plantations and colonies, nothing was omitted. "Touching war, the best way to continue a secure peace, is to be prepared for a war. Security is an ill guard for a kingdom. But this kingdom, where the seas are our walls, and the ships our bulwarks, where safety and plenty, by trade, are concomitant, it were both a sin and a shame to neglect the means to attain unto these ends: let brave spirits that have fitted themselves for command, either by sea or by land, not be laid by, as persons unnecessary for the time; let arms and ammunition of all sorts be provided and stored up, as against a day of battle; let the ports and forts be fitted so, as if by the next wind we should hear of an alarum; such a known providence is the surest protection. But of all wars, let both Prince and People pray against a war in our own bowels: the King by his wisdom, justice, and moderation must foresee and stop such a storm, and if it fall must allay it, and the people by their obedience must decline it. And for a foreign war intended by an invasion to enlarge the bounds for our Empire, I have no opinion . . . Seeing the subjects of this kingdom believe it is not legal for them to be enforced to go beyond the seas without their own consent. . . . But to resist an invading enemy, or to suppress rebels, the subject may and must be commanded out of the counties where they inhabit. The whole kingdom is but one entire body . . . *Dum singuli pugnamus, omnes vincimur* (while we fight alone, we are all vanquished)."

Francis Bacon's advice on trade with colonies and foreign nations is particularly fascinating to the reader of the present day. "Let the foundation of the profitable trade be thus laid that the exportation of home commodities be more in value than the importation of foreign, so we shall be sure that the stocks of the kingdom shall yearly increase, for then the balance of trade must be returned in money or bullion. . . . Let us advance the native commodities of our kingdom, and employ our countrymen before strangers: let us turn the wools of the land into cloths and stuffs of our own growth, and the hemp and flax growing here into linen cloth and cordage, it would set many thousand hands on work. . . . And of all sorts of thrift for the public good, I would above all others commend to your care the encouragement to be given to husbandry, and the improving of lands for tillage. . . . In the last place, I beseech you take into your serious consideration that Indian wealth, which this island and the seas thereof excel in, the hidden and rich treasure of fishing. . . . I may truly say to the English, go to the pismire thou sluggard. I need not expound the text; half a day's sail with a good wind will show the mineral, and the miners."

Francis went on to advise his pupil about behaviour at Court, not to interpose himself in matters proper to the officers of the household, yet to be vigilant in seeing the King was not abused. "But neither in jest nor earnest must there be countenance or ear given to flatterers or sycophants, the bane of all Courts. They are flies who will not only buzz about in every ear, but will blow and corrupt every place where they light."

He concluded by warning George Villiers: "You serve a gracious Master and a good, and there is a noble and a hopeful Prince, whom you must not disserve; adore not him as the rising sun in such a measure, as that you put a jealousy into the father, who raised you; nor out of the confidence you have in the father's affections, make not yourself suspected of the son; keep an equal and a fit distance, so you may be serviceable to both. . . . Thus may you long live a happy instrument for your King and Country; you shall not be a meteor, or a blazing star, but *stella fixa*, happy here, and more happy hereafter."

It might be thought that this letter of advice would have been work enough for the Attorney-General during his leisure hours at Gorhambury that summer of 1616; but no, his mind was ever active; nor must he give way to that fatal habit of "sleeping after dinner or at 4 o'clock." Why not set about revising the whole system of the law in England, which would not only benefit the country but, if the King agreed to the suggested amendments, would prove an added thorn in the flesh of Lord Chief Justice Coke, who had been suspended from office since June for holding certain questionable doctrines of law of which neither his Majesty nor the Council approved? This was the official reason given for the suspension. The Lord Chief Justice had also bungled in the Somerset affair, with his unsubstantiated accusation of treasonable actions on the part of the earl.

Francis's pen, or those of his scribes, was always busy, with advice to George Villiers, amendments of the law, an essay or two, some revision of the great work in progress, the *Novum Organum,* and perhaps a glance back at one of his unpublished Latin works, *A Description of the Intellectual Globe* or the *Theory of the Heaven.* Possibly it was some motion of the planets that brought about the lassitude of afternoon and not the light meal, improperly digested and followed by exercise, up through the grounds to the woods and gardens, his young attendants more exhausted than he was himself, for there was nothing that refreshed him so much as walking in his garden. "There ought to be gardens for all the months in the year. . . . In July come gillyflowers of all varieties; musk roses, the lime tree in blossom, early pears, and plums in fruit. . . . In August come plums of all sorts in fruit, apricots, pease, barberries, filberts, musk-melons, monkshoods of all colours. . . ." He was not so partial to ornamental water as he had been a few years past. "For fountains, they are a great beauty and refreshment; but pools mar all, and make the garden unwholesome, and full of flies and frogs. . . ." One can see him waving his tall hat at the buzzing insects, or fluttering his handkerchief. "The main matter is so to convey the water, as it never stay . . . that the water be never by rest discoloured, green, or red, or the like, or gather any mossiness or putrefaction. Besides that, it is to be cleansed every day by the hand: also some steps up to it, and some fine pavements about it doth well. As for the other kind of fountain, which we may call a bathing-pool, it may admit much curiosity and beauty, wherewith we will not trouble ourselves."

His young gentlemen were evidently not encouraged to splash about in the Gorhambury pools. Such pastimes bordered on sluttery. . . .

All in all, it was a pleasant long vacation, and a year he could look back upon with satisfaction. The trial of the Earl of Somerset, which might have had unfortunate implications for his Majesty, had been conducted fairly and honourably; Somerset had been removed with his life spared, his lady likewise. The new favourite Viscount Villiers promised well, and, if he heeded the advice given him, could not harm the monarch—rather the reverse—and would prove an invaluable associate. Prince Charles's boyish dislike would soon be overcome; the jet of water he had turned upon the favourite at Greenwich had been no more than a prank, although the King had boxed his ears for the offence. Charles would be invested as Prince of Wales in November, and this solemn occasion would help him to grow up.

There were various minor affairs to be dealt with during the new term, but the most important was the business of the Lord Chief Justice and his future. Lord Coke had published reports of some hundreds of cases decided in the courts of law, and in these reports he had set down as law doctrines inconsistent, so it was claimed, with the rights of the King, the church and the courts. He had been commanded to correct or withdraw all such matter as might be considered false or objectionable, and had meanwhile been suspended from his office. On October 2nd, by the King's command, Lord Chancellor Ellesmere and the Attorney-General called upon him to hear whether he now retracted these errors. Coke was summoned three times before the Council to give an explanation of his reports, and the points of dispute were then forwarded to the King.

The Attorney-General, who might have been expected to tackle his old opponent with severity, "used him with more respect than the rest," so Chamberlain reported on October 26th. "As for divers speeches he gives out in his favour—as that of a man of his learning and parts is not every day found nor so soon made as marred."

Francis had not been so mild at the preliminary hearings the previous June, when the Lord Chief Justice had first been suspended; but that he had respect for his one-time rival is evident from a paragraph which he wrote in his *Proposal for Amending the Laws of England* during the long vacation, in which he said, "Had it not been for Sir Edward Coke's Reports—which, though they may have errors, and some peremptory and extra-judicial resolutions more than are warranted, yet they contain infinite good decisions and rulings over cases —the law by this time had been almost like a ship without ballast."

Another reason for greater leniency in October may well have been that Francis had been impressed by the conduct of Coke's wife Lady Hatton, who, according to Chamberlain, had stood her husband in good stead by "soliciting at the council table, wherein she hath done herself a great deal of honour." Lady Hatton, who had been on bad terms with the Lord Chief Justice throughout their nineteen years of married life, had thus shown him some loyalty when he was in trouble.

However, it was to no avail. The King, for reasons of his own—perhaps because of the Lord Chief Justice's interference before the Somerset trial, or because he was known to have questioned the royal prerogative—was determined to replace him, and Coke was removed from his office in the third week of November. He received the news, Chamberlain reported, "with dejection and tears." Sir Henry Montague, at the Attorney-General's suggestion, was sworn in as his successor. As for Lady Hatton, her loyalty to her husband had been but temporary, and she removed herself and her belongings from his house at Stoke, while her abandoned spouse retired to his estate in Norfolk.

Both out of the way, the Attorney-General could attend to other pressing business, but first a word to Viscount Villiers, who appears to have been suffering from a chill the very same day that Chief Justice Coke was removed from office.

"My very good Lord,

"I am much troubled in mind, for that I hear you are not perfectly well, without whose health I cannot joy, and without whose life I desire not to be . . . Good my Lord, once again have care of your health; and learn what Cardanus saith, that more men die of cold after exercise than are slain in the wars. God ever keep you.

"Your Lordship's true and much devoted servant."

Sent with a present of fruit, from Gorhambury, medlars, or flowers such as hollyhocks, and "roses that come late."

Then forward to business, with a speech in the Star Chamber against duels, for a gentleman and a peer of the realm had quarrelled, the peer protesting that he had been libelled and that the gentleman was at fault. The Attorney-General made swift work of the pair of them. "The swelling tumours that arise in men's proud affections must be beaten flat with justice, or else all will end in ruin. . . . Will you have the sacrifices of men, not of bulls or oxen?" Both duellists felt the rough edge of the Attorney-General's tongue, and although the gentleman was obliged to pay a modest fine, the nobleman was warned. "God forbid the privileges of the peers should privilege them to wrong any man: yet there ought a distinction to be kept, and because he is a peer his wrong is the greater."

Next Francis Bacon turned his attention to securing a pardon from his Majesty for the last of the accused persons who had been held in the Tower at the time of the Somerset affair, Sir Thomas Monson. The Lord Chancellor was consulted, and on December 7th the Attorney-General and his Solicitor-General (Sir Henry Yelverton) submitted that "it is a case fit for your Majesty's pardon, as upon doubtful evidence, and that Sir Thomas Monson pleads the same publicly, with such protestations of his innocency as he thinks good, and so the matter may come to a regular and just period." (The pardon was, in fact, formally acknowledged by the King's Bench early in the following February.)

Just before Christmas an anonymous letter of advice to the late Lord Chief Justice Sir Edward Coke began to circulate about town, causing general interest and speculation as to the author. Some were inclined to think the writer was the Attorney-General, and certain historians since have held the same view. But the writer, who had strong Puritan sympathies and possessed views on state and political matters quite contrary to those of the Attorney-General, could not possibly have been Francis Bacon, according to his biographer Spedding. Style, language, outlook, all were different, and the supposition seems to have come about because a copy of this letter—of which there were many in circulation at the time it was printed—was found amongst Francis Bacon's papers in 1648, and appeared in a volume entitled *Remains of the Right Honourable Francis Lord Verulam.* Chamberlain, who one might think would have been among the first to pick upon Francis Bacon as the author, had this to say soon after the paper was printed: "I forgot in my last to signify all I could learn touching the author of that discourse to the Lord Coke. Some father it upon Mr Attorney, some upon Joshuah Hall or Dr Hayward, and some upon any one of those you name; but certainly we have none."

A treatise that Francis did circulate at this time was *A True Relation of a most desperate Murder,* illustrated with woodcuts of the actual murder in Lincoln's Inn and the suicide of the murderer (he hanged himself in jail before he could be brought to trial). The treatise had been written, possibly at Francis's dictation, by his lawyer friend Mr Nicholas Trott. "I have put a little pamphlet, prettily penned by one Mr Trott, that I set on work touching the whole business," the Attorney-General informed Viscount Villiers; but doubtless such matters "were but toys," for the Christmas festivities were upon them, a new honour was to descend upon the favourite, and on January 5th 1617 he was created Earl of Buckingham.

It was Twelfth Night, and a masque was given. The new earl danced with the Queen. So did an earlier favourite, who had never quite made top grade, the Earl of Montgomery. The masque was repeated towards the end of the month when the Spanish ambassador was present, and there began to be talk of a royal betrothal, that of the newly invested Prince of Wales and the Infanta of Spain. Such a match, should it come about, was hardly likely to be popular, either with the people or with the House of Commons, for the Infanta was a Catholic. His Majesty was known to favour it, while the opinion of his Council was more reserved. In any event, an alliance between the two royal houses would take time to negotiate, and his Majesty himself had a more immediate project for which preparations were already under way—his first journey into Scotland since he had been crowned King of England in 1603.

His departure was fixed for the second week in March, and while he was absent the business of the Crown and government must be carried on by the Council. Lord Ellesmere, Lord Keeper of the Great Seal and Lord Chancellor, had been ill since the new year, and was now confined to his room. He told the King he was too infirm to continue his duties, and begged to be replaced. On March 7th his Majesty, having personally visited the sick man at York House, gave the Great Seal of office as Lord Keeper to the Attorney-General, Sir Francis Bacon. That same evening the Earl of Buckingham received a letter.

"My dearest Lord,

"It is both in cares and kindness, that small ones float up to the tongue, and great ones sink down into the heart with silence. Therefore I could speak little to your Lordship today, neither had I fit time: but I must profess this much, that in this day's work you are the truest and perfectest mirror and example of firm and generous friendship that ever was in court. And I shall count every day lost, wherein I shall not either study your well doing in thought, or do your name honour in speech, or perform you service in deed. Good my Lord, account and accept me

"Your most bounden and devoted friend and servant of all men living,
"Fr. Bacon. C.S."

Queen Elizabeth's little Lord Keeper had risen to his father's place.

Chapter XII

Three days after he had become Lord Keeper of the Great Seal
Francis Bacon went to visit his old friend Lord Ellesmere, whom he
had succeeded, bearing with him a promise from the King that on his
retirement he would shortly receive an earldom and a pension of
£3,000 a year for the remainder of his life. The honour came too
late. The aged statesman, who had combined the office of Lord
Keeper with that of Lord Chancellor, could only murmur his thanks
and ask that title and pension should be inherited by his son. Francis
sat by his bedside, and assured him that his Majesty would respect his
last request. Even he did not expect that the end would come so soon,
but in less than half an hour Lord Ellesmere was dead.

He had held his office for over twenty years, and was loved and respected by all who knew him. He had been a good and dear friend
both to Francis and to his brother Anthony, and if Francis had wept
when he visited his sick bed nearly a year ago—as he had told George
Villiers in a postscript to a letter at that time—he undoubtedly did so
again now.

Lord Ellesmere died in York House, perhaps in the very bedroom
where Francis and Anthony's father Sir Nicholas Bacon had also died;
and memories of those times, of his boyhood, of his father in his robes
of state bearing the seal of office, must surely have filled Francis's
mind as he sat beside the dying man. No private memoranda, alas,
exist for the year 1617. If they did once, they have disappeared, or
been destroyed. But one thing is certain; Francis Bacon, now Lord
Keeper of the Great Seal, determined this day that he would hold his
office with the same dignity and respect as had not only his immediate
predecessor, and Lord Keeper Puckering before him, but especially
the man who had won the position on Queen Elizabeth's accession to
the throne in 1558, his own father.

York House had been their home, the first home Francis ever knew.
Here he had been born fifty-seven years ago. He could remember his

mother presiding over the vast retinue of servants, his father's cousin Kemp acting as steward. There were ushers, waiters, servers, cooks, and superior officials forever in attendance, a chaplain, clerks. . . . The impression now, in retrospect, was one of pageantry, of colour. There by the river steps he and Anthony would stand, watching the Thames tide seep over the mudflats to course past the palace of Whitehall, and at high flood, when the wind blew strong, the water would break against the defending wall and nearly breach it.

Francis would return: he would come home. York House was the property of Tobie Matthew's father, the Archbishop of York—it had been the residence of the Archbishops of York in old days—but was now leased out to the holder of the Great Seal. Yes, he would come home, but not until the bereaved family of the late Lord Keeper had time to adjust to the change. He remembered the indecent haste with which his mother had been obliged to pack her things and depart in order to give way to her husband's successor thirty-eight years ago. This time courtesy would prevail, and that promise of an earldom to Lord Ellesmere's son would help to temper sorrow.

Meanwhile Francis and his wife must find somewhere to live. His train of followers would increase of necessity, as suitable to his new status. What had passed for an Attorney-General would not do for the Lord Keeper, who, with his Majesty absent on his progress to Scotland, as the principal officer of the kingdom would find himself presiding at the head of the Council table; indeed, with the King absent for several months all matters pertaining to government would be referred to him. He would be every day in the palace of Whitehall; he would, in all senses, stand in for the monarch. Rumour had it that the Queen, who was not accompanying his Majesty to Scotland, was disappointed that she had not been made regent so that she could conduct the business of the state herself. Perhaps. Homage and respect would be due to her, but it was a relief to the Lord Keeper that she had decided, with the Prince of Wales, to retire to her new house at Greenwich while the King was in the north; her courtiers and other members of the Council could attend her there.

So where to live? Part of Salisbury House, where his cousin had lived, was available, but no, it was too small. Essex House? Overfull of memories. Dorset House, the property of the Earl of Dorset, was then offered him free until York House should become vacant. This should content his wife and her own swelling train for the time being, but first—and doubtless at her own request, prompted by her interfering mother—a warrant was drawn up for his Majesty's signature declaring that "Lady Bacon shall be ranked in place and precedency in all places and at all meetings, as well public as private, next to the ladies or wives of the Barons of this our realm." Thus honoured, Alice could not play the shrew and complain that at Court functions she was ignored and overlooked.

State business claimed Francis's attention: a project to erect staple towns in Ireland for the export of wool; precautions to be taken against disorder in the city of London, for there had been too much of this of late, and trained bands must be increased to keep the peace; measures set in motion against piracy at sea, where sea-captains and merchants were suffering much damage to ships and cargoes, and must have protection, as well as the assistance, if possible, of the King of Spain, whose goodwill might depend upon the negotiations for the marriage of his daughter to the Prince of Wales. . . .

Six days at Gorhambury over the Easter break had renewed Francis's energies. One of his new secretaries was Edward Sherburn, who had frequently corresponded with Dudley Carleton and John Chamberlain during the past year, and had reported most ably and accurately on the trial of the Earl of Somerset. Such young men, in touch with many sources of information, were useful to the new Lord Keeper.

On May 7th 1617 Sir Francis Bacon, Keeper of the Great Seal and, until a successor should be appointed to the late Lord Ellesmere, representing the Lord Chancellor and the absent monarch, took his seat in the Court of Chancery and delivered his first speech of office. The gossips made fine play of the great occasion. "Our Lord Keeper," said one, "exceeds all his predecessors in the bravery and multitude of his servants. It amazes those that look on his beginnings, besides never so indulgent a master." (The correspondent appeared not to know that Francis Bacon held the office his father held.) "On the first day of term he appeared in his greatest glory; for to the Hall, besides his own retinue, did accompany him all the Lords of his Majesty's Council and others, with all knights and gentlemen that could get horses and footcloths." And John Chamberlain reported, "There was a great deal more bravery and better show of horse than was expected in the King's absence; but both Queen and Prince sent all their followers, and his other friends did their best to honour him. He made a speech in Chancery; the substance of which was some reformation in that court, not without glancing at his predecessor, whose beginnings he professed he would follow; but excepted against some of his latter courses; yet would not undo anything he had done. He pleased himself much in the flourishing of the law; and remarked that great lawyers' sons have the way to succeed their fathers. . . . The greatest part of his train dined with him that day, which dinner cost him, as is generally reported, £700."

The speech, which dealt throughout with legal matters pertaining to the Court of Chancery, included the following words: "Because justice is a sacred thing, and the end for which I am called to this place, and therefore is my way to heaven, and if it be shorter is never a whit the worse, I shall by the grace of God, as far as God shall give me strength, add the afternoon to the forenoon, and some fourth night of the vacation to the term, for the expediting and clearing of the causes of the court. Only the depth of the three long vacations I would reserve in some measure free for business of estate, and for studies, arts, and sciences, to which in my nature I am most inclined."

An interesting observation by that first correspondent, who had exclaimed at the multitude of the train which had followed the Lord Keeper into Palace Yard, was that he was dressed, as he had been at his wedding in 1606, in a suit of purple satin. Did Francis Bacon, at fifty-six, still cling to boyhood fantasy, the regal purple a remnant of an unconscious dream? If so, it was in total contrast to his other self, for the next day he wrote to the Earl of Buckingham, who was with the King on his progress, "Yesterday I took my place in Chancery, which I hold only from the King's grace and favour, and your constant friendship. There was much ado, and a great deal of world. But this matter of pomp, which is heaven to some men, is hell to me, or purgatory at least." The magnificence and the splendour thus cloaked and concealed the inner man, or, as he had said in other words in his *Redargutio Philosophiarum,* "Every man of superior understanding in contact with his inferiors wears a mask."

It was not surprising that during the following week he was absent from the Council and the Star Chamber with a fit of the gout—or such was the excuse. Indisposition on becoming Solicitor-General. Indisposition on becoming Attorney-General. "Strangeness, clouds, inclined to superstition. . . ." His absence caused some talk amongst the gossips. "But in truth the general opinion is that he hath so tender a constitution both of body and mind," said John Chamberlain, "that he will hardly be able to undergo the burden of so much business as his place requires; and that if he do not rouse and force himself beyond his natural inclination, both private subjects and the commonwealth will suffer much."

Chamberlain need not have concerned himself. Fit of the gout or fit of the clouds, the Lord Keeper was able to compose a speech on the appointment of the new Lord Chief Justice of Ireland, Sir William Jones, in which he told him, "Ireland is the last *ex filiis Europae* which hath been reclaimed from desolation and a desert, in many parts, to population and plantation; and from savage and barbarous customs to humanity and civility. . . . So as that kingdom, which once within these twenty years wise men were wont to doubt whether they would wish it to be in a pool, is like now to become almost a garden, and a younger sister to Great Britain . . . My last direction, though first in weight, is, that you do all good endeavours to proceed resolutely and constantly, and yet with due temperance and equality, in matters of religion; lest Ireland civil become more dangerous to us than Ireland savage."

It is unfortunate that greater heed was not taken of the Lord Keeper's advice during succeeding years. They were certainly not the words of a man whose mind was in the clouds.

When he did return to the Council in the third week in May it is very possible that he wished he could have prolonged his fit of the gout. He found that a furious altercation had been in progress between his old love Lady Hatton and her husband Sir Edward Coke. Accompanied by her brother Lord Burghley and a number of friends, she had come to the Council and flung a petition upon the table, accusing Coke of desiring to rob her of her personal estate, inherited from her first husband Sir William Hatton. It was said afterwards, by those present, that the actor "Burbage could not have acted better, she declaimed so bitterly against him." Counsel for Sir Edward countercharged that Lady Hatton "had disfurnished and taken away out of three of his houses all hangings, plate and household stuff, and also that she gave him to his face or by letter these unfit words of false treacherous villain." The Lord Keeper may have been reminded of his description of Scylla in *Cogitata et Visa*—"her loins were girt about with yelping hounds." If so we have, alas, no private memoranda to tell us of it, nor any letter from the Lady Hatton warning her former suitor that she had given tongue and expected him to support her. He refused to become involved, and made a motion to the Council referring the whole matter to Lord Carew and the Chancellor of the Exchequer.

The business was settled for the time being, but Francis Bacon was very well aware that trouble might break out again at any moment between husband and wife, and this time he himself would have to exercise the utmost discretion, or he would give offence to his young friend the Earl of Buckingham. The fact was that Buckingham's elder brother, Sir John Villiers, had been negotiating a marriage with Frances, the younger of the two daughters of Sir Edward Coke and Lady Hatton. Coke was in favour of the match, for an alliance with the favourite's brother would surely bring him back into favour with his Majesty. His wife, Lady Hatton, was against it. She had other plans for her daughter.

It is exasperating, for the modern sleuth, that no letters have survived between Francis Bacon and Elizabeth Hatton; there must have been several in existence once, dating back to the original courtship in 1597—when the lady disdained the young lawyer from Gray's Inn and married his rival—down to this period of 1617, when her own fifteen-year-old daughter, singularly enough named Frances, was sought in marriage by someone of whom she disapproved. Francis Bacon was no longer an impecunious lawyer. He was Lord Keeper of the Great Seal, and as such could prove a most valuable ally in her cause. Had she some secret hold upon him? We shall never know.

Someone who might have had access to letters at this time, if they existed, was the new secretary Edward Sherburn, for in early June John Chamberlain told his friend Dudley Carleton, "I saw not Master Sherburn these three weeks. He is grown so inward with his Lord that he is about him in his chamber, and during his indisposition hath waited at an inch; which I hope will turn to his good."

Possibly it was young Sherburn who was Chamberlain's informant later that month about domestic trouble with the Lord Keeper's in-laws. Alice Bacon's mother, Lady Packington, was once again suing her husband Sir John, but, said the gossip, "The Lord Keeper deals very honourably in the matter, which though he could not compound being referred to him, yet he carries himself so indifferently that he wisheth her to yield, and tells her plainly and publicly that she must look for no countenance from him as long as she follows this course."

Disputes and squabbles between man and wife were something Francis Bacon could not stomach. Hence his discreet silence where his own wife was concerned. If, during the eleven years they had been married, there should have been anything untoward to report, assuredly John Chamberlain would have had wind of it. It was from him, and others, that we hear of the next round in the contest between Sir Edward Coke and Lady Hatton, and this time neither gout, nor clouds, nor matters of State could prevent the Lord Keeper from becoming involved.

The actual date of the opening battle seems to be uncertain, but at some point in the latter part of June Sir Edward Coke informed his wife—who with their daughter Frances was living with him once again—that he had now settled the business of the marriage between Sir John Villiers and Frances: she should have a dowry of £10,000

101

and an allowance of £1,000 a year. Sir John was agreeable, and his mother Lady Compton satisfied. Arrangements for the wedding could be set in motion.

All hell and fury were let loose. Never, never would Lady Hatton give her consent. Daughter Frances burst into tears. She did not want to marry a dull stick like Sir John Villiers. When she did marry, she would marry for love. How many days the storm lasted we are not told, but the resourceful Lady Hatton, still in the prime of life (she had not yet turned forty), had plans of her own. One night, when Sir Edward was asleep, she and her daughter left Stoke by coach for the house of her cousin, Sir Edmond Withipole, at Oatlands. They arrived at dawn, and were received kindly, if perhaps with embarrassment, by host and hostess, who promised secrecy.

Lady Hatton then did rather a foolish thing. She decided she must have a rival claimant for her daughter's hand, and one of equal, or rather higher, status than Sir John Villiers. Henry de Vere, Earl of Oxford, would do—his father's first wife had been a cousin of hers. He was absent in Italy, and letters would take too long to reach him, but no matter: she would promise him two houses, and an income of £4,000 to £6,000 a year. She then set herself to persuade her daughter to favour the match, but, seeing that Frances was neither impressed nor very willing, she composed a letter, saying that it had come from the Earl of Oxford, asking for the honour of Frances's hand. Such subterfuges had been in fashion once (possibly Lady Hatton remembered the time when her former suitor Francis Bacon had written a letter to the Earl of Essex, at the time of the earl's disgrace, pretending that it came from his brother Anthony, hoping, by such means, to move the Queen). Her daughter showed some interest, on the strength of which Lady Hatton composed yet another document, which the naïve Frances signed, stating that she plighted her troth to Henry Vere, Earl of Oxford, and if she broke her vow she would beseech God that the earth might open and swallow her up.

Certainly Lady Hatton had a vivid imagination. Acting in all those masques at Court had whetted her appetite for drama. But she had reckoned without her husband. Sir Edward Coke, as furious as his wife, applied to the Council for a warrant to recover his daughter from Oatlands. Here, once again, the dates are confusing. It seems to have been in the first week in July, and both the Lord Keeper and Sir Ralph Winwood, his Majesty's Secretary of State, were at the Council table when the application for the warrant was received. The Lord Keeper refused to sign it. Sir Ralph Winwood, who was a friend of Sir

Edward Coke, protested. There was mutual antipathy between the two men, but whether the question of the proposed marriage between Sir John Villiers and Coke's daughter was discussed that day, and whether the right of Lady Hatton to keep her daughter at Oatlands led to words between them, we do not know.

That there was trouble, but of a different kind, was reported not by the usual gossips but by a Bishop Goodman. "The difference fell out upon a very small occasion," says the prelate, "that Winwood did beat his dog from lying upon a stool, which Bacon seeing said that every gentleman did love a dog." A small occasion, indeed, but an instant impression is created of the Secretary of State, irritated, brushing the unfortunate animal from his seat, and the Lord Keeper looking upon him with his hazel eyes, coldly, contemptuously: "Every gentleman loves a dog," with just the slightest emphasis on that word gentleman, calculated to sting the pride of Sir Ralph Winwood. And imagination goes further, to picture the many dogs there surely must have been at Gorhambury, to welcome their master's return.

Bishop Goodman continues, "This passed on; then at the same time having some business to sit upon, it should seem that Secretary Winwood sat too near by Lord Keeper, and his Lordship willed him either to keep or to know his distance. Whereupon he arose from table."

The upshot was that the Secretary of State, either then or shortly afterwards, signed the warrant for Sir Edward Coke to recover his daughter. It is possible he did not have the right of signature. If so, Sir Edward Coke disregarded the fact. Accompanied by his sons by his first marriage and several attendants, he rode to Sir Edmond Withipole's house at Oatlands. But the birds had flown. Someone must have warned Lady Hatton and her daughter that he was on his way. Who? We do not know. They had fled to a house at Hampton Court belonging to the Earl of Argyle. Someone, a servant perhaps from Oatlands, gave away their whereabouts, upon which Sir Edward rode straight to the new hiding-place, broke down the doors, discovered his wife and daughter hiding in a closet, and seizing his weeping daughter from her mother's arms departed for Stoke Poges, his own estate.

"His Lady was at his heels," reported Chamberlain, "and if her coach had not tired in the pursuit after him there was like to be strange tragedies." In fact, Lady Hatton's coach either overturned or lost a wheel, which gave her ladyship time to think again. She must have realised that it would be useless to follow her husband and his train to Stoke; the doors would be barred, and alone she would achieve nothing. Her coach repaired, she decided to go straightway to

London to see the only man who could help her—her friend and former suitor, the Lord Keeper. It was Saturday, July 12th. No report of this manœuvre from the gossips, who would have seized upon it had they known. The source of information is Mrs Sadler, one of Sir Edward Coke's daughters by his first marriage.

"At last to my Lord Keeper's they come, but could not have instant access to him for that his people told them he was laid at rest, not being well. Then my Lady Hatton desired she might be in the next room where my Lord lay, that she might be the first that should speak with him after he was stirring. The door-keeper fulfilled her desire and in the meantime gave her a chair to rest herself in, and there left her alone; but not long after, she rose up and bounced against my Lord Keeper's door, and waked him and affrighted him, that he called his men to him; and they opening the door, she thrust in with them, and desired his Lordship to pardon her boldness, but she was like a cow that had lost her calf."

That fatal habit of sleeping in the afternoon . . . "I do find nothing to induce stopping more and fill the head and to induce languishing and distaste and feverous disposition more I say than any manner of offer to sleep at afternoon, either immediately after dinner or at four o'clock. And I could never yet find resolution and strength enough in myself to inhibit it."

No word in Mrs Sadler's account as to whether the Lord Keeper had moved to York House or was still at Dorset House. In either case, had his wife Lady Bacon been in residence the servants would presumably have warned her of this sudden intrusion, and confrontation would have taken place. An interesting encounter! But it is likely that, with trouble brewing in her own parents' case, Lady Bacon was out of town and with her mother.

The scene enacted between Francis Bacon and Elizabeth Hatton was surely one that Mr Shakespeare, deceased, could have turned to good account had he lived to edit and amend the publication known as the First Folio, which was printed six years later. Francis, asleep, dreaming of the young woman he had courted in the past, awaking, not to any shadow or even a statue, but to a mature lady standing on his threshold: "Hermione was not so much wrinkled, nothing so aged as this seems." A remark which would certainly have roused Lady Hatton to even greater anger as she thrust herself in at the door, until, remembering her cause, she asked pardon for her boldness. "When she was young, you woo'd her; now, in age, is she become the Suitor?"

Francis recovered himself, dismissed his men, and listened to what the intruder had to say, but alas, we have the remainder of the scene only in Mrs Sadler's words. "And she so justified herself and pacified my Lord's anger, and got his warrant and my Lord Treasurer's warrant and others of the Council to fetch her daughter from the father and bring them both to the Council."

We are not told at what hour Lady Hatton took her departure, but that same day, July 12th, the Lord Keeper penned a letter to the Earl of Buckingham.

"My very good Lord,

"I shall write to your Lordship of a business which your Lordship may think to concern myself; but I do think it concerneth your Lordship much more. For as for me, as my judgement is not so weak to think it can do me any hurt, so my love to you is so strong, as I would prefer the good of you and yours before mine own particular.

"It seemeth Secretary Winwood hath officiously busied himself to make a match between your brother and Sir Edward Coke's daughter: and, as we hear, he doth it rather to make a faction, than out of any great affection for your Lordship. It is true, he hath the consent of Sir Edward Coke, as we hear, upon reasonable conditions for your brother; and yet no better than without question may be found in other matches. But the mother's consent is not had, nor the young gentlewoman's, who expecteth a great fortune from her mother, which without her consent is endangered. This match, out of my faith and freedom towards your Lordship, I hold very inconvenient both for your brother and yourself.

"First, he shall marry into a disgraced house, which in reason of state is never held good.

"Next, he shall marry into a troubled house of man and wife, which in religion and Christian discretion is never good.

"Thirdly, your Lordship will go near to lose all such your friends as are adverse to Sir Edward Coke; myself only except, who out of a pure love and thankfulness shall ever be firm to you.

"And lastly and chiefly, I believe it will greatly weaken and distract the King's service; for though, in regard to the King's great wisdom and depth, I am persuaded those things will not follow which they imagine, yet opinion will do a great deal of harm, and cast the King back, and make him relapse into those inconveniences which are now well on to be recovered.

"Therefore my advice is . . . your Lordship signify unto my Lady your mother, that your desire is that the marriage be not pressed or proceeded with without the consent of both parents; and so either break it altogether, or defer any further dealing in it till your Lordship's return: and this the rather for that, besides the inconvenience of the matter itself, it hath been carried so harshly and inconsiderately by Secretary Winwood, as for doubt that the father should take away the maiden by force, the mother, to get the start, hath conveyed her away secretly; which is ill of all sides. Thus hoping your Lordship will not only accept well, but believe my faithful advice, who by my great experience in the world must see further than your lordship can, I ever rest

"Your Lordship's true and most devoted,
"friend and servant,
"Fr. Bacon. C.S."

The earl, who was travelling with his Majesty in the west of Scotland, would not receive the letter for several days, even if the messenger bearing it set forth immediately.

The following day, Sunday July 13th, Lady Hatton appeared at the Council table, and told the members in "a passionate and tragical manner that . . . she was by violence dispossessed of her child; and informing us that in regard of her daughter's weak constitution she had sent her to Sir Edmond Withipole's house for a small time, and that it was not done in any secret manner. Whereupon Sir Edward Coke . . . pretending warrant, as he said, from the Board, with his son and 10 or 11 servants, weaponed, in violent manner repaired to the house where their daughter was remaining, and with a piece of timber or form broke open the door, and dragged her along to his coach; with many other circumstances too long to trouble his Majesty withal."

The Council appointed the following Tuesday to hear further on the matter, together with Sir Edward Coke's own complaint. But Lady Hatton was not content to wait. She appeared once more at the door of the Council chamber, and asked for a warrant for her daughter to be brought to London from Stoke Poges that night, because of the weakness of her state and the fright that had been occasioned her. "Which," the Council agreed, "being thought reasonable in humanity, and for avoiding other inconveniences, a letter was written from the Board to Sir Edward Coke, acquainting him with his Lady's complaint and desire, and requiring him to deliver his daughter to Mr Edmondes, Clerk of the Council, to be brought by him to London, and kept in his house until the hearing of the cause."

This was quick work for a Sunday, and one can see the Lord Keeper's hand in the arrangement of it. No after-dinner sleep that afternoon. By nightfall the Clerk of the Council had arrived at Stoke, only to be told by Sir Edward that his daughter "was in no such extremity, and that upon his peril he would deliver her to Mr Edmondes' house the next morning."

Monday dawned. No daughter appeared, and the Council sent a

7. Sir Edward Coke, Lord Chief Justice of the King's Bench, attributed to the British School *(reproduced by permission of the Earl of Leicester, photo Courtauld Institute)*

8. Robert Carr, Earl of Somerset, after J. Hoskins *(photo National Portrait Gallery, London)*

YORK HOUSE

This mansion was auntiently the town inn,or residence of the bishops of Norwich, and changed its name to YORK HOUSE in the reign of Queen
Mary, when Abp Heath purchased it for the use of that see. In the reign of James I.being exchanged with the crown,it was granted to George Villiers,
Duke of Buckingham who rebuilt it in the magnificent manner above re presented After the restoration it was destroyed and the site laid out
in several streets,bearing the names and titles of its former owner. YORK STAIRS *still remain and are universally admired.*

Published.Dec 1 1808.by Wᵐ Herbert.Lambeth. and Robᵗ Wilkinson Nᵒ 58 Cornhill.London.

9. York House, c. 1623, from a nineteenth-century print based on a drawing by Hollar, now in the Pepysian Library at Magdalene College, Cambridge (*photo Greater London Council Print Collection*)

10. Sir Tobie Matthew in late middle age. Frontispiece from the Collection of his Letters, 1660

11. George Villiers, Duke of Buckingham, in 1626 *(photo Mansell Collection)*

further warrant "with a clause of assistance" should it be needed. Lady Hatton herself set forth on the road to Stoke, with several friends, all armed, hoping for a battle with her husband; but the wily Coke had taken another route, possibly scenting trouble, and delivered the exhausted Frances into the hands of the Clerk of the Council. In his house, it appears, she spent the remainder of the day and that night. "Doubting some disorder," the Council "gave directions that she should be kept private until the hearing, which was the next day, and two gentlewomen only to be admitted to her company, such as Sir Edward Coke and his Lady should choose; which was accordingly performed, Sir Edward Coke choosing the Lady Compton and his lady the Lady Burghley."

It is to be hoped Frances had some sleep, but her aunt, Lady Burghley, possibly passed a restless evening, for Lady Compton, mother of Sir John Villiers and the Earl of Buckingham (she had been married three times, her third husband being Sir Thomas Compton), was one of the most formidable women of her day, and could hardly be vanquished in argument by anyone, unless it were my Lady Hatton herself.

On Tuesday July 15th Sir Edward Coke appeared before the Council. He immediately brought a counter-charge against his wife, accusing her of wishing to carry their daughter off into France, so that the marriage arranged between her and Sir John Villiers should not take place. The Council declined to discuss the marriage, and pressed the ex-Lord Chief Justice to answer the charge brought against him, that of "riot and force." Sir Edward Coke replied that he had a legal right to recover his daughter. Whereupon the Council ordered that he should appear before the Court of the Star Chamber at some date unspecified, and in the interim his daughter should be placed under the care of the Attorney-General, Sir Henry Yelverton.

Then, on July 18th or 19th, Sir Ralph Winwood turned up a trump card at the Council table. He produced a letter from the King himself, approving of all that he, Winwood, had done to further the marriage of Sir John Villiers and Frances Coke. Consternation at the Council table. If his Majesty were at one with Sir Ralph Winwood and Sir Edward Coke, his Councillors would change their attitude. Action in the Star Chamber must be suspended. The Attorney-General undertook the thankless task of endeavouring to bring about some reconciliation between Sir Edward Coke and his lady. How far he succeeded we learn from a postscript in a letter sent to his Majesty from the Council immediately afterwards:

"But now since, this matter seemeth to have had a fairer conclusion;

for that we find that the writings are perfected, and not only so, but the parties, Sir Edward Coke and his Lady, reconciled, and the daughter with both their good likings sent to live with her father and mother in Sir Edward Coke's house. Which good end hath been much furthered by the charitable endeavour of his Majesty's Attorney-General. And the information, and all other proceedings in the business, is suspended and left wholly to his Majesty's pleasure."

John Chamberlain, writing a full account of the affair to his crony Sir Dudley Carleton, says, "She [Frances Coke] was sent home to Hatton House, with order that the Lady Compton and her son should have access to win her and wear her."

How long husband and wife remained together under the same roof we are not told, but certainly not more than a fortnight. In any case Hatton House was the property of her ladyship, and not Sir Edward—though doubtless this was another matter for dispute. By early August Coke had removed his daughter to stay with his son by his first marriage, Sir Robert Coke at Kingston, upon which Lady Hatton took a lodging in the town in order to visit her every day, and confront Lady Compton and her son Sir John Villiers, the hopeful bridegroom, whenever they appeared to press the suit.

And what of Francis Bacon, the Lord Keeper? Frustrated, exhausted, he left London for Gorhambury as soon as the Council business was concluded. We may hope, for his sake, that his wife was away from home visiting her mother; for there at Gorhambury to join him, to share his relaxation, to renew his inspiration, to read his *magnum opus* in manuscript, to laugh, to sympathise, to converse on every topic in the world but marriage, was the friend he had not seen for ten years, that exile and recusant from the continent of Europe, permitted at last to return under his personal supervision and assurances of good behaviour—Tobie Matthew.

Chapter XIII

Tobie would be forty in October. His friend and mentor was fifty-six. One wonders how changed in appearance, and perhaps in manners, they seemed to each other after ten years of separation. Francis had undoubtedly aged: greying hair, furrows running from nose to mouth, and a suspicion of bags beneath the eyes suggested a man in his mid-sixties. Too much working at all hours of the day and night had taken their toll. The humour still lurked, though, in the corner of the eyes, the hint of mockery.

The only description we have of Tobie is contained in a postscript from Charles Prince of Wales to his father the King in 1623, where he mentions "little pretty Tobie Matthew." Fair of face and small of stature. Yet a man of the world, who in his ten years' absence from England had travelled extensively, chiefly in Italy and Spain, and had formed a wide circle of friends in Madrid, probably owing to his Catholic faith. His father the Archbishop of York had not yet forgiven him for changing his religion, and, in hopes that his eldest son would be converted back to the Church of England, had urged his return home. It was the Earl of Buckingham who had persuaded his Majesty to relent, and it was assumed that Tobie would now conform and in due course take the oath of allegiance.

These matters were inevitably discussed at Gorhambury, and Tobie was hoping that the influence of the Lord Keeper would stand him in good stead. When he had left England in 1607 Francis had not yet been appointed Solicitor-General; now he held one of the most important posts in the kingdom. The retinue of servants and attendants had doubled, trebled; the rooms at Gorhambury no longer held them all, there was talk of building another house in the grounds for the personal use of the master, and the grounds themselves, walks, gardens, woods, had altered beyond recognition. And in a few weeks' time, when the Lord Keeper returned to London, York House would be ready for him, with new furnishings, new appointments, and a further retinue of servants.

Tobie Matthew was impressed. His dear friend had certainly advanced since the early days when Tobie had been a young law student at Gray's Inn and Francis a barrister with few briefs. It was unfortunate therefore that, just as he had returned from abroad, the Lord Keeper should have found himself involved in this marriage dispute between Sir Edward Coke and his wife Lady Hatton, and have fallen out with the Secretary of State Sir Ralph Winwood in consequence. It might have ill effects upon his friend's relationship not only with the Earl of Buckingham but with his Majesty himself.

For of course, once the first delight at meeting had subsided, the renewing of their friendship, the discussion of old times, and Tobie had unburdened himself of all he had to say about life in Europe, the talk eventually came round to what had just taken place at the Council table; the rumour of dissension and trouble had greeted Tobie when he arrived in London. It was the talk of the town. And he could tell, from the Lord Keeper's preoccupation, although he made light of it, that he was seriously disturbed. It was, in fact, now two weeks since Francis had written to the Earl of Buckingham, giving his reasons for opposing the marriage of Sir John Villiers to Frances Coke, and he had received no reply. He had not expected one for five or six days, but a fortnight was excessive. He must write again, and compose a letter to his Majesty at the same time, repeating much the same arguments he had used to the earl, so that there should be no misunderstanding. It was intolerable that the Secretary of State should profess to know the King's mind upon the infernal marriage question, while he, the Lord Keeper, had not been kept informed. Something was amiss somewhere.

Francis wrote, therefore, at some length on July 25th, particularly asking that his Majesty should let him know his own wishes regarding the match, rather than that he, the Lord Keeper, should receive them through a third party. He added, "Though I will not wager upon women's minds, I can prevail more with the mother than any other man," which suggested that should the King be strongly in favour of the marriage, then the Lord Keeper would trim his sails accordingly and endeavour to persuade Lady Hatton that she must withdraw her objections. He wrote to the Earl of Buckingham on the same day, saying, "I do think long to hear from your Lordship touching my last letter, wherein I gave my opinion touching your brother's match." The delay, he reassured himself, had come about by the King travelling south from Scotland, and the earl with him; they must by now have reached Carlisle.

Then, in early August, the long-awaited reply came from the Earl of Buckingham, written in a very different tone from any of those Francis had received before.

"To the Lord Keeper Bacon.
"My Lord,
"If your man had been addressed only to me, I should have been careful to have procured him a more speedy dispatch: but now you have found another way of address, I am excused; and since you are grown weary of employing me, I can be no otherwise in being employed. In this business of my brother's that you overtrouble yourself with, I understand from London by some of my friends that you have carried yourself with much scorn and neglect both towards myself and my friends; which if it prove true I blame not you but myself, who was ever
                              "Your Lordship's assured friend,
                                        "G. Buckingham."

A cold rebuke, and no mistake about it. The favourite was deeply offended, apparently on two counts: that the Lord Keeper had written direct to the King in the matter, and—which of course was hearsay and malicious gossip—that he had spoken scornfully of the earl himself.

The shock Francis received on reading this letter was considerable. He needed all the comfort Tobie Matthew was able to offer. But worse was to follow. A letter arrived from his Majesty himself, also blaming the Lord Keeper for interference. Unfortunately this letter can no longer be traced, but Francis replied to it about August 12th, and from the tenor of his reply it would seem that the King had not only upbraided him for going against his wishes by opposing the marriage but had accused him of criticising the Earl of Buckingham. Sir Ralph Winwood had obviously given his own version of how events had gone at the Council table in July, and since he was a friend of Sir Edward Coke and of Sir John Villiers' mother Lady Compton, it is not difficult to see how both the King and Buckingham had been prejudiced against the Lord Keeper.

One thing strikes the observer today, which is that Francis Bacon, despite his vast retinue, had a poor system of intelligence. His brother Anthony, had he found himself in similar circumstances, would have had secret agents following the King's train and reporting back almost daily. It is almost as though Francis had too great a faith in his own judgement; yet his own vast experience should have warned him that during their absence his Majesty and Buckingham would come under other influences besides his, and that the favourite, despite his previous amiability, was now fully conscious of his own power and had begun to resent advice from any quarter. One wonders, furthermore, who was the attendant "your man" who had carried the Lord Keeper's letters north. It was not Edward Sherburn, because Chamberlain mentions seeing him in town around this time, and he was known to have been down at Gorhambury. In 1618, a year later, we have a list of all the attendants, some seventy-five of them, but this does not help us in July–August of 1617.

Whoever the bearer of the letters may have been, his method of approach must have been unfortunate. His employer was obliged once again to write a long letter to his Majesty, expressing deep apology for the stand he had taken. "And now that your Majesty hath been pleased to open yourself to me, I shall be willing to further the match by any thing that shall be desired of me, or that is in my power." (And how he must have cursed inwardly for ever having become involved!) "I do humbly acquiesce and anchor upon your Majesty's judgement. . . . For the interest which I have in the mother, I do not doubt but it was increased by this, that I in judgement, as I then stood, affected that which she did in passion."

In a previous paragraph he said, "For the manner of my affection to my Lord of Buckingham, for whom I would spend my life . . . I must humbly confess that it was in this a little parent-like, this being no other term than his Lordship hath heretofore vouchsafed to my counsels, but in truth, without any grain of disesteem for his Lordship's discretion. For I know him to be naturally a wise man, of a sound and staid wit, and again I know he hath the best tutor in Europe. But yet I was afraid that the height of his fortune might make him too secure, and, as the proverb is, a looker-on sometimes seeth more than a gamester."

Next a letter to Sir Henry Yelverton, the Attorney-General, explaining that Francis was now resolved to further the match, and another one to Lady Hatton pressing the same sentiment. Couched in what language, and with what regrets, alas, we do not know. Finally, a letter of apology to the Earl of Buckingham.

"I do hear my Lady your mother and your brother Sir John do speak of me with some bitterness and neglect. I must bear with the one as a lady and the other as a lover, and with both for your Lordship's sake. . . . But I hope, though I be true servant to your Lordship, you will not have me vassal to their passions, especially as long as they are governed by Sir Edward Coke and Secretary Winwood;

the latter of which I take to be the worst; for Sir Edward Coke, I think, is more modest and discreet . . . God keep us from these long journeys and absence, which makes misunderstandings and gives advantages to untruth, and God ever prosper and preserve your Lordship."

It would have been better to have named no names. Secretary Winwood was not likely to forgive this allusion, when it came to his ears. Then another error of judgement, though very probably at the time it was thought to be an excellent move. The King was to be a guest on his journey south at the house of Sir Thomas Wilbraham at Townsend, near Nantwich. He was there, in fact, on August 25th. And a guest at the same time was none other than Mr Tobie Matthew, obviously hotfoot from Gorhambury. This coincidence seems to have escaped Francis Bacon's biographer James Spedding, who covered every aspect of his life with such meticulous care and accuracy, but it could be that if he knew of it he did not think the event of much significance.

If Tobie Matthew was not presented to his Majesty at Nantwich he would certainly have sought out the Earl of Buckingham, whose patronage had brought him, a recusant, home to England; and it must have been with this encounter in mind that he had either asked for, or received, an invitation to stay with Sir Thomas Wilbraham. Tobie's experience on the continent should have put him on his guard, but one cannot help wondering if his friendship with the Lord Keeper, and his very recent visit to Gorhambury, had made him a trifle too enthusiastic when talking of these matters to the favourite. An incautious word here, another there, how he and his friend the Lord Keeper had sat up half the night discussing world affairs, and how they had corresponded regularly through the years, he was even permitted to read his manuscripts . . . this would be quite enough to touch the pride of the young favourite who had hitherto been under the impression that Francis Bacon had reserved his *billets doux* for him alone. A whiff of jealousy, perhaps? We cannot tell.

It is significant, however, that on the night his Majesty spent at Nantwich he found time to indite another long letter to the Lord Keeper, in reply to his of August 12th, taking him to task for having spoken of his "parent-like affection" for the Earl of Buckingham and similar expressions, which leads one to suppose that his Majesty himself had some feelings of jealousy where the Lord Keeper and his favourite were concerned, a sentiment which, if fanned by the gossip over-prevalent amongst his courtiers, would be quite enough to stir the embers of mistrust. This letter could well have been dictated later on his progress south, so why especially upon that night in Nantwich, when Tobie Matthew was a fellow-guest?

The remainder of the King's letter concerned the marriage business once again, upbraiding the Lord Keeper for not having signed the warrant for Sir Edward Coke to recover his child, but all particulars would be left until the proper time. And, "We commend you to God. Given under our signet at Nantwich, in the fifteenth year of our reign of Great Britain."

So Francis's letter of apology to his Majesty had done little good, rather the reverse. And Tobie Matthew had achieved even less. It needed a man of real authority, whom he could trust implicitly, to meet the King on his progress south and report back to the Lord Keeper. Such a man was Sir Henry Yelverton, the Attorney-General, and so he travelled north to Coventry. Unfortunately Sir Edward Coke had the same idea, and was first on the scene, as the Attorney-General told Francis in his very full report. "I dare not think my journey lost, because I have with much joy seen the face of my master, the King, though more clouded towards me than I looked for. Sir Edward Coke hath not forborne by any engine to heave both at your Honour and myself; and he works by the weightiest instrument, the Earl of Buckingham, who as I see sets him as close to him as his shirt, the Earl speaking in Sir Edward's phrase, and as it were menacing in his spirit."

The Attorney-General found that the earl had been "misled by misinformation which he embraced as truth." Yelverton stood his ground firmly and boldly, and desired the earl not to give credit to slander. He then approached his Majesty, who "graciously gave me his hand to kiss," but was too pressed with other business to listen to explanations then. Not exactly a rebuff, but not far off it, whereupon the Attorney-General proceeded to glean further information from the gossiping courtiers which he relayed to Francis:

"Every courtier is acquainted that the Earl professeth openly against you as forgetful of his kindness, and unfaithful to him in your love and actions . . . not forbearing in open speech (as divers have told me, and this bearer, your gentleman, hath also heard) to tax you . . . to be as unfaithful to him as you were to the Earls of Essex and Somerset. That it is too common in every man's mouth in court, that your greatness shall be abated, and as your tongue hath been a razor to some, so shall theirs be to you.

"That there is laid up for you, to make your burden the more grievous, many petitions to his Majesty against you. Sir Edward Coke, as if he were already upon his wings, triumphs exceedingly; hath much private conference with his Majesty. . . .

"My noble Lord . . . I would humbly desire that your Lordship fail not to be with his Majesty at Woodstock; the sight of you will fright some. That you single not yourself from the other Lords [Yelverton refers to the Council] but justify all the proceedings as all your joint acts; and I little fear but you pass conqueror. That you retort the clamour and noise in this business upon Sir Edward Coke, by the violence of his carriage. That you seem not dismayed, but open yourself bravely and confidently, wherein you can excell all other subjects; by which means I know you shall amaze some and daunt others.

"I have abused your Lordship's patience long, but my duty and affection towards your Lordship shall have no end; but I shall still wish your Honour greater, and rest myself,

"your Honour's servant,
"Henry Yelverton.

"Daventry, September 3rd.
"I beseech your Lordship burn this letter."

Truly a faithful friend, though we should not have had proof of it had this postscript been obeyed. In the event, Francis did not travel to Woodstock, but the Attorney-General had certainly made an impression upon the Earl of Buckingham, and presumably upon his Majesty as well, for the earl wrote to the Lord Keeper from Warwick two days later in a far more conciliatory tone, expressing his hope that he would shortly see him, "where will be better trial of all that hath passed than can be made by letters."

The King returned to London on September 15th, and at some moment between then and the 21st a meeting took place between Francis and the earl—professedly upon a matter relating to a threat against the King's life. The encounter was evidently successful, the Lord Keeper's charm of manner and powers of persuasion prevailing upon the favourite, for the following day he wrote very fully to Francis:

"Your offer of submission unto me . . . battered so the unkindness that I had conceived in my heart for your behaviour towards me in my absence, as out of the sparks of my old affection towards you I went to sound his Majesty's intention how he meant to behave himself towards you. . . . The sight of his deep-conceived indignation quenched my passion, making me upon the instant change from the person of a party into a peace-maker; so I was forced upon my knees to beg of his Majesty that he would put no public act of disgrace upon you. And as I dare say no other person would have been patiently heard in this suit by his Majesty but myself, so did I, though not without difficulty, obtain thus much. That he would not so far disable you from the merit of your future service, as to put any particular mark of disgrace upon your person. Only . . . he cannot omit, though laying aside all passion, to give a kingly reprimand at his first sitting in council to so many of his councillors as were then here behind and were actors in this business, for their ill behaviour in it. . . .

"I protest all this time past it was no small grief unto me to hear the mouth of so many upon this occasion open to load you with innumerable malicious and detracting speeches, as no music were more pleasing to my ears than to rail of you; which made me rather regret the ill-nature of mankind, that like dogs love to set upon him that they see once snatched at. And to conclude, my Lord, you have hereby a fair occasion so to make good hereafter your reputation by your sincere service to his Majesty, as also by your firm and constant kindness to your friends, as I may, your Lordship's old friend, participate of the comfort and honour that will thereby come to you.

"Your Lordship's faithful friend and servant,
"G.B."

Yes . . . A decidedly better tone and atmosphere, but Francis could not ignore the fact that he had come very near to losing his place. The King's absence and his position of authority had accustomed him to power, a dangerous responsibility too easily misused, as he knew very well when other men possessed it. And it had all come about through loyalty to Elizabeth Hatton—memories shared, sweet friendship's sake —and, he must not deny it, mounting irritation at the conduct of the Secretary of State who presumed too much at the Council table.

Now, it seemed, his Majesty was pacified, the Earl of Buckingham was reconciled, but things would never be quite the same again; that parent-pupil relationship belonged to the past, and any attempt to renew it would not be favoured. Such intimacy was frowned on by the King, and the pupil appeared to have outgrown it. Francis must tread more warily in future, bearing in mind that a careless or too confident step forward upon that winding stair might cause a man to slip and fall headlong.

Back-tracking was not pleasant for him. He must make overtures to Lady Compton, and to Sir John Villiers. Edward Sherburn, that able young secretary, could be employed on this as go-between, and in return Francis would stand godfather to his newly-born son. Sir Edward Coke must be welcomed back to the Council table, to which he had been restored, but hardest of all was Sir Edward's request that his wife Lady Hatton should be held in preventive custody prior to an examination as to the truth or forgery of documents pretending to be from the Earl of Oxford. She was permitted to lodge with first an Alderman Bennet, and later with Sir William Craven, but once separated from her daughter her influence had gone, and Coke was able to have his way at last, and insist upon the wedding taking place as soon as possible.

Whether Francis Bacon was obliged to swallow pride and attend we are not told, but on Michaelmas Day Sir John Villiers, elder brother of the Earl of Buckingham, was married to Frances Coke, daughter of Sir Edward Coke and Lady Hatton. The wedding took place at Hampton Court, and his Majesty gave away the bride. The Queen and the Prince of Wales also attended the ceremony in the private chapel of the palace. Lady Hatton had been invited, but prayed to be excused, through sickness.

One of the gossips, writing to Dudley Carleton, had this to say of the affair, "My Lord Coke gave his daughter to the King with some words of compliment at the giving. The King gave her to Sir John Villiers. The Prince sat with her to a grand dinner and supper to many Lords and Ladies, my Lord Canterbury, my Lord Treasurer, my Lord Chamberlain, etc. The King dinner and supper drank health to the bride, the bridegroom stood behind the bride; dinner and supper. The bride and bridegroom lay next day a-bed till past 12 o'clock, for the King sent word he would come and see them, therefore would they not rise. My Lord Coke looked with a merry countenance and sat at dinner and supper, but my Lady Hatton was not at the wedding, but is still at Alderman Bennet's a prisoner. The King sent for her to the wedding, but she desired to be excused, saying she was sick. My Lord of Buckingham, mother, brethren, their sons and sisters were throughout day at Court, my Lord Coke's sons and their sons, but I saw never a Cecil."

If it was not a case of all's well that ends well for the marriage itself, which later proved to be extremely unhappy, the immediate consequences were not unfortunate for the Lord Keeper. That thorn in his flesh, the Secretary of State, Sir Ralph Winwood, fell ill, very suddenly, in the third week in October, and, despite bloodletting and the usual remedies, died on the 27th of the month. "Upon the opening of his body," reported John Chamberlain, who was a close friend, "it appears he could not possibly have lasted long, having his heart withered almost to nothing, his spleen utterly rotten, one of his kidneys clean gone, the other perished, his liver full of black spots, his lungs not sound, besides divers other defects." Sir Ralph can therefore be forgiven for his interference at the Council table, and for beating his dog; he had good reason.

The King did not at once appoint a successor to his place, but in the meantime handed over the seals of office to the Earl of Buckingham, who, possibly at the discreet suggestion of the Lord Keeper and anyway hoping to restore good relations with his new sister-in-law's family, drove himself on Lord Mayor's Day to set Lady Hatton at liberty, and conduct her to her father (who had been created Earl of Exeter in 1605) at Cecil House in the Strand.

All was forgiven. Lady Hatton went to Court, and was reconciled both to his Majesty and to the Queen, who had always been fond of her. Lady Compton was also present. That evening there was a great feast at Cecil House, and a week later Lady Hatton entertained the royal party at Hatton House. "My Lord Coke only was absent," went the report, "who in all vulgar opinions was there expected. His Majesty was never merrier nor more satisfied, who had not patience to sit a quarter of an hour without drinking the health of my Lady Elizabeth Hatton, which was pledged first by my Lord Keeper and my Lord Marquis Hamilton, and then by all the lords and ladies with great gravity and respect, and then by all the gallants in the next room."

Everyone was happy, except perhaps Sir Edward Coke, who dined alone in his chambers in the Temple. As for the Lord Keeper, he had every reason, like his Majesty, to be satisfied. He too, like his former love, the Lady Hatton, was restored to favour. Letters once more passed almost daily between him and the Earl of Buckingham. His opponent at the Council table, Sir Ralph Winwood—God rest his soul— had gone to his Maker, and his old rival, ex-Lord Chief Justice Coke, although a Councillor, had been outwitted. Young Edward Sherburn had the makings of a most excellent secretary, and Tobie Matthew was a constant visitor ("grown very gay or rather gaudy in his attire," so Chamberlain observed, "and noted for certain night walks to the Spanish Ambassador"), but most satisfying of all was that once again, at long last, the Lord Keeper was living where he most wished to be, under the roof of his old home, York House.

Chapter XIV

On New Year's Day, 1618, his Majesty was pleased to create George Villiers Marquis of Buckingham, which seems to have caused something of a surprise in circles about the Court, the honour not having been expected. John Chamberlain reported that "no such matter had been spoken of," but the King "professed to do it for the affection he bear him, more than he did to any man, and for the affection, faith, and modesty that he found in him." And on the Sunday following the new year, the same writer announced that "the Lord Keeper was made Lord Chancellor, wherein he has this advantage that it is for life, with £600 a year increase. The speech goes that he shall be made a baron, and hath the making of another given him to discharge his debts; which in courtesy he hath offered to his eldest brother [half-brother Sir Nicholas Bacon of Redgrave, now seventy-eight years old] for £1,000 less than another should give; which he will not accept: mindful perhaps of his father's motto or posy, *mediocria firma*. His Lordship hath of late much insinuated into the King's and Lord Marquis's favour; and takes a new course of thriving; having at one clap cashiered sixteen of his gallants."

John Chamberlain, who, as we know, had been a close friend of the late Sir Ralph Winwood, seldom lost an opportunity to take a dig at Francis Bacon.

That same evening the new marquis gave a great dinner, with his Majesty and the Prince of Wales present, and undoubtedly the Lord Chancellor also—surely with his lady taking precedence over the wives of barons—and we are told seventeen dozen pheasants and twelve dozen partridges were served at table.

The Lord Chancellor had presented the marquis with a "plain cup of essay" as a new year's gift, the wording of his accompanying note suggesting a play on words, "in token that if your Lordship in any thing shall make me your sayman, I will be hurt before your Lordship shall be hurt." The Prince of Wales received "a pair of small candlesticks of gold, in token that his light and the light of his posterity upon church and commonwealth may never fail." There is no record of a present to his Majesty, but, remembering the gift of a petticoat which Francis once sent as a new year's token to Queen Elizabeth, perhaps King James was offered some article of wearing apparel to adorn his person in the royal bedchamber.

The Prince of Wales presented a masque on Twelfth Night, written by Ben Jonson, *Pleasure Reconciled to Virtue*, but for once it failed to please, despite the prancing of the two marquises, Buckingham and Hamilton, with the Earl of Montgomery and divers ladies. Lady Hatton was not present, neither was the Queen, who had been unwell for some little time. Both she and the King appear to have had circulatory trouble in their legs, and anything of this nature was invariably put down to gout. It was said that his Majesty had to be tied to his horse when hunting, but stiffness afterwards could be relieved by placing both his legs into the corpse of a disembowelled deer. His Lord Chancellor would not have recommended this doubtful remedy. His own treatment, "which hath seldom failed, but driven it away in twenty-four hours," was "first to apply a poultice . . . of manchet boiled in milk, and a powder of red roses, and ten grains of saffron." Then after the pores were open apply a "fomentation of sage leaves . . . root of hemlock, and water wherein steel hath been quenched." Finally a "plaster, dissolved with oil of roses, spread upon a piece of holland, and applied." Certainly a more pleasant prescription than bathing his legs in deer's blood, but then, his Majesty's tastes in many things were a little less refined than those of his Lord Chancellor.

Tobie Matthew was in the news again, in close attendance upon the Countess of Exeter, who was thirty-eight years younger than her husband the earl, now seventy-six. He had married her as his second wife in 1612, so she was stepmother to a large family of sons and daughters considerably older than herself; one of them was Lady Hatton. Tobie Matthew was said to be "perverting" the countess to become a Roman Catholic, but she was in some trouble anyway, having been accused of attempting to poison Lady Roos, wife of her husband's grandson.

This delicate matter was handed over to the Lord Chancellor to examine. He was obliged to tread warily, knowing both families well, for he had on the one side Sir Thomas Lake, a member of the Council and the father of Lady Roos, and on the other the outraged Earl of Exeter, who considered that his wife had been slandered, and who was determined to bring the whole affair before the Star Chamber. This necessitated several months of delay, and the Lord Chancellor was able to concentrate on more immediate matters connected with

Chancery, finding time also to further certain suits of the Marquis of Buckingham, who was writing weekly from Newmarket or Theobalds, wherever the King should be, desiring him to favour various gentlemen in various affairs, "which I will not fail to acknowledge as done to myself." Frequently these "suits" concerned members of Buckingham's own family, and the Lord Chancellor had to exercise the utmost care and discretion that when there was any controversy between rival parties he judged such cases on their merit alone.

The King, despite his hope for a marriage between the Prince of Wales and the Infanta of Spain, still held to a policy of dealing firmly with recusants, in which he differed from his Lord Chancellor, who took a more moderate line. Perhaps his many conversations with Tobie Matthew had influenced him in this, for Tobie would have reported back to him the hopes of his many Spanish friends and others at the Spanish Court. However, Francis was obliged to abide by his Majesty's commands, and on February 13th, before the judges went out on circuit, he made a speech in the Star Chamber giving them instructions that they should be more definite in finding out how many recusants there were throughout the country, "in what corners and where their nests are, and where it is that they do abound. . . . None shall be a justice of peace whose wife is a recusant," he went on, which seems rather a harsh measure for an otherwise law-abiding Catholic.

The Lord Chancellor also gave instructions that justices should be firmer in dealing with thieves; he would not have tolerated the modern custom of letting the offender off with a fine. "There is a rising of robberies more now than in former times was wont: and there are two causes hereof; the one is that men are too loose in taking of the committers of them, and the other is they are negligent in suffering them to go away; for now hue and cries are of no consequence, only a little paper is sent up and down with a soft pace, whereas they should be prosecuted with horse and foot, and hunted as a thief."

Something that concerned him more personally was the case of Lord Clifton, who had been prosecuted for some fault before Francis became Lord Chancellor, imprisoned in the Fleet, and ordered to pay of fine of £1,000. Furious, this nobleman threatened to kill the Lord Keeper, and was transferred to the Tower. Francis, magnanimous as always, was prepared to intercede for him and he was released, but the unfortunate nobleman appears to have been unbalanced, for some months later he stabbed himself in his Holborn lodgings.

Meanwhile, during the early part of the year and into the spring Francis continued his sittings in the Court of Chancery, present every day, recording every fact, never rising until all business had been concluded; while for information of a more personal kind we have to turn to John Chamberlain, who now and again mentions the Lord Chancellor, or his friends, in his numerous letters to Dudley Carleton in Venice.

We hear in early February that Tobie Matthew is "going to a play at Blackfriars but methinks playing and Friday's fasting agree not so well together as praying in a man of so much profession." Chamberlain obviously disapproved of Tobie; possibly he was still sporting his "gaudy attire" and paying nightly visits to the Spanish ambassador.

There was some disagreement between the Lord Chancellor and the Archbishop of Canterbury about the appointment of a new provost at Oriel College, Oxford. The Archbishop wanted a man of "years and gravity," and that "striplings should not be made heads of houses." Francis favoured a younger man, saying he "respected not minority of years when there was majority of parts." His protégé was only twenty-six, and in the event he was appointed.

In April the Lord Chancellor attended a sermon at Mercers' Chapel to hear the Archbishop of Spalato speak. Francis came "in all his pomp of the Council, which was not so strange as, not a month since, to see him in the same state go . . . to cheapen [bargain for] and buy silks and velvets."

John Chamberlain may have sneered at the Lord Chancellor buying his clothes at bargain prices; he would surely have itched to get his fingers on the personal statement of receipts and disbursements for that same year, from June to September, had he known they existed amongst the private papers. Like the private memoranda for 1608, these lists of ten years later were presumably never intended for any eyes except those of Francis Bacon and his personal secretaries, but preserved they were, and eventually found their way amongst the state documents.

The biographers Spedding and Dixon repeat them in full, but here a selection has been made for the purpose of revealing the more intimate side of Francis Bacon, Lord Keeper and Lord Chancellor, in the year 1618. Under "receipts" for the four months, for instance, we find:

		£	s	d
June 27	Of your Lordship from Mr Tobie Matthew by your Lp. order	400	0	0
July 23	Of Mr Edney [groom of the chamber, and one of Francis Bacon's original attendants]	209	0	0
	Of Mr Young, your Lp. secretary	300	10	0
	Of Mr Hatcher [seal-bearer] from the Hamper	680	0	0

The following items were listed under the heading "Gifts and Rewards":

June 26	To one that brought your Lp. cherries & other things fom Gorhambury by four Lp.'s order	0	6	0
29	To an Italian by your Lp. order	5	10	0
30	To Mr Butler by your Lp. order as a gift	22	0	0
July 1	To my La. Hatton's man that brought your Lp. garden seeds	0	11	0

So the bond of friendship had not been severed, and the gardens of Hatton House were filled with lilies, rosemary, cloves, strawberries, which evidently found their way either to York House or down to Gorhambury.

July 5	To Mr Matthew's man that brought your Lp. sweetmeats	0	5	0
	To Mr Recorder's man that brought your Lp. a salmon	0	10	0
July 6	To Mr Trowshaw, a poor man & late a prisoner in the Compter by your Lp. order	3	6	0
	To the Washwoman, for sending after the crane that flew into the Thames [A delightful image! Had Francis observed the scene from his window in York House, and the washwoman, knowing his affection for birds, halloo'd to a nearby waterman?]	0	5	0
July 8	To my Lady's footman that brought your Lp. cherries from Gorhambury [Alice was evidently in the country, and Francis could entertain his friends to salmon and cherries without her.]	0	5	0
July 30	To Sir Samuel Paton's man that brought your Lp. 12 dozen of quails	1	2	0
	To Mr Jones the apothecary his man [Indigestion must have followed upon the quails!]	0	5	0
July 31	To Sir Edward Carew's man that brought your Lp. boxes of orange flowers, by your Lp. order	9	10	0
August 1	To a poor pilgrim by your Lp. order	2	4	0
August 2	To a poor man at St Albans by your Lp. order	0	2	6
	To Mr Gibson's maid of St Albans that brought your Lp. six turkies	0	5	6

The vacation had started, and the Lord Chancellor was now settled at Gorhambury. Bucks, stags and salmon follow in quick succession, all unsolicited gifts from noblemen, but the apothecary of St Albans was summoned immediately afterwards, and received £1 2s od. Indeed, the apothecary was usually summoned the day after a good dinner, and he pocketed another £1 2s od when Francis had been made a present of some ducks.

The Lord Chancellor was in London in mid-August, and several rewards are listed for this period, all dated August 19th, amongst them being:

To the several servants of your Lp. house at Gorhambury at your Lp. coming from thence at your Lp. order	15	14	0
To the carters that came up to London with the trunks	0	10	0
To him that came with the confectionery glasses	0	3	0
To him that came with the sumpters	0	2	6
To the woman that washed & starched your Lp. lining at Gorhambury	0	6	0
To the Prince's trumpeters by your Lp. order	2	4	0
To old Mr Hillyard by your Lp. order	11	0	0

This last item is of special interest. "Old Mr Hillyard" would be Nicholas Hilliard, the famous painter of portraits and miniatures, who had painted a miniature of Francis Bacon at eighteen, and had been in financial distress for some time. He was now seventy-one, and was to die the following year.

The list of modest rewards for services rendered continues until the end of September, and usually consists of a few shillings paid to a man who had brought a gift of birds or fruit from his master to the Lord Chancellor.

The list of "Disbursements and Payments" is not so modest, although to the present-day eye they do not seem excessive.

June 25	Paid the lining draper and sempster's bill for cloth and lace and making your Lp. ruffs, & cuffs, & shirts	29	8	10
July 4	Paid for a looking-glass for your Lp. case	0	18	0
July 8	Paid Mr Young your Lp. secretary by your Lp. order	66	0	0
	Paid the Steward by your Lp. order	200	0	0
	Paid Mr Neave the upholster in part of his bill	200	0	0

July 9	Paid the Steward by your Lp. order	400	0	0
July 23	Paid the Steward by your Lp. order	200	0	0
July 24	Paid the Steward by your Lp. order	200	0	0

It will be seen from the above that the steward must have been responsible for many of the household bills, food, servants' wages, etc. His name at this time was Mr Sharpeigh, and he appears to have lived up to it. Certain of the tradesmen sent in separate bills, as below:

August 15	Paid Mr Wells your Lp. butcher at Gorhambury in part of his bill of a greater sum due	100	0	0
August 17	Paid the Clerk of the Kitchen at Gorhambury by your Lp. order	50	0	0
September 11	Paid Mr Miller the woolen draper by your Lp. order in part of his old bill	100	0	0

—and, continually, the sum of £200 to Mr Sharpeigh, Steward.

The roll of attendants, grooms of the chamber, gentlemen waiters, pages, ushers, and lesser fry amounted at this time to seventy-three. Certainly an enormous retinue, but the steward may not have been accountable for the salaries of the personal attendants.

Entertaining at York House and Gorhambury must certainly have increased from July onwards, for on the twelfth of that month Lord Keeper Lord Chancellor Sir Francis Bacon was created Baron Verulam of Verulam, and from henceforward signed his name Fr. Verulam, Canc. He took his name from the Roman city of Verulamium three-quarters of a mile away, and it was about this time that he began building his new house, set in the north-east corner of the park at Gorhambury. It was supposed to be a place of retreat, but as it was set near the main turnpike road it could not have been as quiet, even in those days, as the old house in the grounds above. Verulam House was planned to be small and compact, with high rooms, a grand staircase, and a flat leaded roof from which his lordship could enjoy the views over the various walks, gardens and lakes. The kitchens were placed in a basement, a novel idea at that time, and water was piped up to the house from the ponds nearby.

We can tell that building was under way this summer from items listed in the payments.

August 17	Paid Mr Dobson by your Lp. order to discharge areas of workmen's bills left unpaid at Whittide last	100	0	0
September 17	Paid the Steward by your Lp. order for Mr Styles the mason for the works at Verulam	50	0	0

Francis designed the house himself with the help of an assistant, Mr Dobson from St Albans, and the cost of the building was said to be around £ 10,000. This was three times what his father, Lord Keeper Sir Nicholas Bacon, had spent when he built Gorhambury. The ruins of the old house stand today, but—alas for explorers—not a stone remains of Verulam House, which was pulled down some forty years after Francis died. John Aubrey saw it in 1656, ten years before it was demolished, and described it in his *Brief Lives,* in which he said it was "the most ingeniously contrived little pile that ever I saw . . . there were good chimney pieces; the rooms were very lofty, and all were very well wainscotted. There were two bathing-rooms or stuffes, whither his Lordship retired afternoons as he saw cause. All the tunnels of the chimneys were carried into the middle of the house; and round about them were seats. . . .

"In the middle of this house was a delicate staircase of wood, which was curiously carved, and on the posts of every interstice was some pretty figure, as of a grave divine with his book and spectacles, a mendicant friar, etc., not one thing twice. On the doors of the upper story on the outside, which were painted dark umber, were the figures of the gods of the Gentiles; viz, Apollo . . . Jupiter, with his thunderbolt, bigger than the life, and done by an excellent hand; the heightenings were of hatchings of gold, which when the sun shone on them made a most glorious show.

"The upper part of the uppermost moor on the east side had inserted into it a large looking-glass, with which the stranger was very gratefully deceived, for, after he had been entertained a pretty while, with the prospects of the ponds, walks, and country, which this door faced, one would have sworn at first glance that he had beheld another prospect through the house; for as soon as the stranger was landed on the balcony, the concierge that showed the house would shut the door to put this fallacy on him with his looking-glass."

The "stuffes" John Aubrey mentions were heated rooms, in other words a form of Turkish bath. Possibly an antidote to that fatal sleep of afternoon.

After visiting Verulam House Aubrey walked up to Gorhambury, a mile distant, and saw the gardens and the woods, but from his description both were already in decline, and "east of the parquet, where his Lordship much meditated, his servant Mr Bushell attending him with his pen and ink horn, and in his Lordship's time a paradise, now is a large ploughed field." There were some four acres of fish-ponds, "pitched at the bottom with pebbles of several colours, as of fishes, etc., which in his Lordship's time were plainly to be seen through the clear water, now overgrown with flags and rushes."

Thus even in a short space of time the garden and surroundings of Gorhambury that Francis had planted and laid out with so much love and care had gone to waste; something which happens with such frequency in the present day, but is somehow unexpected in the seventeenth century.

Mr Bushell, with his pen and ink-horn, figures in the roll of attendants in 1618 as "gent. usher." He had, in fact, served Francis Bacon since 1608 as a lad of fifteen, and stayed with him until his death, when he became a mining engineer in Somerset and Cardigan, basing his knowledge on all that he had learnt on minerals from his master.

The two chief secretaries in the rolls are Mr Young and Mr Thomas Meautys. Thomas Meautys was later to become secretary-in-chief and a close personal friend, and was to marry the granddaughter of Sir Nicholas Bacon, half-brother to Francis. Edward Sherburn is entered as a groom of the chamber, and there are some twenty-five gentlemen waiters; one would like to know their precise duties. Mr Percy is there, that "bloody Percy" so much detested by the first Lady Bacon. He must by now have been advanced in years, like his master. There is a Mr Nicholas Bacon, very probably the son of half-brother Edward Bacon, and—possibly the most intriguing gentleman waiter of them all—Mr John Underhill, at that time twenty-six years old, of Loxley in Warwickshire, a few miles from Stratford-on-Avon, and kinsman to William Underhill who had sold New Place to Mr William Shakespeare.

This gentleman waiter would presently rise to become steward to the new Baroness Verulam and enter into a very close relationship with her indeed. They were the same age, and one cannot help wondering if Lady Hatton, whose first husband was step-brother to Mr William Underhill of Warwickshire, original owner of New Place, introduced young Underhill to the Gorhambury household. A presentable young man might keep Lady Verulam company about the fishponds, while she herself discussed the planting of rosemary for remembrance in the upper walks with his lordship.

Whether she dined with him on a Monday in early August we are not told, but if she did she would have been in company with Lady Compton, her daughter's mother-in-law, who had just been created Countess of Buckingham, a title which gave some concern to the Heralds, as her husband Sir Thomas Compton remained a knight, causing them to wonder whether her daughters should now take

127

precedence over other ladies. Possibly this was discussed at table, for the new countess drove down there for dinner to see her patent sealed and delivered. Bucks, salmon, a stag, and twelve fat wethers (castrated rams) were delivered to Gorhambury during that first week in August, and the apothecary's man called twice. . . .

Lady Verulam was now accustomed to presiding at her husband the Lord Chancellor's table, and assuming that he had indeed chosen her twelve years before for her looks and her wit—and also, of course, her portion—she would have been well able to hold her own with the formidable Countess of Buckingham. Alice, the alderman's daughter, could now boast that all her three sisters had married knights, and her two Packington half-sisters were to do the same. As for her mother, that interfering lady, when her second husband Sir John Packington died, she found herself a Viscount Kilmorey.

It is easy to imagine how Francis Bacon after entertaining the various members of his wife's family, besides visitors from London who had travelled down on other business, would find an excuse, the moment they all departed, to wander in the woods and gardens he so much loved, with young Bushell or another at his side, pen and inkhorn in hand. "God Almighty first planted a garden; and, indeed, it is the purest of human pleasures; it is the greatest refreshment to the spirits of man; without which buildings and palaces are but gross handyworks." As he looked about him, different thoughts would come to mind, comparisons with earlier days, other years when his mother still lived. . . . "They say that every five-and-thirty years the same kind and suit of years and weathers comes about again: as great frosts, great wet, great droughts, warm winters, summers with little heat, and the like: it is a thing, I do the rather mention, because computing backwards, I have found some concurrence."

Then back to the house to more serious work on his *Novum Organum*, which would cover his whole field of thought: "And again, if a man turn from the workshop to the library, and wonder at the immense variety of books he sees there, let him but examine and diligently inspect their matter and contents, and his wonder will assuredly be turned the other way; for after observing their endless repetitions, and how men are ever saying and doing what has been said and done before, he will pass from admiration of the variety to astonishment at the poverty and scantiness of the subjects which till now have occupied and possessed minds of men."

But duty claimed him once again. He must leave Gorhambury and his private pursuits for London. Sir Walter Ralegh, home from his expedition in search of a gold-mine in the new world, whither he had sailed the year before, had returned to report only failure, and was in disgrace not only for this but for having sacked a Spanish settlement. This was a serious offence, in view of the present state of friendship between Great Britain and Spain. He was arrested and imprisoned for the second time in the Tower of London. The Lord Chancellor was one of the members of the Council appointed to examine him.

Chapter XV

Sir Walter Ralegh's expedition had been made in all good faith, and sanctioned by the King himself. His release from the Tower, after fifteen years' imprisonment, had been for the specific purpose of going "unto the south parts of America . . . to discover and find out some commodities and merchandises in those countries that be necessary and profitable for subjects of his Majesty's kingdoms and dominions; whereof the inhabitants there make little or no use or estimation."

Ralegh declared that he knew of one particular gold mine near the banks of the river Orinoco, and this seems to have been the real purpose of his expedition. Vessels were placed under his command, and he sailed from Plymouth in June of 1617 with the goodwill of his Majesty, the Council and all the people. Francis Bacon, Lord Keeper at the time, had discussed the project with him one day at Gray's Inn, and with his interest in mining and in colonisation—he had been one of the first to invest in the Company of Venturers to Virginia and the islands off the coast—was naturally enthusiastic; Ralegh was as forward in science and mineralogy as he was himself.

Francis would have warned him, however, not to play the pirate, or harm any of the King of Spain's subjects who might be in the vicinity. These instructions were implicit in Ralegh's orders from the Council, but whether he misunderstood them, or Captain Keymis under his command disobeyed them, has never been entirely clear; the sequel was that Spaniards were found on the banks of the Orinoco, fighting took place, villages were burnt, no mine was discovered, and the expedition returned to Plymouth in June 1618 having achieved nothing at all except to endanger diplomatic relations between England and Spain.

The Spanish ambassador Count de Gondomar (he whom Tobie Matthew used to visit by night) had objected to the expedition before it set forth, and now found himself vindicated, crying "Piratas! Piratas!" against Ralegh and his fellow adventurers. Unfortunately for

5. George Villiers, Duke of Buckingham, attributed to William Larkin, c. 1616
(photo National Portrait Gallery, London)

6. and 7. Two views of the pond-yards at Gorhambury today
(photo Christian Browning)

8. Sir Francis Bacon as Lord Keeper after Paul van Somer,
artist unknown *(photo National Portrait Gallery, London)*

the ambassador, one of his train had the misfortune to run down a child with his horse just about this time, which so infuriated the people of Chancery Lane, where the accident occurred, that some five thousand citizens living in the neighbourhood besieged the count's house, and a near-riot took place. Sir Walter Ralegh's arrest and imprisonment in the Tower, clashing with the arrest of the rioters, instantly turned him into a popular hero amongst the ordinary people, everything Spanish was detested, and diplomatic relations became more delicate than ever.

The Council of six appointed to examine Ralegh included Sir Edward Coke, who had uttered vituperation against him sixteen years before at Winchester, and condemned him to death for treason; but then his Majesty had intervened, and spared his life. The examination continued throughout September and into October, and the recommendation of the Council was that Sir Walter should be brought before the whole Council, the judges, and some of the nobility and gentry. The King disagreed: he wished for no one other than the original examiners to be present, and for the Attorney-General and Solicitor-General to prefer the charges against Ralegh and those committed with him. After which the sentence, so long suspended, would be put into execution.

The King knew only too well that Sir Walter Ralegh, now a popular figure, would win even more esteem amongst the people and the nobility and gentry if he was allowed publicly to speak in his own defence. If he were pardoned twice, and imprisoned for life rather than suffer the supreme penalty, relations with Spain would seriously deteriorate, and negotiations for the Spanish marriage be broken off.

The Queen, by now seriously ill with dropsy at Hampton Court, did everything she could to spare Ralegh's life. She had never forgotten the friendship that had existed between him and her eldest son Henry Prince of Wales. The Marquis of Buckingham would surely speak for him, and she wrote as she had done in the past, beginning her letter, "My kind dog, if I have any power or credit with you, I earnestly pray you let me have a trial of it at this time, in dealing sincerely and earnestly with the King that Sir Walter Ralegh's life may not be called in question. . . ." But the Marquis, like his Majesty, had no desire to make trouble with the Spanish ambassador and the King of Spain; he, like Charles Prince of Wales, favoured the marriage at all costs.

The trial took place in private, as the King had demanded. Ralegh denied all allegations save one, that he had attempted to escape from the Tower when first arrested. On October 28th he was brought to the bar of King's Bench and sentenced to death. That night he was taken from the Tower to Westminster gatehouse, and the following morning, the 29th, he was beheaded in Old Palace Yard.

Sir Walter Ralegh spoke for half an hour on the scaffold, and won respect from everyone who heard him. Even that cynic John Chamberlain was impressed. "He spake and behaved himself so, without any show of fear or affectation, that he moved much commiseration, and all that saw him confess that his end was *omnibus numeris absolutus,* and as far as man can discern every way perfect." He was sixty-six years old. Soldier, seaman, courtier, individualist throughout his life, with many friends and many enemies, he was the last of that gallant breed of men who had won the favour and affection of Queen Elizabeth.

Popular indignation was great. There was a man like the Earl of Somerset, still living in comfort at the Tower—in Ralegh's old lodgings, which made comparisons the more odious—while a courageous adventurer like the brave man just beheaded, who had served monarch and country in many an expedition in the past, and had voyaged overseas to bring back wealth to all, was made to die the death of a traitor; just, so it was said, to pacify the blood-lust of Spain.

Something had to be done to reassure the people. Since there had been no public trial they were ignorant of all the aspects of the case. There had been errors of judgement, failure to obey instructions, and many other faults on the part of Ralegh and his commanders of which the people should be told. His Majesty must by now have realised that he had been in error when he insisted on a private trial. The facts must be set out plain and clear for all to know.

So far Francis Bacon had taken no prominent part in the proceedings beyond having been one of the six Councillors appointed to examine Sir Walter Ralegh in the Tower. Now he was desired by the King, with others of the Council, to draw up an official declaration of the *True Motives and Inducements which occasioned his Majesty to proceed in doing justice upon him, as hath been done.*

This extensive document, which was printed in London by his Majesty's printers, and appeared on November 28th, was attributed by John Chamberlain and others to "the Lord Chancellor, Master Attorney, and Secretary Naunton." (Sir Robert Naunton had succeeded to the late Sir Ralph Winwood's place earlier in the year.) If all three Councillors were blamed for salving the King's conscience at the expense of the popular hero, it was something to which the Lord Chancellor had become accustomed. Indeed, he had been commanded to do the same some seventeen years before, after the Earl of Essex had been condemned to death. It was no light thing to serve a monarch who ruled by divine right. Obedience to royal command came before any personal obligation to former friends.

The effort required to assist in the compiling of the declaration took its usual toll upon the Lord Chancellor's health; there was no meeting of the Star Chamber during the week previous to its publication because of his "indisposition," and no meeting early in December either, the excuse being "that he cannot endure the cold." The weather had certainly turned bitter, with the Thames frozen over and impassable for boats, while the smallpox raged in London at the same time. These natural hazards were hardly likely to have kept Francis from the usual routine, and one cannot help wondering whether he felt that Ralegh's execution had been a grave error of judgement and would reflect badly upon the monarchy and the person of the King himself, whose popularity with the ordinary people had never been high.

The "indisposition" continued off and on throughout the winter, and for almost the first time since her marriage Lady Verulam is mentioned in one of John Chamberlain's letters in December, appearing at a large funeral cortège for one of the nobility, a victim to smallpox, "with a world of other Ladies." Perhaps she was deputising for her husband, and found satisfaction in her new status.

Something that certainly saddened Francis was that Tobie Matthew had still not taken his oath of allegiance, and early in the new year his Majesty once more ordered him to leave the country. "What offence was done or taken I know not," observed John Chamberlain, "but it seems for all his great friends he was commanded away." Correspondence between the two friends would continue, with Tobie writing from Brussels, but this was not the same as seeing one another continually at York House and Gorhambury, and there was no one, not even among his secretaries and attendants, to whom he could open heart and mind as he did to Tobie Matthew. It was not a happy start to 1619.

Then on January 12th there was a great fire at Whitehall. The banqueting-house was burnt out, and many Council papers that had been kept in the room beneath the gallery were destroyed. Mercifully no lives were lost in the fire, but the disappearance of so many important records and documents came as a great shock to those who, like the Lord Chancellor and other members of the Council, held high office.

Foreign intelligence was another cause for concern. Early in February Tobie Matthew reported to the Lord Chancellor from Brussels that "in Spain there are very extraordinary preparations for a great Armada." Where this fleet was to be employed no one knew.

It was about this time, between winter and spring, that Francis drew up a paper entitled *A Short View to be Taken of Great Britain and Spain,* evidently to be shown to his Majesty as a summing up of the relative power of the two countries. This paper was found after his death, and we have no means of knowing whether in fact it was ever shown to the King. It is worth quoting for its forthright views, which may well have been expressed at the Council table.

"His Majesty now of England is of more power than any of his predecessors . . . Ireland is reduced into a more absolute state of obedience and increase of revenue than heretofore. . . . The joining of Scotland hath made us an entire island, which by nature is the best fortification and the most capable of all the advantages of strength that can by art be added unto nature; whereby we may be able at one and the same time both to undertake any action abroad and defend ourselves at home without either much danger or great cost. . . .

"Now for Spain, his Majesty there, though accounted the greatest monarch of Christendom, yet if his estate be enquired through, his root will be found a great deal too narrow for his tops. . . . The policy of Spain hath trodden more bloody steps than any state of Christendom. Look into the treaties and the negotiations of his ministers abroad. You shall find as much falsehood in these as blood in the other. . . . And [his Spanish Majesty] hath an ambition to the whole empire of Christendom. . . . Who hath been so thirsty of our blood as Spain? And who hath spilled so much of it as he? And who hath been so long our enemy? And who hath corrupted so many of our nation as Spain?"

What is particularly fascinating to the modern reader is to find Francis Bacon revealing himself in the plumage of what we are pleased to call in present-day phraseology a "hawk." For the enterprise which he suggested in his pamphlet was no less than the conquest of the Indies for Great Britain, with the accompanying risk of a war with Spain—if, in fact, the King of Spain had resources enough to face such an encounter by sea.

The King of Great Britain, on the contrary, was a "dove." He had no desire for war of any kind; the role of mediator was more agreeable to him. So the Lord Chancellor's "hawk-like" project—inspired, one cannot help thinking, by regret at Ralegh's execution—was laid aside; and then the events at home preoccupied his Majesty and all his loyal subjects.

The Queen, who had been failing for some months, died early in the morning of March 2nd at Hampton Court. The Prince of Wales was at her bedside. The King was at Newmarket with a "fit of the stone," and became so weak himself that his doctors feared for his life also and would not permit him to travel.

By a coincidence, the Lord Chancellor was ill of the same disease, more seriously than was supposed at the time. He referred to it later in a letter to Tobie Matthew, "when once my master and afterwards myself, were both of us in extremity of sickness, which was no time to dissemble, I never had so great pledges and certainties of his love and favour." It is unfortunate for us that the messages from the sick sovereign to his equally sick subject do not seem to have survived.

The Queen's body was brought to Denmark House in the Strand and lay there for more than two months, the excuse being, so rumour had it, that there was no ready money available for the funeral. The London crowds, hoping for the customary stately spectacle, became restless. Entertainments were forbidden, and all play-houses were closed, the ban coinciding, strangely enough, with the death of London's most famous and best-loved actor-manager, Richard Burbage.

Finally, on May 13th, the Queen's coffin, drawn by six horses, was escorted to Westminster Abbey. The Prince of Wales walked before it, deputising for the King, who was at Theobalds. John Chamberlain did not think much of the procession. "The funeral was but a brawling, tedious sight, more remarkable for number than for any other singularity . . . and though the number of Lords and Ladies were very great, yet methought altogether they made but a poor show, which was perhaps because they were apparelled all alike, or that they came laggering all along even tired with the length of the way and weight of their clothes, every Lady having twelve yards of broad cloth about her and the countesses sixteen." Lady Verulam would have been one of these, and Lady Hatton.

Queen Anne's had been a sad, lonely life, despite her many ladies, since the death of her beloved son Prince Henry; and with her husband the King, who had his own separate household, his own pursuits and his own favourites, there had for many years been little companionship. Her happiest time had surely been when she first came to England, to be acclaimed by the crowds, and when her children were still young, and she herself twenty-nine years old, throwing herself with delight and gaiety into those frequent masques at Court which she enjoyed so much. She lies somewhere beneath the Henry VII chapel in Westminster Abbey, but no monument was ever placed to mark her grave.

The Lord Chancellor sent a tribute to her memory when he wrote to her brother King Christian of Denmark, first mentioning that he himself had "newly recovered from a sickness of some severity . . .

and yet I am so pressed and distracted with infinite business that I seem hardly to breathe, or live. I have moreover a new and great grief continually recurring for the death of my most serene mistress Queen Anne, from whose constant favour ever flowing and accumulated upon me I was wont to find myself much refreshed and strengthened. . . . Wherefore it will be my part to cherish continually her most happy memory."

The rumour that the Exchequer was so low that it could not find the money for the Queen's funeral had evidently been unfounded, for on May 21st the Lord Chancellor was able to tell his Majesty that "his resources and expenses were now equalled for the ordinary, and there was £120,000 now yearly for the extraordinaries; but he prayed it might be taken but as an estimate."

His own finances had also improved, since he had lately received a grant of £1,200 a year out of the office of alienations.

The exact pressure of business of which he had complained to the King of Denmark was probably connected with the Star Chamber. The quarrel between the Countess of Exeter and her granddaughter Lady Roos had been settled in February, in favour of Lady Exeter. Lady Roos's parents Sir Thomas and Lady Lake were imprisoned in the Tower, and their unfortunate maid Sara publicly whipped and branded in the face with the letters F and A as a false accuser. A condition of the Lakes' release was to be an acknowlegment of their offence and an apology to Lady Exeter. In June Sir Thomas was too ill to appear before the Star Chamber, and he made acknowledgement by letter to the King.

Another offender at this time was the Lord Treasurer, the Earl of Suffolk, who was accused of misconduct in his office. He was dismissed and ordered to appear before the Star Chamber later in the year.

It was never pleasant to see fellow Councillors fallen from high position; and what with these unfortunate affairs, his own recent illness and the death of the Queen, Francis was thankful when further business could be deferred until the autumn, the King set forth on his summer progress, and he himself could retire to Gorhambury.

"I hope to give the King a good account of my time this vacation," he wrote to the Marquis of Buckingham of July 19th, telling his lordship at the same time, "I can but be yours, and desire to better myself, that I may be of more worth to such an owner."

The relationship seemed almost re-established on the old footing; and with a few weeks of repose at Gorhambury, dictating through long hours to his willing secretaries—amongst whom he was pleased to count his chaplain William Rawley, a most trustworthy young clergyman from Corpus Christi whom he had known a number of years—it might be he could bring his *Novum Organum* to near completion.

The King was at Windsor by the end of August, where Francis waited upon him, and a consultation seems to have been held on the vexed question of the trouble in Bohemia. The Habsburg King of that country, Ferdinand, who was much disliked by his subjects, had been deposed, and his throne offered to James's son-in-law, the Elector Palatine Frederick. The Elector had, rather ill-advisedly, accepted the offer, and had set off for Prague with his consort Elizabeth. Ex-King Ferdinand was cousin and elected successor to the German Emperor, who had promptly declared war on Frederick. The new King of Bohemia very naturally hoped for aid from Great Britain. His position was not an easy one. He had little or no experience of his new kingdom and had never commanded an army in the field; but so great was his faith in the Protestant cause that he was ready to oppose the armies of the Emperor and the King of Spain.

We have seen what opinion the Lord Chancellor had of Spain. Unfortunately no document has been discovered giving an account of the interview between him and his Majesty at Windsor, and whether he advised the King to support his son-in-law or to continue in the role of mediator which he had pursued hitherto. Possibly those weeks at Gorhambury had helped Francis to modify his hawk-like attitude. Seizure of the Indies was one thing, but strife on the continent of Europe and against the Emperor of Germany quite another. That he did advise the King one way or the other we know from a letter which he received from Buckingham in September, mentioning the "discourse at Windsor," which, "though I heard not myself, yet I heard his Majesty much commend it both for the method and affection you showed therein to his affairs."

The Council met shortly afterwards at Wanstead, where the King was by now staying, to discuss the Bohemian question. They tended towards suggesting that support should be given to Frederick; but whether this was the opinion of the whole Council, or of a majority of members, is uncertain. His Majesty disagreed. He saw himself as the peace-maker of Christendom, and had no wish to stir up other princes in Europe or to be thought the aider and abettor of one of them because he happened to be his own son-in-law. So his Majesty temporized, as was his custom in a difficult situation, and declared that nothing could be decided until the legal validity of Frederick's accession to the throne of Bohemia had been proved. This would take several weeks, so the matter was postponed, probably to everyone's relief except that of Frederick and his Queen Elizabeth, who had left England with high hopes and expectations of a peaceful life at the time of her marriage in 1613.

The case of the Earl of Suffolk came up for discussion in the Star Chamber in October, with the Lord Chancellor reporting upon each day's hearing to the Marquis of Buckingham, who was at Royston with the King. The charges were rather more serious than was originally supposed. The ex-Lord Treasurer, having had access to Crown finances, was accused of having misappropriated certain sums, which accusation was found to be substantiated. Sir Edward Coke, rather typically, wished a fine of £100,000 to be imposed and both the earl and his lady to be imprisoned in the Tower. Lord Chief Justice Hubbard, with the Lord Chancellor, concurred in imprisonment, but desired the fine to be reduced to £30,000.

This was the course adopted, and to the Tower in November went the earl and his countess, to join the select group of those already enjoying the riverside air of his Majesty's fortress, including the Earl of Somerset and Sir Thomas Lake.

The Lord Chancellor also found himself in need of riverside air early in December, though rather more upstream than either the Tower of London or his own residence York House, for on the 12th he wrote to the Marquis of Buckingham, "On Friday I left London to hide myself at Kew; for two months and a half together to be strong-bent is too much for my bow." He took with him Sir Giles Mompesson, to confer with him on matters of finance pertaining to his Majesty. He and Sir Giles may have lodged in the building at Kew known as Dutch House, belonging to Sir Hugh Portman, a Dutch merchant, the final case heard in the Star Chamber that December having been proceedings taken against certain merchants for exporting gold to Holland.

Christmas was upon him once again, and, his bow no longer at full-stretch, it is to be hoped that he was able to pass the new year at Gorhambury, perhaps at Verulam House, amid "things as are green all winter: holly, ivy, bays, juniper, cypress trees, yew, pineapple trees, fir trees. . . . And myrtles, if they be stoved; and sweet marjoram, warm set." He was entering his sixtieth year, and pressure of public work seldom relaxed; he remembered how it had aged his father prematurely, that and the agony of gout and increasing weight; he must watch his diet.

One thing was certain: he would refuse all invitations to Hatton House when he returned to London. The pace had become too fast for him. Her ladyship had given out, even before Christmas, that she would feast with dancing and revelling every Thursday night until Lent—his former love was indefatigable—and if dance she must then she could foot it with younger men like her son-in-law John Villiers, now Viscount Purbeck, or her stepson-in-law Robert Rich, Earl of Warwick.

"Discern of the coming on of years, and think not to do the same things still; for age will not be defied."

Chapter XVI

The spring of the year 1620 had come, and the King had made no attempt to recall Parliament, or to fill the office of Lord Treasurer which
had remained vacant since the disgrace of the Earl of Suffolk. Nor had
he made any decision as to whether or not to support his son-in-law
Frederick of the Palatinate in his claim to the throne of Bohemia.

The government of the country was not as it should be, certainly
not as it had been under Queen Elizabeth; and because he loved his
country well, and was loyal in all things to the reigning monarch, the
Lord Chancellor was much concerned. The ordinary day-to-day routine of government could be greatly improved, in his opinion, if there
were set up various commissions to deal with specific matters, such as
the export and import of grain; setting the people to work on manufacture; encouraging husbandry and preventing depopulation in rural
areas; recovering drowned lands; proceeding with greater care in the
plantations of Ireland; and in the provision of the realm with all kinds
of warlike defences, ordnance, powder, munition and armour. He drew
up a list of such particulars with meticulous care, and forwarded it to
his Majesty, but nothing came of it; Francis Bacon was too far ahead
of his time.

Next he urged the appointing of a new Lord Treasurer. The national debt had been reduced, but not far enough, and Francis drew
up recommendations to deal with this matter of extreme importance.
A commission here was not enough; it needed "an officer of understanding and authority with his ministerial assistants," for there had
been "great loss in the inning of your Majesty's harvest, whereof I see
no cause, except it should stay for fouler weather. . . . Your Majesty's
estate requires in point of treasure not only fidelity and judgement,
but invention and stirring and assiduity and pursuit, with edifying one
thing upon another; all which cannot possibly be done by a commission where the care lies not principally upon one or two men. . . .

"Your business in this kind goes on by one and by one, and not at once, and rather by shifts to stop gaps from time to time, than by any sound establishments; so that according to the ordinary proverb of the woman that roasted her hen by faggot-sticks, stick after stick, the faggot is burnt and the hen not roasted. This is but to let unto your Majesty a lease for life of want and misery. . . . It is good for your Majesty, nay necessary as the case is, that your business be set forward in many parts at once, and that you be kept from straights afar off, and not only eased a little when they press you."

On the question of suits, those endless pressing demands for favour that came in every day, he advised, "To grant all suits were to undo yourself, or your people. To deny all suits were to see never a contented face. . . . But to make sorted and distributed references, and to let every man bear part of the envy; and likewise to encourage your officers in stopping suits at the seals. . . . But above all to make a good Lord Treasurer, whose proper duty is . . . to stir in these cases, and to stop suits, put back pensions, check allowances, question merits . . . and in short to be a screen to your Majesty in things of this nature; such as was the Lord Burghley for many years."

Francis had someone for the office in mind, the Lord Chief Justice of the King's Bench, Sir Henry Montague, but he was not appointed until late November. As to the trouble in Bohemia, here King James was so harried on the one side by the Spanish ambassador, and on the other by his son-in-law, that Francis let it alone; all his Majesty could say was "he hoped God would arrange everything for the best." A pious maxim, but not the best way to conduct his foreign policy. Small wonder, with all these matters still unsettled, that Francis told the Marquis of Buckingham in July, "The King's state, if I should now die and be opened, would be found at my heart, as Queen Mary said of Calais." (Buckingham, incidentally, had married Lady Katherine Manners, daughter of the Earl of Rutland, at the end of May. There is no reference to the marriage in this or subsequent letters to Buckingham from the Lord Chancellor.)

His Majesty was obliged to make up his mind after September 2nd, when news came that the Spanish army, with the backing of the Emperor, had marched into the Palatinate, and Prince Frederick—or the King of Bohemia, as he liked to term himself—was now hard-pressed. James could no longer stand aside. Though he regarded his son-in-law as a usurper of the Bohemian throne, aid must be given to him, and Parliament must be recalled for this purpose. Francis Bacon, thankful that action was to be taken at long last, set about drafting a proclamation for a new Parliament.

"We have resolved, by the advice of our privy council, to hold a

Parliament in our city of Westminster . . . and do require the Lower house, at this time, if ever, to be compounded of the gravest, ablest, and worthiest members that may be found . . . experienced parliament-men . . . wise and discreet statesmen, that have been practised in public affairs . . . substantial citizens and burgesses . . . well affected in religion, without declining either on the one hand to blindness and superstition, or on the other hand to schism or turbulent disposition."

It was decided that Parliament would be summoned in January of 1621; and now, with three months to wait, another disagreeable duty had to be performed. The Lord Chancellor must sit in judgement with his colleagues upon his friend and associate Sir Henry Yelverton, Attorney-General, who some months earlier had been suspended from his office. The charge was that, in a new charter granted to the City of London, he had inserted, without warrant, certain clauses held to be objectionable. This was a serious offence, and he was summoned to appear before the Star Chamber. The Lord Chancellor made a note of what he intended to say; "Sorry for the person, being a gentleman that I lived with in Gray's Inn; served with him when I was attorney; joined with since in many services, and one that ever gave me more attributes in public than I deserved; and besides a man of very good parts; which with me is friendship at first sight; much more joined with so ancient acquaintance. But, as a judge, I hold the offence very great, and that without pressing measure . . . for if it be suffered that the learned counsel shall practice the art of multiplication upon their warrants, the crown will be destroyed in small time. The great seal, the privy seal, signet, are solemn things; but they follow the King's hand. It is the bill drawn by the learned counsel and the docket, that leads the King's hand."

The Attorney-General made a humble submission when he appeared before the Court, acknowledged his error, but denied corruption. Judgement was given on November 10th, Sir Edward Coke proposing a fine of £6,000. The Lord Chancellor, with the rest of the Court, suggested £4,000, which was adopted. Sir Henry Yelverton was dismissed his post, and sentenced to imprisonment in the Tower at his Majesty's pleasure.

Yet another colleague, through miscalculation, error of judgement or sheer carelessness, had fallen into disgrace; it was not a happy thought or a pleasant occasion. All in all, it had been a trying year, with trouble and threat of war abroad and the King's indecision here at home, and although, God be praised, there had been no major event to disturb the nation like the Powder Treason of 1605, Francis was reminded of that particular year because he had chosen to publish then his major work *Of The Advancement of Learning,* which had fallen flat in consequence. Now he was equally unlucky in the appearance of his unfinished *Novum Organum,* forming an introduction to the *Instauratio Magna,* on which he had been working for years, and which contained a series of aphorisms on "the interpretation of nature and the kingdom of man." While *Of The Advancement of Learning* can be read and enjoyed by the unscholarly, the *Novum Organum,* especially the second book, even in translation defies the patient application of the ordinary reader, being a work of immense erudition that can only appeal to, and be understood by, those who have already made a profound study of logic, philosophy and science.

The work was dedicated to his Majesty, and in the letter accompanying the copy which Bacon sent to the King he said, "This work is but a new body of clay, wherein your Majesty by your countenance and protection, may breathe life . . . I am persuaded the work will gain upon men's minds in ages, but your gracing it may make it take hold more swiftly; which I would be glad of, it being a work meant not for praise or glory, but for practice, and the good of men. One thing, I confess, I am ambitious of, with hope, which is, that after these beginnings, and the wheel once set on going, men shall suck more truth out of Christian pens, than hitherto they have done out of heathen. I say with hope, because I hear my former book of the *Advancement of Learning* is well tasted in the universities here, and the English colleges abroad; and thus is the same argument sunk deeper."

His Majesty, in his reply, promised "to read it through with care and attention, though I should steal some hours from my sleep; having otherwise as little spare time to read it as you had to write it." Hardly an encouraging response, and it is to be hoped that Francis was never aware that the King said later, "His last book is like the peace of God, that passeth all understanding."

King James, "the wisest fool in Christendom," and no mean scholar himself, could well have risked loss of sleep by reading the Preface, and the Plan, and the First Book of Definitions or Aphorisms, without too much scratching of his head, for much of this Francis had already said both in the *Advancement of Learning* and in *Cogitata et Visa,* though in them, it must be confessed, with greater clarity. The false notions that possess men's minds had always been one of his main preoccupations, and those philosophical systems that have perverted the scholar since the dawn of history. "Four out of the five and twenty centuries over which the memory and learning of man extends, you can hardly pick out six that were fertile in sciences or favourable to

143

their developments. . . . For only three revolutions and periods of learning can properly be reckoned; one among the Greeks, the second among the Romans, and the last among us, that is to say, the nations of Western Europe; and to each of these hardly two centuries can justly be assigned. . . .

"Again there is another great and powerful cause why the sciences have made but little progress; which is this. It is not possible to run a course aright when the goal itself has not been rightly placed. Now the true and lawful goal of the sciences is none other than this: that human life be endowed with new discoveries and powers. . . . Men have been kept back from progress in the sciences by reverence for antiquity, by the authority of men accounted great in philosophy, and then by general consent. . . . But by far the greatest obstacle to the progress of science and to the undertaking of new tasks and provinces therein, is found in this—that men despair and think things impossible. . . . And therefore it is fit that I publish and set forth those conjectures of mine which make hope reasonable; just as Columbus did, before that wonderful voyage of his across the Atlantic, when he gave the reasons for his conviction that new lands and continents might be discovered besides those which were known before. . . . There is much ground for hoping that there are still laid up in the womb of nature many secrets of excellent use, having no affinity or parallelism with any thing that is now known, but lying entirely out of the beat of the imagination, which have not yet been found out."

So far so good. Whoever has read *Valerius Terminus, Of The Advancement of Learning* and *Cogitata et Visa* can follow Bacon's thought in the first book of the *Novum Organum*, and cannot fail to be impressed by the magnitude of his survey, which stepped beyond the bounds of his own century, forever seeking and probing the future and what it might bring to the benefit of mankind. What fascination he would have found in telecommunication, the landings of men on the moon, the exploration of space: had these been foretold in prophecy in 1620 he would not have shaken his head as his Majesty might have done, and murmured "witchcraft," but smiled and assented possibility.

The second book of Aphorisms is best left to the specialist. Forms of heat and cold, the nature of whiteness, the velocity of light . . . here, with King James, without scientific training our patience is limited; nevertheless, turning the pages at random, the modern eye is caught by a speculation that had evidently struck Francis one evening, perhaps, at Gorhambury, which we in the twentieth century know to be proven fact.

"A strange doubt; viz, whether the face of a clear and starlight sky be seen at the instant as it really exists, and not a little later; and whether there be not, as regards our sight of heavenly bodies, a real time and an apparent time, just like the real place and apparent place which is taken account of by astronomers in the correction for parallaxes. So incredible did it appear to me that the images or rays of heavenly bodies could be conveyed at once to the sight through such an immense space, and did not rather take a perceptible time in travelling to us."

Today we accept as natural that the brightness of a star is so many "light years" away; Francis Bacon already suspected it was so in 1620.

A copy of the *Novum Organum* was sent to Cambridge University. "As your son and pupil," ran the accompanying letter, "I desire to lay in your bosom my new-born child. Otherwise I should hold it for a thing exposed. Let it not trouble you that the way is new; for in the revolutions of time such things must needs be. Nevertheless the ancients retain their proper honour—that is, of wit and understanding; for faith is due only to the Word of God and of Experience. Now to bring the sciences back to experience is not permitted; but to grow them anew out of experience, though laborious, is practicable. May God bless you and your studies. Your most loving son, Fr. Verulam, Canc."

In late November the country was shocked by the news that Frederick of Bohemia, Elector Palatine, had been defeated at Prague, and was a fugitive, the Palatinate being occupied by the armies of the King of Spain and the Duke of Bavaria. The King was now prepared to send his son-in-law aid, on the understanding that he gave up all claim to Bohemia. This condition would enable Britain to remain on friendly terms with Spain, and would not affect the marriage negotiations. The trouble was that the raising of an army would cost money, and England's finances were once more at a very low ebb indeed. More than £1,000,000 would be needed, and although the people were ready enough for war, the Protestant cause being a popular one, they were not prepared to be taxed for it—a fact of life that has continued through the centuries.

"It is most certain," wrote John Chamberlain, "that England was never generally so poor since I was born as it is at this present; inasmuch as all complain they cannot receive their rents. Yet there is plenty of all things but money; which is so scant that country people offer corn, cattle, and whatsoever they have else in lieu of rent, but bring no money . . . I fear when it comes to trial, it will appear as some merchants, which, having carried a great show a long time, when they are called on too fast by their creditors, are fain to play bankrupt. But the strangeness of it is how this great defect should come and be perceived but within these two or three years at most. Divers reasons are devised, as some say the money is gone northward, some eastward, and I know not whither."

Parliament met, for the first time in seven years, on January 30th 1621. His Majesty made a long speech, which was well received, and asked for supplies to be granted so that the debts the Crown had perforce incurred could be repaid and an army raised to send to the Palatinate.

The case for the Palatinate was referred to a committee of the whole lower House, and later a bill was passed and received the royal assent. But a debate in early February on the causes of the scarcity of money brought up all the old complaints of the previous Parliament— patents, monopolies, prerogatives. Once more the heated arguments broke forth, and a Committee of Grievances, convened to deal with them, continued through February into March.

Francis Bacon had listened to it all before, as Solicitor-General in 1610, when the question of the Great Contract and subsidies had been argued in the House. With his acute political and legal sense, it is a curious anomaly in his character that now, as Lord Chancellor, he seems to have been completely unaware of the direction which these various arguments were taking, and how they were likely to affect his own position.

He had celebrated his sixtieth birthday on January 21st, giving a banquet at York House on the occasion. His Majesty had created him Viscount St Alban, and a week later Francis went down to Theobalds to be invested with coronet and robe. The King, the Prince of Wales, the Marquis of Buckingham and many peers of the realm were present to applaud him.

His friend Ben Jonson, poet, dramatist and masque-maker, had written him an ode, *Lord Bacon's Birth-day*, beginning,

> Hail, happy genius of this ancient pile!
> How comes it all things so about thee smile?
> The fire, the wine, the men! And in the midst
> Thou stand'st as if some mystery thou didst!
> Pardon, I read it in thy face, the day
> For whose returns, and many, all these pray:
> And so do I . . .

Francis Bacon, Lord Verulam, Viscount St Alban, Keeper of the Great Seal, Lord Chancellor; never had he been held in higher esteem by the King, or by his patron the Marquis of Buckingham. He had turned the final corner of that winding stair to great place, and had reached the peak of his career.

"This is now the eighth time, that your Majesty hath raised me . . . the eighth rise or reach," he told King James, "a diapason in music, even a good number and accord for a close. And so I may without superstition be buried in St Alban's habit or vestment."

The first intimation of trouble, that the Committee of Grievances had found abuses in the matter of patents—for which, of course, the Court of Chancery was responsible—did not worry him unduly. He told Sir Edward Sackville, Chairman of the Committee on the Courts of Justice, that "any man might speak freely anything concerning his Court of Chancery." A letter from Tobie Matthew in Brussels warning him that his friends believed him to be in danger of attack from sources within both Houses received the answer, "I would not have my friends, though I know it to be out of love, too apprehensive either of me, or for me; for I thank God my ways are sound and good, and I hope God will bless me in them." Even the indictment of his friend Sir Giles Mompesson for irregularities concerning patents seemed of little concern, although it had been referred to him at the time. No, all was well, and the only thing of real concern was that the subsidy bill should be passed, and his Majesty's affairs settled to his satisfaction.

Then, in early March, Francis Bacon was informed that two former suitors were accusing him of taking money for the furthering of their suits some years previously, and that a charge of bribery and corruption was formally to be brought against him in both the lower and the upper Houses.

147

Chapter XVII

The shock was profound. Francis Bacon was stunned into disbelief. It could not possibly be. Pressure had never been put upon him to give a favourable or an adverse verdict. What was this all about? Presents? Yes, he had accepted presents, new year gifts, birthday gifts, many gifts of various kinds from satisfied suitors, but never as a bribe; never had he allowed such presents to affect his judgement.

Names of the two complainants were shown to him. Christopher Awbrey, who was he? Then he remembered, yes, the man had had a suit pending in the Court of Chancery, which Francis had hastened. One of his gentlemen had attended to it, Sir George Hastings. A hundred pounds in recompense? Completely false. Possibly Sir George knew the truth of the matter.

Edward Egerton? Yes, another case of delay. Egerton had had many suits in Chancery and Francis may have forwarded a few of them. A basin and ewer worth fifty guineas? Very possibly. He had been moving into York House then, so many people had presented him with gifts about that time. There was no act in the statutes of the realm forbidding a Lord Chancellor to accept presents. He would produce evidence to prove his point . . . but could he? More names were being brought forward, more witnesses against him, a commission was set up to examine these witnesses under oath, and the truth dawned on him at last; he was in trouble, deep trouble. No "strangeness or clouds" now, no "melancholy or distaste," but genuine sickness from grave shock.

The Lord Chancellor took to his bed in York House, physicians were called, and for a few days he believed himself on the point of death. It was within a week of Good Friday, and the two Houses agreed that they would adjourn for Easter on March 27th, and continue with their examinations during the recess. This gave the sick Lord Chancellor three weeks to prepare his defence, and he would

148

need all that time and more, for he still did not know how and when he had transgressed the law, who were his many accusers. Names, particulars, the sums involved, all these must be checked by his secretaries and submitted to his scrutiny. On March 24th, the anniversary of the King's accession, he was sufficiently recovered to sit up in bed and write a letter to his Majesty.

"Time hath been when I have brought unto you *gemitum columbae* from others. Now I bring it from myself. I fly unto your Majesty with the wings of a dove, which once within these seven days I thought would have carried me a higher flight. I have been no avaricious oppressor of the people. I have been no haughty or intolerable or hateful man, in my conversation or carriage. I have inherited no hatred from my father, but am a good patriot born. . . .

"For the House of Commons, I began my credit there, and now it must be the place of the sepulture thereof. . . . For the Upper House, even within these days before these troubles, they seemed to take me into their arms, finding in me ingenuity which they took to be the true straight line of nobleness, without crooks or angles.

"And for the briberies and gifts wherein I am charged, when the book of hearts shall be opened, I hope I shall not be found to have the troubled fountain of a corrupt heart in a depraved habit of taking rewards to pervert justice; howsoever I may be frail, and partake of the abuses of the times. And therefore I am resolved when I come to my answer, not to trick up my innocency by cavillations or voidances, but to speak to them [the Lords] the language that my heart speaketh to me, in excusing, extenuating, or ingenuous confessing; praying to God to give me the grace to see the bottom of my faults, and that no hardness of heart do steal upon me, under show of more neatness of conscience than is cause."

Francis travelled down to Gorhambury for Easter, still very frail, but possibly not so troubled physically as by extreme nervous exhaustion, for, like all highly-strung individuals, his sudden reverse of fortune made the approach of death appear very near, so much so that on April 10th he drew up a hasty will, in which he bequeathed "my soul to God above, by the oblation of my Saviour.

"My body to be buried obscurely.

"My name to the next ages, and to foreign nations.

"My compositions unpublished, or the fragments of them, I require my servant Harris to deliver to my brother Constable, to the end that if any of these be fit in his judgement to be published, he may accordingly dispose of them. And in particular I wish the Elogium I wrote *In*

149

felicem memoriam Reginae Elizabethae may be published. And to my brother Constable I give all my books; and to my servant Harris for this his service and care 50 pieces in gold, pursed up."

All his lands, leases, goods and chattels were bequeathed to his executors in payment of his debts, and after the death of his wife—to whom he gave a box of rings—he desired that the first offer of the reversion of Gorhambury and Verulam House should be made to the Prince.

Then he pushed the document aside. His mood was such that he wanted everything earthly to be blotted out, all that he had ever created, thought or done. In his extremity, like many other religious men before and since, he felt his only recourse was to God, his Creator, Redeemer and Comforter, who would not forsake him; and the prayer he wrote at this time was a strong exposition of what he felt himself to be, a sinner, naturally, yet free from malice, cruelty and guile. Humble, yes, but proud of the qualities God had given him. "Remember, O Lord, how thy servant hath walked before thee: remember what I have first sought, and what hath been principal in mine intentions. . . ." (This jogging of the Almighty's memory is almost as if he were reminding a fellow judge of past occasions.)

"The state and bread of the poor and oppressed have been precious in mine eyes: I have hated all cruelty and hardness of heart: I have, though in a despised weed, procured the good of all men." (Does he refer to his lawyer's gown or to his writer's mask?) "If any have been mine enemies, I thought not of them; neither hath the sun almost set upon my displeasure; but I have been as a dove, free from superfluity of maliciousness . . . Thousand have been my sins, and ten thousand my transgressions; but thy santifications have remained with me, and my heart, through thy grace, hath been an unquenched coal upon thy altar. . . .

"I confess before thee, that I am debtor to thee for the gracious talent of thy gifts and graces, which I have neither put into a napkin nor put it, as I ought, to exchangers, where it might have made best profit; but misspent it in things for which I was least fit; so as I may truly say, my soul hath been a stranger in the course of my pilgrimage."

No bowing of the head, no beating of the breast, no bending of the knee; the prayer reads almost as a challenge. Did Francis see himself as Prometheus, who had fashioned men of clay and stolen fire from heaven to give them the means of survival, and had then been bound to a rock, preyed upon by an eagle until Hercules had freed him?

Now he must review other cases of bribery and corruption, to see if they in any way resembled those with which he was shortly to be charged, and when this was done request, through his Majesty, that he might have the full particulars of all the charges, for if there were so many his memory could well be at fault in respect of some of them, dating back, as they were said to do, through the years. His Majesty granted him an interview, but, although his manner was gracious, he referred the Lord Chancellor to the House of Lords. The matter was in their hands, and he could not interfere.

The examination of the various witnesses continued, and by April 19th Francis learnt that twenty-seven charges were to be brought against him, all concerning gifts of money or in kind that he had received either as Lord Keeper of the Seal or as Lord Chancellor; suits that had been brought before him in the courts, by parties he had long since forgotten, opposing parties he had reconciled, cases he had dismissed; and all these persons had sworn upon oath that he had been recompensed for his pains.

The cause of Hodie versus Hodye—yes, he had received a dozen buttons. . . . A hundred pounds from Sir John Trevor? But he thought it had been a new year's gift. . . . Quarrel between Kenneday and Van Lore, true, he was made a present of a fine cabinet, Sir John had begged him in his own hand to accept it—it was standing in York House today. . . . Some hangings from Sir Edward Shute, also at the time of moving, but in no way relating to the cause heard. . . . A diamond ring from Sir George Reynell, and more furniture for the house, but this again a new year's gift . . . and on and on. The list was endless, overwhelming. Francis realised now that any hope of defence was out of the question and it would be better to submit, to admit all the charges. The mood of the House was made up; they were determined to make an example of him, fellow-peers and councillors he had thought his friends; among them the Earl of Suffolk, reinstated after his own disgrace and hoping for revenge; and hovering somewhere in the background, rubbing his hands in satisfaction, the chairman of the Committee of Grievances, Sir Edward Coke.

On April 21st Francis wrote a letter of submission to his Majesty, offering to surrender his Seal, and on the following day, the 22nd, another to the upper House in which he said, "I do ingenuously confess and acknowledge, that having understood the particulars of the charge . . . I find matter sufficient and full, both to move me to desert the defence, and to move your Lordships to condemn and censure me."

What is perplexing is that the Lord Chancellor should have readily made this submission without any attempt at self-defence, thus denying himself any right to reply to accusations, or to call witnesses to speak on his behalf. Many of the charges could have been disproved, and much of the smear campaign shown for what it was as though the shame and disgrace of being charged with bribery and corruption had broken any fighting spirit he possessed, and in a state of nigh total nervous collapse he could summon up no will-power to resist.

On April 24th the Prince of Wales rose in the upper House and handed over the letter of submission, which was read to the assembled peers. A committee was then formed to consider the letter. Both the Prince and the Marquis of Buckingham hoped the submission would be accepted and the matter ended without a formal sentence. Others were less lenient, the Earl of Suffolk amongst them. A debate followed, on the question of whether the Lord Chancellor should have a list of every charge sent to him, or whether he should be summoned to answer the charges in person. The House divided on this question, the majority being in favour of the charges being sent, doubtless the more lenient being anxious to spare the accused's state of health. The list of the offences was therefore despatched to York House, despite the fact that the Lords had made no attempt to sift the evidence, to examine the legal aspect of the charges, or to investigate any mitigating circumstances. Nothing had been proved in open court, the witnesses and complainants having been examined in private.

The roll of charges was returned by the Lord Chancellor on April 30th with these opening words, "Upon advised consideration of the charge, descending into my own conscience, and calling my memory to account so far as I am able, I do plainly and ingenuously confess that I am guilty of corruption; and do renounce all defence, and put myself upon the grace and mercy of your Lordships." The twenty-seven charges followed, to each of which he confessed, taking, one could almost swear, a perverse pleasure in his own humiliation. If a man must sink, then let him wallow in the mire. When formally asked, by a deputation from the Lords, whether the signature to his confession was in his own hand, he replied, "My Lords, it is my act, my hand, my heart. I beseech your Lordships, be merciful to a broken Lord."

The upper House accepted the confession. The next procedure was to decide the sentence. Had he been well enough to do so, the Lord Chancellor would have been ordered to appear to hear sentence pronounced, but he was still sick in bed, and it was thought he might not have long to live. By May 3rd the Lords were agreed upon their verdict, and the lower House was informed. The Lords put on their robes. The Speaker came to the bar and, bowing low, demanded in the name of the lower House that the Lord Chief Justice should declare the judgement. This was as follows:

"1. That the Lord Viscount St Alban, Lord Chancell of England shall undergo fine and ransom of forty thousand pounds.
"2. That he shall be imprisoned in the Tower during the King's pleasure.
"3. That he shall for ever be incapable of any office, place, or employment in the State or Commonwealth.
"4. That he shall never sit in Parliament, nor come within the verge of the Court."

How Francis Bacon heard the sentence we do not know. One of his close friends—and he had many in both Houses—must have brought it to his bedside, and would have surely told him how the upper House had been divided in their opinion, the Lords Sheffield, Richmond and Arundel not wishing him to be degraded, and the Marquis of Buckingham dissenting from all punishment. He cannot have been so sick that these names made no impression. And never to be employed again, ineligible for any office in State or Commonwealth—did the full implication of this penetrate his mind? Who was at his bedside? The chaplain Dr Rawley? The very able friend and secretary Thomas Meautys? His old friend and servant Henry Percy? His wife? We do not know.

The Earl of Southampton, remembering his own two years' imprisonment after the Essex rebellion in the time of Queen Elizabeth, asked the Lords in the upper House on May 12th why the Lord Chancellor had not yet been sent to the Tower. The Marquis of Buckingham, now Lord Admiral, informed him that, "The King hath respited his going to the Tower in this time of his great sickness." The answer did not satisfy those peers who, besides rejoicing in Viscount St Alban's downfall, were resentful of Buckingham's own growing power in State affairs, and a warrant was sent committing the late Lord Chancellor to the Tower. The exact date of his imprisonment is uncertain, but that he was there on May 31st is known from his letter to Buckingham on that day, written from the Tower of London.

"Good my Lord,
"Procure the warrant for my discharge this day. Death, I thank God, is so far from being unwelcome to me, as I have called for it, as Christian resolution would permit, any time these two months. But to die before the time of his Majesty's grace, and in this disgraceful place, is even the worst that could be; and when I am dead, he is gone that was always in one tenor, a true and perfect servant to his master, and one that was never author of any immoderate, no, nor unsafe, no—I will say it—not unfortunate counsel; and one that no temptation could ever make other

than a trusty, and honest, and thrice loving friend to your Lordship; and howsoever I acknowledge the sentence just, and for reformation sake fit, the justest Chancellor that hath been in the five changes since Sir Nicholas Bacon's time. God bless and prosper your Lordship, whatsoever become of me.

> "Your Lordship's true friend, living and dying,
> "Fr. St Alban."

Imprisonment had reawakened the fighting spirit; and one is led to speculate whether his judges would have been of another mind, have given another sentence, if Francis Bacon had been sufficiently master of himself at the end of April to have gone to the upper House, confronted his accusers, and stood upon his defence. Skilled orator that he was, with a perfect command of language, he would surely have delivered a speech unsurpassed for eloquence that would have trounced his fellow peers. That he preferred silence is further proof of the extraordinary complexity of the man whose soul was truly, in his own words, "a stranger in the course of my pilgrimage." Not only to the world, but to himself as well.

His appeal to Buckingham, and thence to the King, succeeded. By May 4th he was released from the Tower, and lodging at the house of Sir John Vaughan in Fulham. Sir John was Comptroller to the Prince of Wales, and that this house was immediately put at Bacon's disposal showed that the Prince himself was sympathetic, as well as Buckingham and the King, to the former Keeper of the Great Seal and Lord Chancellor.

On the day of his release Francis wrote letters of gratitude both to his Majesty and to the favourite. To the former, "Let me live to serve you, else life is but the shadow of death"; to the latter, "Now my body is out, my mind nevertheless will be still in prison, till I may be on my feet to do his Majesty and your Lordship faithful service." And on June 7th there was a rather longer letter to the Prince of Wales, extolling his virtues and princely qualities, as well as his religious, moral and natural excellencies. The "sweet air" of Fulham had "already much revived" Francis's languishing spirits, and he was itching to be at work again, on the King's business, on State business—but of course this was denied him. Debarred from approaching his Majesty's presence, he must attend to his own affairs. His creditors were pressing heavily upon him, more especially since his fall, and he was reminded of how it had been when the Earl of Essex was first disgraced, and brother Anthony was obliged to bolt his door against the tradesmen. What would become of York House, of all the servants, many of whom, had he chosen to do so, he could have blamed for his present

12. The Strand in 1700
(*photo National
Monuments Record*)

13. Coat of Arms of
Francis Bacon, Baron Verulam,
Viscount St Alban
(*photo H. Graeme, Fowey*)

14. Verulam House, after
a drawing by John Aubrey
(*reproduced by courtesy
of Basil King*)

15. Charles, Prince of Wales, by Mytens, 1623 *(copyright reserved)*

16. Tomb of Francis Bacon, Baron Verulam, Viscount St Alban, in St. Michael's Church, St Albans *(photo Christian Browning)*

17. Title-page of the first edition of the *Novum Organum*, 1620

18. Title-page of *Valerius Terminus*. The list of contents and the word "philosophy" are in Bacon's handwriting

state? Some of them must go, had already gone. He no longer had the wherewithal to pay their wages. There was no money, none. Poor Ned Sherburn had already been arrested for debt, whether his own or his master's neither of them could say.

In mid-June Francis petitioned his Majesty that he might stay in London until the end of July, to clear up his affairs, but his request could not be granted. Doubtless the King felt that clemency had gone far enough and the peers and Parliament might protest; so by June 23rd Francis Bacon was home at Gorhambury.

"He is gone this day, as I hear," John Chamberlain wrote to Sir Dudley Carleton, "to his own house at Gorhambury, having, as should seem, no manner of feeling of his fall but continuing as vain and idle in all his humours as when he was at his highest, and his fine of £40,000 to the King is so far from hurting him, that it serves for a bulwark and protection against his creditors." Gossip about those who have lost position does not much alter through the centuries. The wording may differ, but the sneer remains.

There was little that was either vain or idle where Francis Bacon was concerned during the next few months. A man who is no longer employed by his sovereign or by Parliament, with a fine hanging over his head and creditors snapping at his heels, must turn to work of a different kind to keep himself from stark ruin. And the ex-Lord Chancellor was a writer, first and foremost. He realised now that to continue immediately with the next part of his *Instauratio Magna* would not bring him in a penny—the publication of the *Novum Organum* was proof of this: a more popular work, written in English, was more likely to produce the cash. He had often considered writing a history of Henry VII, a monarch for whom he had always had a high regard, and who was, moreover, great-great-grandfather to the present King. This would surely please. He would set to work at once. Yet isolation down at Gorhambury, without access to papers, documents and everything else needed for such a task, made the undertaking well-nigh impossible, and by September he was once more imploring both his Majesty and the Marquis of Buckingham for permission to return to London, and for some financial aid to enable him at least to live. The ex-Lord Chancellor, who in the recent past had given good advice to the sovereign upon state finances, was now at his wit's end how to manage his own. Verulam House was not completed, bills were outstanding.

"As for my debts," he told Buckingham, "I showed them to your Lordship, when you saw the little house and the gallery, besides a little wood or desert, which you saw not." He knew only too well the gossip spoken of him, how he had squandered with a lavish hand, and at the State's expense. "I never took penny for any benefice or ecclesiastical living, I never took penny for releasing any thing I stopped at the seal, I never took penny for any commission or things of that nature, I never shared with any servant for any second or inferior profit. My offences I have myself recorded, wherein I studied, as a good confessant, guiltiness and not excuse."

He thought back into history, and how another statesman, also Lord Chancellor and a cardinal of the church, had been disgraced almost a hundred years before. Had he not been brought up on the story of how his own great-grandfather, Sir William Fitzwilliam, had received the fallen prelate Wolsey at his home at Milton? He could not help thinking of this when he penned his letter to his Majesty on September 5th: "The misery I am fallen into hath put me below the means to subsist as I am . . . I have been the keeper of your seal, and now am your beadsman." He added in a postscript, "Cardinal Wolsey said, that if he had pleased God as he pleased the King, he had not been ruined. My conscience saith no such thing; for I know not but in serving you I have served God in one. But it may be, if I had pleased men as I have pleased you, it would have been better with me."

Familiar words, surely. The reader looks again, and turns to Act III, Scene II, and Cardinal Wolsey's concluding speech in Shakespeare's *King Henry VIII.*

> There take an Inventory of all I have,
> To the last peny, 'tis the Kings. My Robe,
> And my Integrity to Heaven, is all,
> I dare now call my owne. O Cromwel, Cromwel,
> Had I but serv'd my God, with halfe the Zeale
> I serv'd my King: he would not in mine Age
> Have left me naked to mine Enemies.

Yet *King Henry VIII*, though acted on the stage, was not published until the First Folio in 1623. Curious. . . .

Francis's letter so moved his Majesty that on September 16th he issued a licence permitting him to come to London and reside at Sir John Vaughan's house once again for six weeks, and on the 20th of the month he was pleased to assign the fine imposed by Parliament to four trustees of Francis's own choosing; Sir Richard Hutton, Justice of Assize; Sir Thomas Chamberlain, Justice of the King's Bench; Sir Thomas Crewe, a barrister; and Sir Francis Barnham, Lady St Alban's cousin.

The significance of this was that it made the trustees responsible for the £40,000 debt to the Crown, and meant in effect that it would not be exacted. Moreover, the trustees had authority to keep other creditors at bay, so that what the gossips had predicted back in June had proved correct.

There remained one final hope, which was that Francis Bacon would be granted a full pardon; although he would never again be employed by King or Parliament, he would at least be free to travel as he wished, and when he wished, between London and Gorhambury, with the stigma of disgrace removed, no longer an exile from the world and from his friends.

It seemed as if fortune was about to smile on him once more, for on October 12th his Majesty had desired the Attorney-General, Sir Thomas Conventry, to draw up a pardon, and present it to the new Lord Keeper of the Seal, the Bishop of Lincoln. The Lord Keeper was reluctant. Parliament might take offence, he must confer with the Council, there would inevitably be some delay. Francis, who had meanwhile worked at his usual pace and finished his *History of Henry VII* in a matter of weeks, sent a copy of it to the King, and at the same time pressed the Marquis of Buckingham to speak for him to the Lord Keeper about the pardon.

There came an unexpected hitch. The Marquis, who had been so warmly in his favour throughout his impeachment and disgrace, turned suddenly cool. A misunderstanding had arisen. The truth of it seems to have been that Buckingham, believing that Viscount St Alban, now fallen from office, would be content to live down at Gorhambury and when in London lodge in some smaller residence, wanted York House for himself. Francis, whose affection for his birthplace was even greater than it was for Gorhambury, demurred.

His six weeks in London, some of which had actually been spent at York House, had come to an end, and he was back in Hertfordshire once more. Letters to the Marquis went unanswered. Nor had the King's pardon received the official seal. "Twice now at my being in London, your Lordship did not vouchsafe to see me," Francis wrote to the favourite. "The cause of change is either in myself or your Lordship. I ought first to examine myself, which I have done, and God is my witness, I find all well, and that I have approved myself to your Lordship a true friend, both in the watery trial of prosperity and the fiery trial of adversity. If your Lordship take any insatisfaction touching York House, I pray think better of it. . . . For that motion to me was a second sentence more grievous than the first as things then stood, and do yet stand."

He was referring, one supposes, to banishment from his London home; and when the King's pardon received the seal in late November it seems to have been only partial, for he was still excluded from living in London, and letters from the Marquis of Buckingham remained cool.

Perhaps a petition to the House of Lords would achieve success. Francis began to draft a note of what he might say, his mood obviously one of frustration and irritability. One can picture him in mid-December, staring out of the windows at Verulam House on a grey cold winter's day, his digestion playing havoc, an attack of gout threatening, and somewhere, not far away, the plaintive sound of her ladyship's voice.

"I am old, weak, ruined, in want, a very subject of pity. My only suit to your Lordships is to show me your noble favour towards the release of my imprisonment, for so every confinement is, and to me, I protest, worse than the Tower. There I could have company, physicians, conference with my creditors and friends about my debts and the necessities of my estate, helps for my studies and the writings I have in hand. Here I live upon the sword-point of a sharp air, endangered if I go abroad, dulled if I stay within, solitary and comfortless without company, banished from all opportunities to treat with any to do myself good, and to help out my wrecks; and that which is one of my greatest griefs, my wife that hath been no partaker of my offending, must be partaker of this misery of my restraint."

Here was perhaps the crux. He could not get away from her, or she from him. The draft was never sent. Parliament was prorogued on December 19th. So it must be Christmas at Verulam House with no thought of festivity, no smiling at the table, his servants and attendants anxious to please but their very solicitude for his welfare irksome, his lady tapping her foot and sighing. What a world away from the atmosphere a year ago, when he, and she, and all their friends were looking forward to the celebrations at York House on his sixtieth birthday and his Majesty was about to create him Viscount St Alban.

> This is the state of Man; to day he puts forth
> The tender Leaves of Hopes, to morrow Blossoms
> And beares his blushing Honours thicke upon him:
> The third day, comes a Frost; a killing Frost,
> And when he thinks, good easie man, fully surely
> His Greatness is a ripening, nips his Root,
> And then he falls as I do.

Her ladyship, exchanging a glance with her steward, Mr John Underhill, declared that she would go up to London immediately after the new year and approach the Marquis of Buckingham herself, to see whether she could achieve in person more than her husband could do by letter. So be it. Let her try. Meanwhile, he would wander about the passages at Verulam House, the pools beneath the windows thick with ice, as hard as the mirror that confronted him in the upper corridor.

"I have been too long a debtor to you for a letter," he had written to Tobie Matthew after his disgrace, "and especially for such a letter, the words whereof were delivered by your hand, as if it had been in old gold. For it was not possible for entire affection to be more generously and effectually expressed. . . . Your company was ever of contentment to me, and your absence of grief: but now it is of grief upon grief. I beseech you therefore haste hither, where you shall meet with as good a welcome as your own heart can wish."

Tobie Matthew, in fact, landed at Dover on December 29th.

Chapter XVIII

Tobie Matthew's banishment from his native land had ended. Permission had been granted for his return for good through the personal intervention of the Spanish ambassador, Count de Gondomar, and Lord Digby, who had both spoken to the King on his behalf. Lord Digby—soon to become Lord Bristol, and with twelve years' experience as ambassador at Madrid—was greatly in favour of the marriage alliance between the Infanta of Spain and the Prince of Wales, and he had come to know Tobie well both at the Spanish court and in Brussels. Here was no hot-headed recusant, he told his Majesty, but a man of parts who would make an excellent diplomat and prove of inestimable worth in his sovereign's service, both at home and abroad. If his Majesty would permit Matthew to return he, Lord Digby, would certainly vouch for his good conduct. Later he could be employed in the marriage negotiations, and when the moment was opportune be sent to Spain.

When Tobie, now forty-four, arrived home in England and paid his first visit to his life-long friend and mentor Viscount St Alban at Gorhambury, it was to find their positions reversed. He was now the diplomat, with powerful friends at Court and the promise of a career ahead of him, and the older man had lost his status and was living in banishment in Hertfordshire. No matter. Their relationship had not altered. No loss of power on the one hand, nor rise of fortune on the other, could mar those sentiments of real affection and friendship that each held for the other; and although doubtless the whole sorry story of the impeachment and its aftermath had to be recounted in detail, which had not been possible by letter, one can be sure that "work in progress," scientific, philosophical and literary, took prior place in the later discussions.

Tobie had translated Francis Bacon's essays into Italian during his previous visit to England, and these had been reprinted twice, besides a translation of *De Sapientia Veterum*. Tobie had dedicated the volume to the Grand Duke of Tuscany, with a preface descriptive of the author, praising his intellect, his virtues, and his desire to adorn the age in which he lived and to benefit the whole human race. "And I can truly say . . . that I never yet saw any trace in him of a vindictive mind, whatever injury were done him, nor ever heard him utter a word to any man's disadvantage which seemed to proceed from personal feeling against that man, but only, and that too very seldom, from judgment made of him in cold blood. It is not this greatness that I admire, but his virtue: it is not the favours I have received from him, infinite though they be, they have thus enthralled and enchained my heart, but his whole life and character; which are such that, if he were of an inferior condition I could not honour him the less, and if he were my enemy I should not the less love and endeavour to serve him."

Tobie had also translated *The Confessions of St Augustine* into English, and was thus proving himself a writer as well as a diplomat.

Meanwhile, back in London he would use what influence he had with Lord Digby and others about his Majesty to see if the enforced exile of his friend could be ended, and Viscount St Alban come and go between Hertfordshire and the capital at will. This was not so easy. His lady was already in London. She had left Gorhambury in the first week in January, and had obtained access to the Marquis of Buckingham himself. After she had waited a whole afternoon he had finally condescended to appear in his room and talk to her. What transpired between them is not, alas, recorded, but Thomas Meautys, Francis's friend and secretary, who was waiting in an adjoining room, reported to his employer that "she found time enough to speak at large," which suggests she was in no way awed by the King's favourite. Meautys adds, "And though my Lord spake so loud as that what passed was no secret to me and some others that were within hearing . . . my Lady told me she purposeth to write to your Lordship the whole passage." Since Francis kept none of his wife's letters, or else gave orders that they should be destroyed at his death, the reader is left to imagine the scene for himself.

The interview over, her Ladyship returned to York House, where Tobie Matthew was waiting to pay his respects before visiting Gorhambury later in the week. We have no record of this brief encounter, the budding diplomat all courtesy, one feels sure, with the lady, shrewd enough to remember he was one of her husband's closest friends, dropping a hint that if she had no satisfaction out of the Marquis of Buckingham she would find means of seeking an interview with the Prince of Wales. So Thomas Meautys informed his em-

161

ployer. The Viscountess St Alban was as determined to live in London as her husband, whether at York House or elsewhere did not matter, anywhere in town would suit her but at the end of January another prospective tenant appeared on the scene. The Duke of Lennox wrote to Francis, "I have resolved to intreat your Lordship that I may deal with you for York-house; wherein I will not offer any conditions to your loss. And in respect I have understood that the consideration of your Lady's wanting a house hath bred some difficulty in your Lordship to part with it, I will for that make offer unto your Lordship and your Lady to use the house at Channon-row, late the Earl of Hertford's being a very commodious and capable house, wherein I and my wife have absolute power; and whereof your Lordship shall have as long time as you can challenge or desire of York House." He added, in a postscript, that he would not have petitioned for the house but for the fact that the Marquis of Buckingham was now provided with one.

Francis had no intention of living in Channon Row. He was a man of habit. It was one thing to explore the unknown in the world of scientific thought and to probe the future, quite another to take up permanent quarters in an unfamiliar atmosphere. He must live where he had already put down roots.

"My very good Lord," he wrote to the Duke, "I am sorry to deny your Grace anything; but in this you will pardon me. York-house is the house where my father died, and where I first breathed, and there will I yield my last breath, if it so please God, and the King will give me leave; though I be now, as the old proverb is, like a bear in a monk's hood. At least no money nor value shall make me part with it. Besides, as I never denied it to my Lord Marquis, so yet the difficulty I made was so like a denial, as I owe unto my great love and respect to his Lordship a denial to all my other friends; among which in a very near place next his Lordship I ever accounted of your Grace."

We hear no more from the Duke of Lennox, but Buckingham, despite his own newly acquired residence off Whitehall, seems determined to have had one of his own closer associates living in York House. His choice fell upon Sir Lionel Cranfield, recently appointed Lord Treasurer. It soon became clear to Francis that only be relinquishing his birthplace and his first home would he be permitted freedom to come to London. York House, or else exile forevermore in Hertfordshire. Tobie Matthew, Lord Digby, Sir Edward Sackville, all did what they could by manœuvre and discretion to change the favourite's attitude, but to no avail. Buckingham was adamant. His influence and power was such now with both his Majesty and the

Prince of Wales that to thwart his wishes would be to court disaster. As a final gesture Francis was willing to give up Gorhambury and all his estates in Hertfordshire to Buckingham if only he could keep York House. The favourite did not want Gorhambury. He wanted York House for the Lord Treasurer. . . .

The business dragged on through February to March, with Sir Edward Sackville acting as chief go-between, finally urging Francis Bacon to reconcile himself to parting from York House in order to obtain his freedom. There was no other way out of exile. Lord Falkland made an offer to Francis of his own house at Highgate, and Sir Edward Sackville suggested this would make a good alternative.

"My Lord Falkland," he wrote to Francis, "by this time hath showed you London from Highgate. If York-house were gone, the town were yours, and all your straightest shackles clean off, besides more comfort than the city air only. . . ." But Francis had no more desire to live at Highgate than Buckingham had to live at Gorhambury. Finally, in mid-March, he came to terms with the inevitable. The Lord Treasurer should have York House if he would at the same time consider "the relief of my poor estate . . . I humbly pray your Lordship to give it dispatch, my age, health, and fortunes making time to me therein precious. . . . As for somewhat towards the paying off my debts, which are now my chief care, and without charge of the King's coffers, I will not now trouble your Lordship; but purposing to be at Chiswick, where I have taken a house, within this seven-nights, I hope to wait upon your Lordship, and to gather some violets in your garden, and will then impart unto you, if I have thought of any thing of that nature for my good."

The paying off of his debts was possibly helped by the sale of his *History of Henry VII*, which was published at the end of March and sold for the sum of six shillings; but the "relief of his estate" would have to await the consideration of Lord Treasurer Cranfield after he had moved into York House. As for the house at Chiswick, Thomas Meautys reported, "My Lady hath seen the house at Chiswick, and can make a shift to like it"; which was very considerate of her, only "she means to come to your Lordship thither, and not to go first, and therefore your Lordship may please to make the more haste, for the great Lords long to be in York house."

His Lordship Viscount St Alban would not move from Gorhambury until his warrant of release and freedom from exile was signed, sealed and delivered and he was legally a free man once more. On March 27th he told Tobie Matthew, "I do make account, God willing, to be at Chiswick Saturday, or because this weather is terrible to one that hath kept much in, Monday. . . . If on your repair to the court, whereof I am right glad, you have any speech with the Marquis of me, I pray place the alphabet, as you can do it right well, in a frame to express my love faithful and ardent towards him. And for York-house, that whether in a straight line or a compass line, I meant it his Lordship, in the way which I thought might please him best."

And so to Chiswick, with copies of his volume of Henry VII dispatched to all his friends, as well as to those in high places, amongst them the King's daughter the former Queen of Bohemia, with a letter saying, "Time was, I had Honour without Leisure; and now I have Leisure without Honour. . . . But my desire is now to have Leisure without Loitering, and not to become an abbey-lubber, as the old proverb was, but to yield some fruit of my private life. . . . If King Henry the Seventh were alive again, I hope verily he would not be so angry with me for not flattering him as well-pleased in seeing himself so truly described in colours that will last and be believed."

The Queen was pleased presently to reply, "My Lord, I thank you very much for your letter and your book, which is the best I ever read of the kind . . . and I am very sorry that I cannot show otherwise but by my letters my gratitude for this and other benefits for which I am beholden to you: and though your fortunes are changed, for which I grieve, believe that I shall not change to be what I am, your very affectionate friend."

So the Princess Elizabeth had not forgotten his worth, any more than her late beloved brother Henry Prince of Wales would have done; and although his *History of Henry VII* bore a dedication to the present Prince, Francis could have wished the elder had lived and bore the title still.

As to the work itself, although later historians may have discounted it, Francis Bacon's biographer Spedding found "it comes nearer to the merit of Thucydides than any English history that I know," and certainly to the layman there is nothing tedious, exaggerated or biased in its two hundred and fifteen pages. On the contrary, Henry VII and the times in which he lived are as vivid and alive to the reader of today as they must have seemed to Francis Bacon himself, separated as he was from them by some hundred and fifty years, while the speed with which it was written and completed—all in the space of a few months—leaves one astounded that this man, who had so recently suffered supreme disgrace, could find the energy and will-power to execute his task.

Even John Chamberlain found words of praise at last. "The late

Lord Chancellor hath set out the life or reign of Henry the Seventh. It is pity he should have any other employment. I have not read much of it yet, but if the rest of our history were answerable to it, I think we should not need to envy any other nation in that kind."

Francis was already planning further histories. The reign of Henry VIII, a complete history of England, a dialogue on the Holy War, in which he envisaged an alliance between Christian peoples against the Turk, a complete digest of all the laws of England; and if this was not enough he was preparing at the same time another work in Latin, to be published in monthly instalments later in the year, entitled *Historia Ventorium* (*The History of Winds*) and *Historia Vitae et Mortis* (*The History of Life and Death*) whilst adding further parts to his original *Advancement of Learning*.

Whether all this could be attempted from Chiswick remained to be seen—it is to be hoped her ladyship had quarters well away from her husband's library. Books of reference were essential to the labours to come, with willing secretaries and attendants travelling to and fro, all of whom must be recompensed for their services, and who would have to possess genuine ability for the labour of research. Francis Bacon could not possibly have undertaken all the necessary listing and sorting of the very specialized subjects he wished to write about without such assistance, and although Thomas Meautys, his chaplain William Rawley and doubtless Edward Sherburn and Thomas Bushell, later to be a mining engineer, would have been available, they had also to deal with domestic matters—correspondence, the running of the household, and so on. It is regrettable that Rawley, who published so much of Francis Bacon's work after his death, with a brief life of his greatly loved and respected employer, gave no details of the manner in which he set about his writing.

The History of Winds, intended to be the third part of his *Instauratio Magna,* is positively encyclopedic in its information. Every conceivable source is quoted, and one can picture Francis seated at desk or table, pointing to a pile of volumes near at hand: "There, third volume on the left, Pliny," "Fourth from the right, Acosta, *Histoire des Indes,*" "Top shelf, Herodotus"; and when the mass of detail had been sorted, the wheat separated from the chaff, he would decide what must be set down and what omitted. On what occasion, one wonders, with the good chaplain Rawley by his side, did he dictate, "In a south wind the breath of men is more offensive, the appetite of animals is more depressed, pestilential diseases are more frequent, catarrhs common, and men are more dull and heavy; whereas in a north wind they are brisker, healthier, and have a better appetite"? A south wind was surely blowing that day in Chiswick, and the Master moved his chair. . . .

"In a water thermometer dilated air depresses the water as with a blast; but in a glass filled only with air and capped with a bladder the dilation of the air blows out the bladder perceptibly, like a wind.

"I made an experiment of this kind of wind in a round tower that was completely shut up on every side. A chafing dish of coals thoroughly ignited so that there might be no smoke was placed in the middle of the room. At one side of this, but some distance from it, I suspended a thread, with a cross of feathers fastened to it to make it more susceptible of motion. After a short time, therefore, when the heat had increased and the air dilated, the cross of feathers with its thread began to wave about, first to one side and then to the other. And further, when a hole was made in the window of the tower, a warm gust of air passed out, not continuous, but intermittent, with undulating currents."

The reader is more intrigued by the where and when than by the experiment itself. One of the three towers at Gorhambury? Was Francis young at the time, and seized suddenly with a desire to investigate curious phenomena? Or already middle-aged, with his lady tapping her foot in an adjoining room awaiting dinner? His knowledge of sailing cannot have been obtained except through close observation of a vessel at sea—and he had crossed the Channel once only, back and forth, as a young man attending the ambassador Sir Amias Paulet—or by long consultation with an experienced mariner. He describes in minute detail not only the exact rigging of a ship of his day under full sail, and how the sails should be adjusted to meet the ever-changing wind direction, but how, by altering the designs of certain sails, they could be made more efficient—something that was not put into practice until at least two centuries later.

Challenge this brain on any topic and he had an answer for it, almost invariably correct; yet he had not possessed the foresight to steer clear of that charge of impeachment, or to evade the ever-mounting claims upon his purse. It was now eighteen months since he had spoken to his Majesty, and despite the handing over of York House to the Lord Treasurer and the bunch of violets proffered from the garden, Lord Cranfield, 1st Earl of Middlesex, had done nothing for him. His pension of £800 was in arrears, his income from Petty Writs had been confiscated. His friend and supporter Lord Digby, now Lord Bristol, was in Spain. In a moment of despair, Francis drafted a letter to the King that summer of 1622 which was never sent.

"Mine own means, through mine own improvidence, are poor and weak, little better than my father left me. The grants which I had from your Majesty are either in question or in courtesy. . . . The poor remnants which I had of my former fortunes in plate or jewels, I have spread upon poor men unto whom I owed, scarce leaving myself bread. . . . Help me, dear sovereign lord and master, and pity me so far, as I that have borne a bag be not now in my age forced in effect to bear a wallet; nor I that desire to live to study, may not study to live."

His Majesty was said to be affected by gout in his arms and in his legs these days, and when in residence at Theobalds was carried around in a litter to see his deer. A chapter on the prolongation of life might be opportune, in the *Historia Vitae et Mortis,* and with his passion for minutiae Francis sat down yet again to his desk.

"Hairiness of the upper parts of the body is a sign of short life; and men with hairy breasts, like manes, are short-lived; but hairiness in the lower parts, as the thighs and legs, indicates longevity. . . . Eyes rather large, with an iris of greenish colour; senses not too acute; a pulse slow in youth, but quicker as age increases; a power of holding the breath easily and long; the bowels more costive in youth and looser in old age, are likewise all signs of longevity. . . .

"I remember a young Frenchman of great wit . . . who argued that the defects of the mind had some parallel with the defects of the body. To dryness of the skin, he opposed impudence; to hardness of the bowels, hardness of the heart; to blear eyes, envy and the evil eye; to sunken eyes and bowing of the body to the ground, atheism; to the bending and clutching of the fingers, rapacity and avarice; to the tottering of the knees, timidity; to wrinkles, cunning and crooked ways."

Such passages might induce his Majesty to look a little harder at his courtiers, and perhaps to examine his own features in a mirror. But stay, what was this? Francis turned to a passage from the Italian humanist Ficino: "Old men, to comfort their spirits, should frequently recall and ruminate on the acts of their childhood and youth." Very true. Hence his own sentiment for York House, which was now denied him. Was it not the Emperor Vespasian who had this feeling so strongly that he could not bear to change his father's house, and on holidays used to drink out of a wooden cup, tipped with silver, which had belonged to his grandmother?

Francis was fretting for familiar sights and sounds. Chiswick was too far out of town. The southerly wind might suit his lady, but it poisoned the atmosphere for him. Besides, she was forever plagueing him as to when the money for York House would be forthcoming, for half this sum would be due to her. Perhaps if he could arrange accommodation for himself and his attendants in Bedford House on the Strand the matter could be brought to a successful conclusion.

The reader is indebted to the gossip John Chamberlain for the following information, writing, as usual, to his friend Dudley Carleton. "Not long since I met with your old friend Tobie Matthew and we had long conference. He continueth his course and lodgeth at Bedford House with the late Lord Chancellor." The letter is dated June 22nd 1622.

A week later he reports, "The Lord of St Alban hath put a bill into the Chancery against the Lord Marquis Buckingham which the world will not believe but to be done with consent. The substance is that having contracted for the lease of York House for the sum of £1,300 where of £500 was to be paid to the Lady of St Alban, the time of payment being past and no money appearing the poor Lady is in fear to be defrauded by her Lord for whose satisfaction he desires the Lord Marquis may show cause why he goeth not on with the contract as agreed."

John Chamberlain makes a valid point. Francis would never have put a bill into Chancery without Buckingham's agreement, but we are left in ignorance as to how and when the bill was passed, if it was passed. Though the favourite and the ex-Lord Chancellor were no longer on the intimate terms they had been once, there was no open rupture between them, and certainly by the autumn Buckingham had moved his Majesty to sign a warrant for the payment of the arrears of pension, telling Francis in a letter dated November 13th, "I have likewise moved for your coming to kiss his hand, which he is pleased you shall do at Whitehall when he returneth next thither."

Whether advance copies of *The History of Winds* and *The History of Life and Death* had helped to smooth the path we do not know, but on January 20th 1623 Francis Bacon, Viscount St Alban, was conducted by the Marquis of Buckingham to kiss his Majesty's hand.

It is to be hoped for all concerned, that the wind was in the north.

Chapter XIX

Restored once more to favour, prospects for the future seemed brighter than they had done for many months. He must not expect continual access to the monarch, but at least the first interview had been granted, and with Buckingham in good humour once more greater progress would be made in time. The eight books of *De Augmentis Scientiarum*—the Latin additions to *The Advancement of Learning*—were with the printers, and his leisure hours, apart from other work, could be spent on a life of Henry VIII, a fitting sequel to the *History of Henry VII*.

Living at Bedford House was expensive, though, and it was difficult to keep her ladyship at bay. His finances were still at a low ebb, and there appeared to be one answer to this, ensuring privacy at the same time. He would move back to his old quarters at Gray's Inn. Here he would have all the books he needed, students going to and fro at his bidding, friends and associates calling with no questions asked, the life that had suited him admirably when young now adjusting to his needs as he grew old. Every corner was familiar: the entrance through the court, his rooms above, the furniture that had been his father's and his half-brothers' before him—no whining creditor could take these from him.

At Gray's Inn he was known, loved and respected, his very name a legend; and if he needed a nosegay on his table and the fragrance of fresh-cut flowers, he need not send to Gorhambury but to Lady Hatton within strolling distance, and her garden there. She had sold the house itself to the Duke of Lennox for £2,000 in ready money, with £1,500 a year for her lifetime, but had wisely kept the lodgings over the gate and a door into the gallery. His Grace would never dare deny her access to her garden. So, when he felt in the vein, talks over old times, without mentioning his rival, her husband Sir Edward Coke, who had been in disgrace himself the past year and committed to the Tower, but was now released.

Juggling for position was long over, they could call it quits. The power game had ended for the ex-Lord Chancellor and the ex-Lord Chief Justice. Their advice in Council, usually on opposing sides, was no more than a memory. Sir Edward, an exile in his turn, was living with one of his married daughters, and was likewise over-burdened with his own and his family's debts. Neither man, any longer, could do the other harm.

Francis at least could follow each turn in the political game through his informant Tobie Matthew, who, moving with ever-growing involvement in diplomatic circles, and in constant touch with the Spanish ambassador Count de Gondomar, was one of the first to report that a plan was afoot for the Prince of Wales and the Marquis of Buckingham to travel incognito to Spain. Once there it was hoped they could enlist the co-operation of King Philip in the recovery of the Palatinate, and in return conclude the marriage negotiations between the Infanta and the Prince of Wales. In short, an alliance would be cemented between Catholic Spain and Protestant Britain.

The reason for secrecy was that such an alliance was likely to be unpopular at home. Parliament, prorogued the year before without the subsidy granted, had not been recalled, nor was the Council briefed on this sudden project. The Prince of Wales and his companion Buckingham, wearing false beards, were ferried from Essex to Gravesend, and thence to Dover, sailing on February 21st 1623; but the secret was out. According to John Chamberlain the world was talking of it the following day and doubts were expressed about the mission which was likely to prove "costly and hazardous."

Francis would have discussed the likelihood of success or failure privately with Tobie Matthew, but to Buckingham he wrote, "Though your Lordship's absence fall out in an ill time for myself, yet because I hope in God this noble adventure will make your Lordship a rich return in honour abroad and at home, and chiefly in the inestimable treasure of the love and trust of that thrice-excellent Prince; I confess I am so glad of it, as I could not abstain from your Lordship's trouble in seeing it expressed by these few and hasty lines. I beseech your Lordship of your nobleness vouchsafe to present my most humble duty to his Highness, who I hope ere long will make me leave King Henry the Eighth and set me on work in relation of his Highness's heroical adventures." And in a note to the gentleman in attendance upon the Prince and Buckingham he wrote, "Myself for quiet and the better to hold out am retired to Gray's Inn: for when my chief friends were gone so far off, it was time for me to go to a cell. God send us a good return of you all."

And her ladyship? Not a word of her since July, when she was demanding half the sum due for the sale of York House lease. It was now the end of February. She can hardly be blamed if she relied rather more for companionship upon her steward John Underhill than her husband, safely installed at Gray's Inn, either knew or cared. She had her freedom. He had his work.

The question is, on what particular work was Francis Bacon engaged during the winter, spring and summer of 1623, and did Tobie Matthew possess the secret? Tobie left for Spain, in the wake of the Prince of Wales and Buckingham, some time in April, bearing letters from his friend and mentor to the Marquis, to the Earl of Bristol (the King's emissary) and to Count de Gondomar. Spedding, Bacon's biographer, prints all three letters, but omits—possibly because he thought it of little interest—a letter from Tobie to Francis which was published in Birch's Collecion of 1762.

The letter reads as follows:

"To the Lord Viscount St Alban.
"Most honoured Lord,
    I have received your great and noble token and favour of the 9th of April, and can but return the humblest of my thanks for your Lordship's vouchsafing so to visit this poorest and unworthiest of your servants. It doth me good at heart, that, although I be not where I was in place [referring obviously to his stay under Francis's roof, either at Bedford House or Gray's Inn], yet I am in the fortune of your Lordship's favour, if I may call that fortune, which I observe to be so unchangeable. I pray hard that it may once come in my power to serve you for it; and who can tell, but that, as *fortis imaginatio generat causam*, so strange desires may do as much? Sure I am, that mine are ever waiting on your Lordship; and wishing as much happiness as is due to your incomparable virtue, I humbly do your Lordship reverence.
                                        "Your Lordship's most obliged and humble servant
                                                        "Tobie Matthew."
    [Postscript.] *"The most prodigious wit, that ever I knew of my nation, and of this side of the sea, is of your Lordship's name though he be known by another."*

Here is food for speculation. To what personal notes and papers, to what manuscripts, had Tobie Matthew been granted access at Gray's Inn? Was something in preparation that was to appear later under a different name? No other inference can be drawn from that cryptic postscript. The Latin *De Augmentis Scientiarum* had been with the printers for months, and would be published in October with the author's name upon it, and the usual copies forwarded to his Majesty and the Prince of Wales. The history of the reign of Henry VIII was no more than a fragment, consisting of a couple of pages, and never finished; besides, when the chaplain Rawley came to publish it, with other of the works, it carried, as the rest did, the author's name, Francis Bacon.

"The most prodigious wit . . . is of your lordship's name, though he be known by another."

Mr William Shakespeare's *Comedies, Histories & Tragedies,* in one volume, was published in November 1623, a month later than *De Augmentis Scientiarum,* and had likewise been in the hands of its printers for something like eighteen months. Printing had started early in 1622, had been interrupted during the summer, and had continued during the following year. The work, which came to be known as the First Folio, consisted of 934 pages, and approximately 1,000 copies were printed, all at the shop of William and Isaac Jaggard. The editors were fellow actors of the dead dramatist, John Heminge and Henry Condell (thus was the spelling of the day), Heminge having also been business manager of the acting company and having large financial interests in the Blackfriars and Globe theatres. It is generally thought that Edward Knight, the book-keeper of the King's Men's company, actually had the exacting task of editing the text, but there is no proof of this. Of the thirty-six plays that the volume contained, eighteen had never before been printed. Performed, yes; yet, again, there is no documentary proof that each of these eighteen plays had been seen in public, nor can any scholar affirm that the acted text was word for word, or scene for scene, the same as that of the printed text of the First Folio in 1623. (A list of these eighteen plays is given in Appendix II.)

The volume also contained laudatory poems to the dead dramatist from Ben Jonson and others, an epistle *To the Great Variety of Readers* from John Heminge and Henry Condell, and a list of the principal actors who had appeared in the plays. Henry Condell, incidentally, had by now retired from the stage and was living on his estate at Fulham, a neighbour to Sir John Vaughan, with whom Francis Bacon had lodged after his disgrace in 1621.

It might be thought the Folio would have been dedicated to the Earl of Southampton, known to have been William Shakespeare's patron in his early days in the theatre, but he is nowhere mentioned. The volume bore the dedication to William Herbert, 3rd Earl of Pembroke, and his brother Philip Herbert, Earl of Montgomery. The former was currently Lord Chamberlain, and his brother succeeded him in this position three years later.

William Herbert was one of those members of the House of Lords who had been more kindly disposed to Viscount St Alban at the impeachment than some others, and there is a memorandum of thanks to him for "his kind remembrance," in the hand of Francis's secretary Thomas Meautys but dictated by his employer: "I cannot but acknowledge the moderation and affection his Lordship showed in my business, and desire that of those few his Lordship will still be one for my comfort, in whatsoever may cross his way, for the furtherance of my private life and fortune." As for his brother, the Earl of Montgomery, it was he who had obtained the interview for Lady St Alban with the Marquis of Buckingham, and a note in St Alban's papers late that year says, "There is not an honester man in court than Montgomery." All three men, Francis Bacon, Pembroke, and Montgomery, had been founders of and had held shares in the Virginia Company and the Newfoundland Company in 1609, and had known one another for years.

It is interesting that the decision to print the volume of plays—the First Folio—had been taken early in 1622, after the Lord Chancellor's disgrace, and when his fortunes were at their lowest ebb. Why had no attempt been made to collect and publish the thirty-six plays immediately after William Shakespeare's death in April 1616? Why the lapse of seven years? Heminge and Condell mention in their epistle to the reader "surreptitious copies, maimed and deformed by the frauds and stealths of injurious imposters, that exposed them": so fraudulent editions had been distributed from time to time; but now at last, in 1623, the genuine and definitive edition was for sale.

It is not intended here to enter into a long and tedious argument as to whether William Shakespeare was indeed the author of all the thirty-six plays published under his name in the First Folio. The original manuscripts, notes and prompt-copies have never been found. It is suggested, however, that some of the themes, plots, scenes and speeches could have been contributed by others, and woven into the necessary form for dramatic presentation by the actor-playwright. Anthony Bacon was living in Bishopsgate, close to the Bull Inn where plays were performed, in 1594; William Shakespeare was living in the same parish, and acting with Richard Burbage and the Lord Chamberlain's Men. It was on December 28th of that year that *The Comedy of Errors* was performed at Gray's Inn. It is furthermore suggested that from this time forward both Anthony and Francis Bacon, and possibly others, were in collaboration with the actor-dramatist on some of the earlier plays, which were issued in quarto and printed, and that, after the Essex débâcle, Anthony's death and the start of the new reign, Francis Bacon continued this collaboration. Anonymity suited both men, William Shakespeare deriving financial advantage and popular success, while the Learned Counsel and politician preferred to be known for his philosophical and literary efforts.

It is interesting that William Shakespeare, despite the performances of his plays often given at Court, seems never to have been officially presented to their Majesties King James and Queen Anne, unlike his contemporary Ben Jonson; and that no new plays were forthcoming from his pen after 1612, when he retired to his birth-place at Stratford-on-Avon, shortly before Francis Bacon became Attorney-General and was occupied with affairs of State.

William Shakespeare left a long and very detailed will when he died four years later, entirely concerning property to be settled amongst his family, but without mentioning any interest he may have had in any of the plays that had been issued in his name. This was because all rights of authorship belonged to the King's Men's company, and to the publishers of those plays that had appeared in quarto. Twenty-five pounds each went to his fellow-actors John Heminge, Richard Burbage and Henry Condell, "to buy them rings."

It was only in succeeding centuries, and particularly during the past one hundred and fifty years, that the astonishing range and versatility of these plays won world-wide recognition, and perhaps in our own time more than ever before, now that they can be seen not only on the stage but on the screen at home as well. There are said to be some 238 copies of the First Folio in existence today. Priced at £1 in 1623, a copy was sold to a book-dealer in 1923 for approximately £25,000. In 1975 it would probably cost a quarter of a million. John Chamberlain, who had at least made an attempt to read Francis Bacon's Latin philosophical works, and had praised his *History of Henry VII*, cannot have thought very much of William Shakespeare's plays. The publication of the First Folio is not even mentioned in his letters. "The most prodigious wit that ever I knew of my nation. . . ."

Tobie Matthew, in Madrid, "is grown extreme lean and looks as sharp as an eyass" reported the Marquis, now Duke of Buckingham, from Spain on May 29th, when thanking Francis for his "hearty congratulation for the great honour and gracious favour which his Majesty hath done me." Negotiations for the royal marriage were apparently progressing well, and frequent letters passed between Matthew and his mentor the Viscount St Alban during that summer of 1623, but there is no further allusion to "the prodigious wit," and if

Francis ever remarked upon that postscript to Tobie's letter the shrewd diplomat destroyed the reference.

By the end of June Francis, still at Gray's Inn, told his friend in Madrid that the essays were being made more perfect, "well translated into Latin by the help of some good pens which forsake me not. For these modern languages will at one time or other play the bankrupts with books; and since I have lost much time with this age, I would be glad as God shall give me leave to recover it with posterity."

"For the essay of friendship, while I took your speech of it for a cursory request I took my promise for a compliment. But since you call for it I shall perform it."

Bacon's essay *Of Friendship*, which he now enlarged from a shorter, earlier version, is one of his longest and most famous, and the more interesting in that Tobie Matthew was the source of inspiration.

"You may take sarza to open the liver, steel to open the spleen, flower of sulphur for the lungs, castoreum for the brain, but no receipt openeth the heart but a true friend, to whom you may impart griefs, joys, fears, hopes, suspicions, counsels, and whatsoever liveth upon the heart to oppress it, in a kind of civil shrift or confession. . . . Certain it is, that whosoever hath his mind fraught with many thoughts, his wits and understanding do clarify and break up in the communication and discoursing with another; he tosseth his thoughts more easily; he marshalleth them more orderly; he seeth how they look when they are turned into words; finally he waxeth wiser than himself; and that more by an hour's discourse than by a day's meditation. . . . I have given the rule, where a man cannot fitly play his own part; if he have not a friend, he may quit the stage."

No man could have wished for a finer tribute than this.

It is possible that Francis was indeed taking sarza for the liver and flower of sulphur for the lungs that summer of 1623, for on August 29th he wrote to the Duke of Buckingham, excusing himself for not having written before. "In truth I was ill in health . . . for I have lain at two wards, the one against my disease, the other against my physicians, who are strange creatures. I do understand from Mr Matthew, which rejoiceth me much, that I live in your Grace's remembrance, and that I shall be the first man that you will have care of at your return, for which I most humbly kiss your hands."

The letter is written from Gray's Inn, which leads one to suppose that he had remained there throughout his sickness, and had not spent any time at Gorhambury. Copies of *De Augmentis Scientiarum*—the Latin translation and additions to *The Advancement of Learning*—

175

were awaiting the Prince of Wales and the Duke of Buckingham on their return from Spain in October, and Francis, who seems to have recovered his health by now, was hoping that Buckingham could obtain for him the position of Provost of Eton. The post had not been filled since the former Provost had died in April, and although Francis had put forth tenders at the time the Secretary of State, Sir Edward Conway, had not been able to hold out any firm promise. A word from the Duke to his Majesty would surely arrange the matter. Francis had never abandoned his desire to help mould the minds of future generations, to watch over the training of the young who would one day, by their birth and upbringing, rise to positions of authority in Parliament and government; besides, Eton's proximity to Windsor Castle would be useful. Unfortunately the Duke had promised the post to another— Sir Henry Wotton had it eventually—and Eton College lost the chance of a provost who possessed "the most prodigious wit . . . this side of the sea."

Meanwhile, what had the Duke and the Prince of Wales actually accomplished in Spain? Not a very great deal, according to the gossip filtering through the pen of John Chamberlain to Dudley Carleton. At first there was great public acclaim. Hogsheads of wine in the streets, butts of sack, bonfires everywhere, and when the Prince and Duke arrived at Royston his Majesty fell on their necks, and everybody wept. But, the celebrations over, Chamberlain reported in the third week of October that "our courtiers and others that were in Spain begin now to open their mouths and speak liberally of the coarse usage and entertainment, where they found nothing but penury and proud beggary, besides all other discourtesy . . . and whereas it was thought the Spaniards and we should have peace and grow together, it seems we are generally more disjointed and farther asunder in affections than ever."

One of the incidents that irritated John Chamberlain most was that Tobie Matthew had been knighted at Royston, "but for what service God knows." For keeping the peace, one assumes, between the high dignitaries of the Spanish court and their English guests, for it was soon learnt that the Duke of Buckingham had fallen out with the Count de Gondomar, the Spanish ambassador, and had returned from Spain no longer in favour of the Spanish treaty of alliance. Francis would have heard of this direct from Tobie Matthew, also that Parliament was likely to be recalled. No longer a member of the Council, or of Parliament, yet he fretted to give advice, the mood of those in power being such that opposing factions might once more develop, and the Duke's own position of authority be placed in jeopardy. He must write a letter of advice to his Grace, first of all jotting down notes in a memorandum of what he intended to say.

"There are considerable in this state three sorts of men. The party of the Papists which hate you, the party of the Protestants, including those they call Puritans, whose love is yet but green towards you, and particular great persons, which are most of them reconciled enemies, or discontented friends. . . . It is good to carry yourself fair . . . to keep a good distance and to play your own game, showing yourself to have, as the bee hath, both of the honey and of the sting. . . . You march bravely, but methinks you do not draw up your troops. . . . If a war be proceeded in, to treat a straight league with France. . . . Above all you must look to the safety of Ireland . . . for the disease will ever fall to the weakest part. . . . You bowl well, if you do not horse your bowl an hand too much. You know the fine bowler is knee almost to ground in the delivery of the cast. Nay, and the King will be a hook in the nostrils of Spain, and lay a foundation of greatness to his children here in these west parts. The call for me, it is book-learning . . . I cannot thread needles so well."

The jottings run on and on, fascinating for the image they give of Francis Bacon, ex-Lord Chancellor, letting his mind leap ahead to a future alliance with France as against a treaty with Spain, ever mindful of Catholic Ireland as a possible base for Spanish invaders. Then, when his thoughts were assembled into some order, they could be translated into a true directive. One jotting only was omitted: "Offer of mine own service upon a commission into France." He had been ill, he was yet frail, his sixty-third birthday was fast approaching, but if there was anything he could still do to serve his King and his country he was ready, despite the humiliation and shame of his disgrace.

Parliament was to be called during February of the new year, 1624, and both Houses would then be informed of all that had taken place regarding the Spanish treaty and the marriage negotiations. According to the terms of his sentence Francis was not permitted to take his seat in the House of Lords; nevertheless he could draw up notes of a speech he would have made had he been present, and, moreover, compose a lengthy document entitled *Considerations Touching a War with Spain* which he addressed specifically to the Prince, beginning with the words, "Your Highness hath an imperial name. It was a Charles that brought the empire first into France; a Charles that brought it first into Spain; why should not Great Britain have his turn?"

The document was an enlargement of his original treatise on the subject, first written in 1619 when he still held high office, and once again Francis Bacon, who had been a man of peace for most of his life, showed himself to be something of a hawk in his last years, with considerable understanding of how the united forces of Great Britain, France and the Low Countries could scatter and overcome the armies and ships of Spain. His comparison with the power which Spain possessed in 1588, Armada year, and now in 1623, is concise and masterly, the balance having shifted in favour of Britain and her nearest neighbours; while any naval or military authority who read the document then—if any did—would surely have warmed to the author (as he would today) for certain of the sentiments expressed.

"Of valour I speak not; take it from the witnesses that have been produced before: yet the old observation is not untrue, that the Spaniard's valour lieth in the eye of the looker-on; but the English valour lieth about the soldier's heart." And he has a splendid tilt at the "doves" who demurred against taking action of any kind, calling them "schoolmen, otherwise reverend men, yet fitter to guide penknives than swords."

He recommended that the Commons should appoint a select committee with power "to confer with any martial men or others, that were not of the House, for their advice and information," but needless to say this suggestion went unheeded. Whether indeed the document was ever shown to the Prince of Wales or anyone else in authority at the time we have no means of knowing. In any event the marriage negotiations were broken off, apparently with the agreement of both parties, and when Parliament met in February 1624 it was observed that the Prince of Wales was in attendance every day. Possibly he had read Viscount St Alban's document after all. When the House voted to end the treaties, and to raise money for the assistance of the Palatinate, the whole British people rejoiced, and bonfires were lighted in the streets once more. Francis Bacon contributed, it was said, four dozen faggots and twelve gallons of wine. He might be without influence or power, but he could still engage in celebration, and damnation to his creditors.

Chapter XX

"We sailed from Peru, where we had continued by the space of one whole year, for China and Japan, by the South Sea; taking with us victuals for twelve months; and had good winds from the east, though soft and weak, for five months' space and more. But then the wind came about, and settled in the west for many days, so as we could make little or no way, and were sometimes in purpose to turn back. But then again there arose strong and great winds from the south, with a point east . . . so that finding ourselves in the midst of the greatest wilderness of waters in the world, without victual, we gave ourselves for lost men and prepared for death."

The start of a nineteenth-century novel by Robert Louis Stevenson, telling the adventures of a barque in the Pacific? Not so. The opening of *New Atlantis,* the fable that Francis Bacon began in 1624 and never finished. Now read on.

"And it came to pass that the next day about evening, we saw . . . as it were thick clouds, which did put us in some hope of land: knowing how that part of the South Sea was utterly unknown; and might have islands or continents, that hitherto were not come to light. . . . And after an hour and a half's sailing, we entered into a good haven, being the port of a fair city . . . but straightway we saw divers of the people, with bastons in their hands, as it were forbidding us to land; yet without any cries of fierceness. . . . There made forth to us a small boat, with about eight persons in it; whereof one of them had in his hand a tipstaff of a yellow cane, tipped at both ends with blue, who came aboard our ship, without any show of distrust at all. . . . He drew forth a little scroll of parchment . . . in which scroll were written in ancient Hebrew, and in ancient Greek, and in good Latin of the School, and in Spanish, these words, 'Land ye not, none of you; and provide to be gone from this coast within sixteen days, except you have further time given you. Meanwhile, if you want fresh water, or victual, or help for your sick, or that your ship

179

needeth repair, write down your wants, and you shall have that which belongeth to mercy.' This scroll was signed with a stamp of cherubins' wings, not spread but hanging downwards, and by them a cross. . . . About three hours after we had dispatched our answer, there came towards us a person, as it seemed, of place. He had on him a gown with wide sleeves, kind of a water chamolet, of an excellent azure colour, far more glossy than ours; his under apparel was green; and so was his hat, being in the form of a turban, daintily made, and not so huge as the Turkish turbans; and the locks of his hair came down below the brims of it."

After swearing they were not pirates, and had not shed blood within forty days past, and were Christians, the ship's company were given permission to land the following day, bringing their sick. This they did, and were taken to a spacious house, built of brick of a blueish colour, known as the Stranger's House. Here they were told they might rest for three days and were given food and drink of a more refreshing kind than any of them had tasted in Europe, and pills to hasten the recovery of the sick. When the three days had passed, the governor of the Stranger's House came to visit them, telling them that he was by vocation a Christian priest, and seeing that his guests were also Christian he would answer their questions, for the state had given them licence to stay for six weeks in the island, which was called Bensalem.

The officers of the ship's company, six in number, then learnt, after further discussion each day, the extraordinary history of the island. How some three thousand years before, although even then an island, it had formed part of the great continent of Atlantis, possessing ships that travelled the world over. Hence their knowledge of Hebrew, Greek and Latin. Then disaster struck. A mighty flood overwhelmed the whole continent, burying its cities and drowning almost all its inhabitants, and the few who survived became, through succeeding centuries, the unlettered and near savage population of what remained of the once proud and powerful continent, namely America.

As for the island of Bensalem, it had survived intact, through the miraculous intervention of the Almighty, and the Apostle of Jesus Christ, Saint Bartholomew, thus enabling the islanders and their descendants to grow in wisdom and culture through the ages, Christian in faith and outlook, while their king and governor had been one they called Solamona, who had created an order of society that was named Salomon's House, dedicated to the study of the works and creatures of God.

Isolated from the rest of the world, the islanders had thus avoided all contamination from outer sources, but certain brethren of Salomon's House were permitted to travel in disguise, wander amongst the peoples of the world, and then return with what they had learnt of the progress of science, art, manufacture and invention, and so improve their own inventions in the island; yet by their very isolation in these unexplored waters of the Pacific Ocean, and the rule of life by which they lived, safeguard their discoveries from man's greed and exploitation.

The visitors to Bensalem were permitted to wander about the town and its neighbourhood as they wished. "We took ourselves now for free men," says the narrator of *New Atlantis,* "and lived most joyfully . . . obtaining acquaintance with many of the city . . . at whose hands we found such humanity, and such a freedom and desire to take strangers as it were into their bosom as was enough to make us forget all that was dear to us in our own countries: and continually we met with many things right worthy of observation and relation; as indeed, if there be a mirror in the world worthy to hold men's eyes, it is that country."

The resemblance to a nineteenth-century novel of adventure ends, and a forerunner of twentieth-century science fiction begins when the narrator is allowed access to one of the Fathers of Salomon's House, who imparts to him all the secrets of the work in progress.

"Caves . . . sunk six hundred fathom. . . . These caves we call the Lower Region. And we use them for all coagulations, indurations, refrigerations, and conservations of bodies . . . and the producing also of new artificial metals . . . and we use them sometimes for curing of some diseases, and for prolongation of life. . . . We have also great variety of composts, and soils, for the making of the earth fruitful.

"We have high towers . . . and these place we call the Upper Region. . . . We use these towers for the view of divers meteors; as winds, rain, snow, hail; and some of the fiery meteors also. . . .

"We have also a number of artificial wells. . . . Chambers of Health . . . gardens where we practise all conclusions of grafting and inoculating . . . parks and enclosures of all sorts of beasts and birds . . . to try poisons and other medicines upon them . . . resuscitating of some that seem dead in appearance. . . .

"We have heats in imitation of the sun's and heavenly bodies' heats. . . . Instruments also which generate heat only by motion. . . . We procure means of seeing objects afar off . . . and things afar off as near, making feigned distances. . . . We have also sound-houses . . . and means to convey sounds in trunks and pipes, in strange lines and distances. . . . Engine-houses, where we practise to make swifter motions than any you have . . . and more violent than yours are, exceeding your greatest cannons and basilisks. . . . We imitate also flights of birds; we have some degrees of flying in the air; we have ships and boats for going under water, and brooking of seas. . . .

"We have also houses of deceits of the senses, where we represent all manner of feats of juggling, false apparitions, impostures, and illusions; and their fallacies.

"These are, my son, some of the riches of Salomon's House."

To the ordinary reader, who is neither scholar nor historian and has yet managed to read *Of The Advancement of Learning* and translations of the Latin works without difficulty, indeed with enjoyment, *New Atlantis* comes as a further shock of surprise and excitement, for here is something quite different again from anything that Francis Bacon had written hitherto. The nineteenth-century Robert Louis Stevenson has been mentioned, and the names of Jules Verne and H. G. Wells could be added; but these were all writers close to our own time and the author of *New Atlantis* preceded them by two and a half centuries.

So what were his sources, and who inspired him? Certainly the style and the opening description of the voyage are reminiscent of *The Principal Navigations, Voyages, Traffics, and Discoveries of the English Nation* by Richard Hakluyt, first published in 1589, with further editions in 1598, 1599 and 1600. Francis, an avid reader, would have seized upon them as a young barrister at Gray's Inn, and undoubtedly made notes of their contents. Moreover, Richard Hakluyt, like Francis, had shares in the Virginia Company; the two men would certainly have met.

Dr John Dee, astrologer, mathematician and alchemist, was another celebrated figure about the Elizabethan Court in those days, one of his obsessions being to discover a north-west passage to the Far East; while later in his career, in Bohemia, he became involved with the curious mystical Rosicrucian movement which spread across the whole of Germany, a "fraternity in learning and illumination," its members secret, known as the Brothers of the Rosy Cross. Their manifestoes, the *Fama* (in German) and *Confessio* (in Latin), were published in 1615, and Francis Bacon would certainly have read the latter and known about the Rosicrucian fraternity. There is a striking resemblance between Salomon's House in his *New Atlantis* and the Brothers of the Rosicrucian movement; and Frances Yates, author of *The Rosicrucian Enlightenment*, believes that Francis Bacon based his fable upon the manifestoes but that he was not himself a member of the fraternity.

Nor is there any proof that Francis Bacon ever belonged to any mystical or other secret society.

In *New Atlantis* Francis Bacon was developing into a fable for the future the dream that had obsessed him all his life. Years before, when he had helped to produce the Revels at Gray's Inn as a young barrister in January 1595, the theme of the *Gesta Grayorum* had been along the same lines: the knightly Order of the Helmet suggesting many of the rules of conduct observed by the Brethren of Salomon's House. It was not by rules of conduct, though, that his dream-world could come into being: it was by a new understanding of natural science, and we have seen how he continually developed this idea in later years, with *Cogitata et Visa* and *The Advancement of Learning*. Thence his desire, forever frustrated, to become vice-chancellor of a university, or, if not vice-chancellor, then master of a college, and finally (though this also was denied him) to be provost of Eton. Students, men of learning, must be directed to research. There must be nothing in heaven or earth, or under the earth, left unexplored. Nobody listened. Nobody cared.

Very well, then. A fable, and in English, about an island in the Pacific, with caverns and towers equipped as laboratories, and the Father of Salomon's House a glorified image of what Francis himself might have been; no Prospero on the stage with a magician's wand and spirits to do his bidding, but the director of an institution for research, and men of goodwill working beside him.

A fable of some thirty pages, left unfinished, put aside. To be published by chaplain Rawley a year after Francis's death, with the preface to the reader: "This fable my Lord devised, to the end that he might exhibit therein a model or description of a college instituted for the interpretation of nature and the producing of great and marvellous works for the benefit of men; under the name of Salomon's House, or the College of Six Days' Works. And even so far his Lordship hath proceeded, as to finish that part. Certainly the model is more vast and high than can possibly be imitated in all things; notwithstanding most things therein are within men's power to effect. His Lordship thought also in this present fable to have composed a frame of laws, or of the best state or mould of a commonwealth; but foreseeing it would be a long work, his desire of collecting the Natural History diverted him, which he preferred many degrees before it. . . ."

Disappointment may also have had its effect. It was reported in April that Sir Henry Wotton was likely to become the new provost of

Eton, and by midsummer the appointment was confirmed; no school-boy, with "his satchel and shining morning face, creeping like snail unwillingly to school," would greet Francis in College Yard to be moulded into a man of science. Instead, he must rest content with those student lawyers at Gray's Inn, and the many other handy pens who loved him well.

And at this point, July and August of 1624, he fell ill once more, as he had done the preceding summer, and his helpers were set to work to copy down, from dictation at his bedside, some 280 apophthegms, or sayings that he had memorised during his lifetime. It was not a fatiguing occupation for a sick man who knew each of the apophthegms by heart, though it may have taxed his attendants. As might be expected from "the most prodigious wit" of this side of the sea, many of the sayings betray a pungent sense of humour. He drew them from every source: classical, historical, his own time, sayings from the previous reign, some spoken by Queen Elizabeth herself, and one or two by his own father. The following happen to appeal to the present writer:

"A great officer in France was in danger to have lost his place; but his wife, by her suit and means making, made his peace; wherein a pleasant fellow said, 'That he had been crushed, but that he had saved himself upon his horns.'"

"There was a young man in Rome, that was very like Augustus Caesar. Augustus took knowledge of it, and sent for the man, and asked him 'Was your mother never at Rome?.' He answered 'No, sir, but my father was.'"

"Alexander was wont to say: 'He knew he was mortal by two things; sleep and lust.'"

"Sir Edward Coke was wont to say, when a great man came to dinner with him, and gave him no knowledge of his coming: 'Well, since you sent me no word of your coming, you shall dine with me; but if I had known of it in due time, I would have dined with you.'"

"There was a gentleman that came to the tilt all in orange-tawney, and ran very ill. The next day he came all in green, and ran worse. There was one of the lookers-on asked another; 'What's the reason that this gentleman in the orange-tawney.'"

"The counsel did make remonstrance unto Queen Elizabeth of the continual conspiracies against her life; and namely of a late one . . . and upon this occasion advised her that she should go less abroad to take the air, weakly accompanied, as she used. But the Queen answered: 'That she had rather be dead, than put in custody.'"

James Spedding was of the opinion that Francis published his apophthegms because he owed both publisher and printer money, which may well have been the case; his debts were piling up as usual.

We do not know which of the many "idle pens" copied the sayings down, to chuckles from the sick bed, but possibly not the chaplain Rawley, who would have preferred the other slim volume that appeared at the same time, the *Translations of Certain Psalms into English Verse*, dedicated to the poet George Herbert as "this poor exercise of my sickness."

One wonders what Tobie Matthew would have thought of them. No evidence of prodigious wit here, or indeed of talent. Is it possible that Francis had been turning over some of the faded effusions of his devout mother, the late Lady Bacon, and then, with judicious alterations here and there, had decided to send them off with the apophthegms for good measure?

Whatever the reason for the publication of both apophthegms and psalms, there is no doubt that Francis Bacon had been seriously ill through summer and autumn, and so had many others, adults and children alike. John Chamberlain reported in September from London that, "We have here but a sickly season, and yet admit of no infection. 407 this week, 150 of them children, most of the rest carried away by this spotted fever, which reigns almost everywhere in the country as well as here." He gives the names of some of those who had died, or been ill, and mentions Lord St Alban amongst them.

Writing three months later, just before Christmas, to Dudley Carleton abroad, he mentions Francis's apophthegms, "newly set out this week, but with so little allowance or applause that the world says his wit and judgement begins to draw near the lees; he hath likewise translated some few psalms into verse or rhyme which shows he grows holy towards his end: if I could meet with a fit messenger you should have them both."

Francis himself, in his very scanty correspondence during the autumn, makes no mention of "spotted fever" in a letter to the Duke of Buckingham, but speaks of "the raving of a hot ague," which sounds equally painful if not so dangerous. He was still without that formal pardon for which he craved, and it seems uncertain whether his pension had been paid. He would have learnt that summer, possibly with mixed feelings and with a certain sense of irony, that Lord Treasurer Cranfield, first Earl of Middlesex, who had succeeded him as the owner of York House, had been accused of certain offences, confined to the Tower, deprived of all his offices and heavily fined, and was now an exile in the country, just as he himself had been three years previously. Few statesmen those days could climb the winding stair without a fall.

Nevertheless, although Viscount St Alban had no more part in the government of the country, his advice regarding a French alliance had not gone altogether unheeded, and he would have heard, with an equally ironic smile, in November of 1624, that negotiations for a marriage between the Prince of Wales and Princess Henrietta Maria, daughter of King Louis XII of France, were nearing completion. The Duke of Buckingham was expected to cross the Channel early in the new year, accompanied by a retinue of peers, and bring the princess to England.

Unfortunately, Bacon's counsel that, before any British army should be sent abroad to help recover the Palatinate, military authorities must be consulted was apparently disregarded. Some 12,000 men, composed of Scots and English regiments, arrived in Holland to take part in a joint expedition with Count Mansfeldt, but without definite orders and under poor leadership. The British contingent was so ill-disciplined that it went on its way looting and despoiling the countryside as if, so John Chamberlain was obliged to report, "it had been in an enemy's country. . . . We hear they have mutinied already so that Count Mansfeldt durst not show himself among them." Later half the number were carried off by disease and privation. Apparently no attempt was made to feed the troops or to organise supplies, and the enterprise was a total failure.

It was not a happy start to the year 1625, and John Chamberlain spoke, for once, for all his fellow-countrymen when he wrote in February, "The time hath been, when so many English as have been sent into those parts within these six or eight months would have done somewhat, and made the world talk of them, but I know not how we that have been esteemed in that kind more than any other nations, do begin to grow by degrees less than the least, when the basest of people in matter of courage dare brave and trample upon us."

On March 5th King James became ill, after hunting at Theobalds. Although he had suffered for some time with gout, and possibly arthritis, it was not at first realised that his condition was now serious. He lingered for some three weeks, unable to speak—perhaps the result of a stroke—and died on March 27th 1625, aged fifty-eight. His body was brought to London and lay in state at Denmark House until the funeral on May 7th, "the greatest indeed that ever was known in England," after which King James I of England and VI of Scotland was buried in the chapel of Henry VII at Westminster Abbey.

His son, who succeeded him as King Charles I, had been married by proxy to the Princess Henrietta Maria on May 1st, but was obliged to wait for his bride six weeks, when he received her at Canterbury on June 13th.

"The Queen," reported Chamberlain, "hath brought they say such a poor pitiful sort of women that there is not one worth the looking after saving herself and the Duchess of Chevreuse, who though she be fair yet paints foully." The Duke of Buckingham gave a magnificent banquet in their honour at York House, but because of indisposition neither of their Majesties was present. We do not know whether Francis Bacon was well enough to attend and to partake of the sumptuous fare that was provided in his old home. A sturgeon "six foot long" that had leapt into a sculler's boat that very afternoon was served at supper.

The new King summoned his first Parliament on June 18th. His speech was short. He told the Members "they had drawn him into a war, and they must find means to maintain it." The means were not forthcoming. His father, as "the wisest fool in Christendom," though he had never won the hearts of his subjects, might have handled the matter with more discretion and been applauded. King Charles was not so fortunate. The reign of that ill-fated monarch, destined to die upon the scaffold in 1649, had now begun. He was at this time twenty-four years old.

Chapter XXI

Plague and sickness raged through the summer of 1625. Nobody stayed in town who could get away. Whether Francis Bacon left his lodgings in Gray's Inn for Verulam House at Gorhambury in spring or later we have no means of knowing, for there is no correspondence from him extant for at least six months, dating from December of the previous year until the following June. He can hardly have remained silent on the death of King James in March, and on the marriage and accession to the throne of King Charles, unless he was himself ill. Whatever the reason, no letters to or from him have survived.

Tobie Matthew was apparently in Boulogne in June, just before the new Queen Henrietta Maria left France to join her husband, for he wrote to the Duke of Buckingham describing her appearance with enthusiasm, despite the fact that the previous year he had done the same about the Infanta. He would undoubtedly have written in similar vein to his close friend at Gorhambury, although with the start of a new reign Tobie was to find himself fresh patrons in Lucy, Countess of Carlisle, and the Duchess of Chevreuse, whose use of cosmetics had been so deplored by John Chamberlain. This invaluable scribe also became silent during 1625, for reasons of failing health, and the gossip of the day, so fascinating to readers in later centuries, went unreported.

As the summer progressed, so did the plague, and the people swarmed out of London, carrying the infection further afield. The King and Queen retired to Hampton Court, then to Windsor, and finally to Woodstock near Oxford, where notices were displayed forbidding anyone from plague-ridden districts to go near. Shops and inns were closed down, graveyards became congested, and to make conditions worse the rain fell ceaselessly day and night, threatening the growing crops. It was said that no letters were delivered from the town to the country during this period, and this may be the most likely reason for Francis Bacon's lack of correspondence. The only surviving letters date from June, soon after the Queen's arrival in Eng-

188

land, one of which welcomes the French ambassador, the Marquis d'Effiat. The others, as might be expected from one whose pension still remained unpaid, were requests to the new Lord Treasurer Lord Ley for financial aid, and to Sir Humphrey May, Chancellor of the Duchy of Lancaster, praying him to "quicken" the Lord Treasurer, "that the King may once clear with me. A fire of old wood needeth no blowing; but old men do."

Thereafter silence until October, when we have a long letter in Latin written to a Father Fulgentio, a divine of the republic of Venice, in which Francis speaks of having suffered "under a very severe illness, from which I have not yet recovered." In the same month he writes from Gorhambury to a Mr Roger Palmer, saying, "I thank God, by means of the sweet air of the country, I have obtained some degree of health. . . . Sending to the court, I thought I would salute you: and I would be glad, in this solitary time and place, to hear a little from you how the world goeth. . . ." It is sad to think of a man of his eminence relying for news from a comparatively obscure correspondent in this final period of his life.

The world, alas, was going rather badly, or those parts of it that Francis had closest to his heart. King Charles had signed a treaty with the Dutch against Spain, and had sent an expedition out to Cadiz in September under the command of Edward Cecil, brother of Lady Hatton, which was an even more disastrous failure than the expedition to Holland the year previously.

As to the Lady Hatton herself, it is very possible that by withdrawing to the sweet air of the country Francis was spared some of the histrionics that might have been inflicted upon him at Gray's Inn, so close to Holborn, for Elizabeth Hatton had been plunged into family troubles for the last three years. Her elder daughter Elizabeth, who had married Sir Maurice Berkeley, had died in November of 1623, while the younger, Frances, about whom there had been so much to-do before her marriage in 1617 to Sir John Villiers, Buckingham's brother, had suffered a series of disasters ever since. Her husband, created Lord Purbeck, became insane and was confined to his house, and Lady Purbeck returned to her mother. Here she was foolish enough to fall in love with her own cousin, Sir Robert Howard. Lady Hatton wisely took her daughter off to Holland on a visit to the exiled Electress Palatine, ex-Queen of Bohemia, but the unhappy girl could not forget her lover, and in 1624 gave birth to a son, whom her husband's family pronounced a bastard, despite the fact that Frances declared she had received visits from her insane lord during the preceding months.

Sir Robert Howard was clapped in the Fleet and Lady Purbeck

placed in confinement. The bitter dispute continued into 1625, with the Duke of Buckingham the most virulent against his sister-in-law, declaring there should be a divorce, although his brother, Lord Purbeck, protested between bouts of insanity that the child born to his wife was indeed his.

The new reign brought some respite for the lovers. Sir Robert Howard was released from the Fleet, and Lady Purbeck from her confinement in an alderman's house. But two years later she was found guilty of infidelity, and was sentenced to a fine of £500 and to do penance by walking barefoot from St Paul's Cross to the Savoy, standing at the door of the church for all to see. She escaped this ordeal by dressing up as a page, and later she, her lover and her baby son went into hiding in Shropshire. Her mother withstood the shock of this second ordeal, and resumed her life of ceaseless activity.

It is small wonder that during the long summers of 1624 and 1625 Francis Bacon pleaded sickness and wrote few letters or none at all, his friendship for Lady Hatton being well known. One can imagine the knock on the door, and one of his numerous attendants announcing, in hushed tones, that the Lady Hatton was without. Then the cry of exasperation from the invalid, and a wave of the hand, "No . . . no . . . I am far too ill to receive her ladyship or any visitor," and the sigh of relief when her departure was confirmed. This would be the moment to reach for his list of herbal remedies. "An orange flower water to be smelt or snuffed up," "to use once during supper time wine in which gold is quenched. . . ." But better still, though this would have been at Gorhambury and impossible at Gray's Inn, "In the third hour after the sun is risen, to take in air from some high and open place, with a ventilation of rose moschatae, and fresh violets; and to stir the earth, with infusion of wine and mint."

He had remedies for the stomach, for gout, for the stone—evidently he suffered from all three—and four precepts of health he upheld firmly: "To break off custom. To shake off spirits ill disposed. To meditate on youth. To do nothing against a man's genius." And, very important indeed, "Never to keep the body in the same posture above half-an-hour at a time." Possibly the astringent he recommended, "which, by cherishing of the parts, do comfort and confirm their retentive power," was noted down for its originality and because it may have shocked his chaplain Rawley. "A stomacher of scarlet cloth. Whelps, or young healthy boys, applied to the stomach. Hippocratic wines, so they be made of austere materials."

The ironic humour of Francis Bacon escaped many of his contemporaries, but not all of them. A contemporary scholar, Thomas Farnaby, published a collection of Greek epigrams three years after Bacon's death, and printed at the same time what he termed a paraphrase in English verse, written by Lord Bacon, of one of the themes in the collection. Even Spedding, who was no satirist himself, did not doubt its authenticity. Farnaby gave no date for the adaptation of the theme into English verse, or of how he obtained the manuscript, but one might hazard a guess that the poem was written in a mood of total disenchantment with the world, when nothing pleased, when news from abroad was as disturbing as news at home, and the Viscountess St Alban was proving more than usually troublesome. It could well have been written during the autumn of 1625.

> The world's a bubble, and the life of man
> > less than a span;
> On his conception wretched, from the womb
> > so to the tomb:
> Curst from the cradle, and brought up to years
> > with cares and fears.
> Who then to frail mortality shall trust,
> But limns the water, or but writes in dust.
> Yet since with sorrow here we live opprest,
> > what life is best?
> Courts are but only superficial schools
> > to dandle fools.
> The rural parts are turned into a den
> > of savage men.
> And where's the city from all vice so free,
> But may be turned the worst of all the three?
> Domestic cares afflict the husband's bed,
> > or pains his head.
> Those that live single take it for a curse,
> > or do things worse.
> Some would have children; those that have them moan,
> > or wish them gone.
> What is it then to have or have no wife,
> But single thraldom, or a double strife?
> Our own affections still at home to please
> > is a disease:
> To cross the seas to any foreign soil
> > perils and toil.
> Wars with their noise affright us: when they cease,
> > we are worse in peace.
> What then remains, but that we still should cry
> Not to be born, or being born to die."

The only work that was definitely published during the year 1625 was the final edition of the essays, enlarged from the volume of 1612 by the addition of twenty new essays (see Appendix I). The work was dedicated to the Duke of Buckingham.

"Excellent Lord,

"Solomon says, *A good name is as a precious ointment;* and I assure myself, such will your Grace's name be with posterity. For your fortune and merit, both have been eminent. And you have planted things that are like to last. I do now publish my Essays; which, of all my other works, have been most current; for that, as it seems, they come home to men's business and bosoms. I have enlarged them both in number and weight; so that they are indeed a new work. I thought it therefore agreeable, to my affection and obligation to your Grace, to prefix your name before them both in English and in Latin. For I do conceive that the Latin volume of them, being in the universal language, may last as long as books last. My *Instauration* I dedicated to the King; my *History of Henry the Seventh,* which I have now also translated into Latin, and my *Portions of Natural History* to the Prince; and these I dedicate to your Grace; being of the best fruits that by the good increase which God gives to my pen and labours I could yield. God lead your Grace by the hand.

"Your Grace's most obliged,
"and faithful servant,
"F. St Alban."

That the dedication still refers to the King and the Prince suggests that the essays were in the press before the spring of the year, when King James died, and that when they were published, possibly some months later, it was too late to alter the wording.

Many of the original essays had also been altered and enlarged, and a comparison between the various editions of 1597, 1612, 1625, is interesting. The 1625 edition opens with the essay *Of Truth,* and the famous sentence, "What is Truth? said jesting Pilate; and would not stay for an answer." Indeed, it had become part of Bacon's method in the writing of essays to begin with a phrase which would hammer home his theme and give a lead to the argument that followed. *Of Revenge,* for instance, the fourth essay in the volume, opens, "Revenge is a kind of wild justice; which the more man's nature runs to, the more ought law to weed it out." And *Of Suspicion:* "Suspicions amongst thoughts are like bats amongst birds, they ever fly by twilight."

The essay on building evidently reflects what he himself put foremost when designing Verulam House: "Houses are built to live in, and not to look on. . . . He that builds a fair house upon an ill seat, committest himself to prison. Neither do I reckon it an ill seat only where the air is unwholesome; but likewise where the air is unequal. . . . Neither is it an ill air only that maketh an ill seat, but ill ways, ill markets, ill neighbours; want of water, want of wood, shade, and shelter . . . too near the sea, too remote . . . too far off from great cities, which may hinder business, or too near them, which lurcheth all provisions, and maketh everything dear." The advice holds good for anyone hoping to possess his own home today, as it did for Francis Bacon and his contemporaries in 1625.

Probably the most famous of all his essays is the one on gardens, with its opening lines, "God Almighty first planted a Garden. And indeed it is the purest of human pleasures." We do not know whether he composed it wandering amongst the shrubs and flowers he had himself planted, sitting down to dictate it from the summer-house or temple that stood below the old house of Gorhambury, with a "fair prospect" all about him; finally retiring in his coach, if walking was now too arduous, the mile or more back to Verulam House. There is little doubt, though, that it was his own garden, or rather gardens, on the Gorhambury estate that had inspired him, gardens which he had laid out and improved upon after his mother's death, and which were to fall into so sad a decline after his own.

We have seen how Francis Bacon made his last will and testament in the April of 1621, at the time of his impeachment. It was short and drawn up in great haste, when he believed himself to be at the point of death. In May 1625, when he was once more ill, plague was raging in London and King James had recently been buried in Westminster Abbey, Francis evidently thought that the moment was now opportune to draw up another, and one of greater length. This will, or the greater part of it, was dated May 23rd, according to a decree of Chancery after his death, but the final version was dated December 19th, seven months later. It is very probably the earlier will of May 23rd, or rather an earlier draft, that Tenison, Archbishop of Canterbury, saw when all the Bacon papers came into his hands at Lambeth Palace, for he quoted the passage relative to "Lord Bacon's writings" which is somewhat changed in the version of December 23rd. The two versions are quoted below:

First version. "But towards that durable part of memory which consisteth in my writings, I require my servant, *Henry Percy*, to deliver to my brother Constable all my manuscript-compositions, and the fragments also of such as are not finished; to the end that, if any of them be fit to be published, he may accordingly dispose of them. And herein I desire him to take the advice of *Mr Selden*, and *Mr Herbert*,

193

of the *Inner Temple,* and to publish or suppress what shall be thought fit."

Second version. "But as to that durable part of my memory, which consisteth in my works and writings, I desire my executors, and especially Sir John Constable and my very good friend Mr Bosvile, to take care of all my writings, both of English and of Latin, there may be books fair bound, and placed in the King's library, and in the library of the university of Cambridge, and in the library of Trinity College, where myself was bred, and in the library of Bennet College, where my father was bred, and in the library of the University of Oxonford, and in the library of my Lord of Canterbury, and in the library of Eton."

It is evident that the December version is very carefully drawn up and worded, whereas the earlier draft is much more akin to the will of 1621 at the impeachment, with the name of "my servant" Henry Percy substituted for "my servant Harris." The matter might seem of small importance but for the fact that, when Henry Percy is named to be the bearer to John Constable, the wording is "all my manuscript-compositions, and the fragments also of such as are not finished." In the final will of December 1625 there is no mention of manuscripts as such, but only concern for his writings "both of English and of Latin," from which there were to be books "fair-bound" for the various libraries.

Mr Harris had a mention in the list of servants of 1618, when Francis was Lord Verulam as well as Lord Chancellor. He is mentioned, with a Mr Jones, in connection with "Remembrances for benefices." Yet in the final will of 1625 his name does not figure in the list of beneficiaries. Henry Percy, the "bloody Percy" so much distrusted by old Lady Bacon as her son's "coach companion and bed companion," received a legacy of £100. More interesting still is the fact that the last letter but one that his master ever wrote in his own hand, addressed to the Secretary of State, Sir Edward Conway, referred to Percy.

"Good Mr Secretary,

"This gentleman, Mr Percy, my good friend and late servant, hath a suit to his Majesty, grounded upon service of profit which he hath done his Majesty, for the making of a friend of his Baronet. I pray, Sir, commend this his petition to his M. I shall account the pleasure all one as done unto myself. I rest

> "Your affectionate friend,
> "to do you service,
> "F. St Alban.

"Gray's Inn, this 26th of January, 1626."

So Henry Percy had finally left his service, after more than thirty-three years, but what became of him, and his petition, we cannot tell. He would have known so many of his master's secrets, had access to his papers. As time went on, and Francis became more concerned with his Latin and philosophical writings, it is at least possible that some manuscripts, of a more private nature, were never placed in the hands of Sir John Constable or any other of the executors, and this might have come about through the personal instructions of Francis himself. Henry Percy, who bore such a distinguished name, remains an enigmatical figure in his master's life.

It is strange that Tobie Matthew, mentioned in the will of 1625 as "my ancient good friend" received, under the terms of this will, no more than "some ring to be bought for him of the value of £30," but then Tobie, now Sir Tobie, was doing well for himself and needed no patronage. A number of the servants who had figured in the will of 1618 are named as beneficiaries: another former servant, Francis Edney, equally detested by Lady Bacon along with Henry Percy, received "£200 and my rich gown." Perhaps the purple one Francis had worn when he rode in state to Whitehall as Lord Chancellor. And "old Thomas Gotherum, who was bred with me from a child, £30." This would be the son of the Thomas Gotherum (then spelt Cotheram) who used to write to Anthony Bacon in France back in 1581 giving him news from home. The poor of various parishes, relatives, godsons, friends, and many of those serving on the Gorhambury estate—none is forgotten. Chaplain Rawley was left £100, "the secretary Thomas Meautys some jewel to be bought for him of the value of £50, and my foot-cloth horse." The bulk of Francis's property—land and goods, personal and otherwise—he did "give, grant, and confirm to my loving wife," and a list follows of all such "to maintain the estate of a viscountess."

There is nothing in this very exhaustive list to lead one to suspect that all was not harmonious within the home, which suggests that this portion of the will at any rate was drawn up in May of 1625. There is, however, a marked change at the conclusion of the will dated December 19th.

"Whatsoever I have given, granted, confirmed, or appointed to my wife, in the former part of this my will, I do now, for just and great causes, utterly revoke and make void, and leave her to her right only."

Just and great causes. . . . So at some moment during that last summer at Gorhambury, when Francis had moved from Gray's Inn with the plague raging in London and himself far from well, he had at last recognised the truth, to which he had probably closed his eyes hitherto, of his wife Alice's relationship with her steward John Underhill. His bequests to Lady Constable remained unchanged. "I give to my brother Constable all my books, and £100 to be presented him in gold; I give to my sister Constable some jewels, to be bought for her, of the value of £50." Evidently they were not held responsible in any way for his wife's infidelity.

The executors, and especially Sir John Constable and Mr Bosvile, were also instructed to "take into their hands all of my papers whatsoever, which are either in cabinets, boxes, or presses and them to seal up until they may at their leisure peruse them." Papers, it will be noted, not manuscripts.

The executors were named as Sir Humphrey May, Chancellor of the Duchy of Lancaster, Mr Justice Hutton, Sir Thomas Crewe, Sir Francis Barn, Sir John Constable and Sir Euball Thelwall. An account of the legal difficulties that ensued after the testator's death will be found in the Epilogue.

The new year of 1626 found Francis Bacon so far recovered that he was back again in London, living at Gray's Inn, and well enough to write to Sir Humphrey May to use his influence with the Duke of Buckingham to procure a pardon from King Charles for his whole sentence. This would have enabled him to take his seat in the upper House when Parliament met on February 6th.

"It is true," he wrote, "that I shall not be able, in respect of my health, to attend in Parliament; but yet I might make a proxy. Time hath turned envy to pity; and I have had a long cleansing week of five years' expiation and more. Sir John Bennet hath had his pardon; my Lord of Somerset had his pardon; and, they say, shall sit in Parliament. My Lord Suffolk cometh to Parliament, though not to Council. I hope I deserve not to be the only outcast."

He foresaw that the next Parliament was likely to be crucial, with a formidable opposition in the Commons led by Sir John Eliot, and others equally strong in the Lords, united against the policies of the Duke of Buckingham, who was to die by an assassin's knife two years later. Whether Francis would have voted by proxy against his former patron we have no means of knowing; his loyalty to his Majesty was such that, even if he had misgivings about his sovereign's policy, he might have abstained.

However, if attendance by proxy in the House of Lords was denied him, he could at least continue his studies in Gray's Inn, and make experiments in natural science. The weather at the end of March was particularly cold, but this did not deter him. It may be that the final break with his wife Alice had given a fillip to his spirits. In early April, on the first or second of the month, he set forth in his coach to take the air, accompanied by a Scots physician, Dr Witherborne, and proceeded out of town towards Highgate.

There had been a fall of snow here, on the higher ground, which Francis could see from his coach, and the thought came to him that this was an invaluable opportunity to make an experiment. He bade his coachman stop at the bottom of the hill, and Francis and his companion knocked on the door of a cottage and enquired if there was any possibility of a hen being for sale. There was indeed, and the obliging woman within at once killed a bird, and with the help of his lordship gutted it. Between them they stuffed the hen with snow which was lying all about her cottage, for, so Francis told her, and his physician, it was very likely that snow could preserve flesh just as successfully as salt, and it would be interesting to put this theory to the test.

The gutting and stuffing took some little while, and, as might be expected in the proximity of Hampstead and Highgate, the air, in late afternoon, turned very cold and keen. The sun was setting in the west behind them. Suddenly Francis became aware of chill. He could not possibly impose upon the woman in her humble cottage, but a hot drink and warm surroundings would restore him. He remembered that his friend the Earl of Arundel, Earl Marshal of England, had a house in Highgate, which he knew well; and although the Earl himself was in temporary confinement in the Tower for having allowed his son Lord Maltravers to marry the daughter of the Duchess of Lennox, whom King Charles had expressly desired should be wedded to another, Francis felt certain that the Earl of Arundel's housekeeper would be delighted to receive him.

He and his companion entered the coach once more, and went on to Highgate. By the time they arrived it was growing dark, and Francis, his clothes clinging to him, half-frozen with the snow, which had penetrated his boots and his hose also, was shivering all over. Doctor Witherborne watched him with an anxious eye. The steward, his master the Earl of Arundel absent in the Tower, received them with consternation but with every attempt at hospitality. His lordship must come within at once. He must not attempt the journey back to London. His master would never forgive him if he permitted the Viscount St Alban to depart in such a state of chill.

A bedroom was made ready. Sheets, hastily warmed with a pan, were laid upon a bed that had not been slept in for over a year. The guest retired to the room which had been prepared for him. He continued to shake all over. He could not get warm. The physician watched him, more anxious than ever. Francis reassured him. He would be better by morning, but first he must make his excuses to his absent host, who was himself suffering surely far worse privation in the Tower. He dictated, from the damp bed in Highgate, the last letter he was ever to compose.

"To the Earl of Arundel and Surrey.
"My very good Lord,
"I was likely to have had the fortune of Caius Plinius the elder, who lost his life by trying an experiment about the burning of the mountain Vesuvius. For I was also desirous to try an experiment or two, touching the conservation and induration of bodies. As for the experiment itself, it succeeded excellently well; but in the journey, between London and Highgate, I was taken with such a fit of casting, as I knew not whether it were the stone, or some surfeit, or cold, or indeed a touch of them all three. But when I came to your Lordship's house, I was not able to go back, and therefore was forced to take up my lodging here, where your house-keeper is very careful and diligent about me; which I assure myself your Lordship will not only pardon towards him, but think the better of him for it. For indeed your Lordship's house was happy to me; and I kiss your noble hands for the welcome which I am sure you give me to it. . . .
"I know how unfit it is for me to write to your Lordship with any other hand than mine own; but in troth my fingers are so disjointed with this fit of sickness, that I cannot steadily hold a pen."

This is all that exists of that last letter. Chaplain Rawley must have been summoned to Highgate during the week, where he found the sick man far from better—indeed, rather worse, suffering from "a gentle fever, accidentally accompanied with a great cold, whereby the defluxion of rheum fell so plentifully upon his breast, that he died by suffocation. . . ."

Francis Bacon, Baron Verulam, Viscount St Alban, ex-Lord Keeper of the Great Seal, ex-Lord Chancellor, died on Easter Day, April 9th 1626, in the early morning, aged sixty-five years.

"First I bequeath my soul and body into the hands of God by the blessed oblation of my Saviour, the one at the time of my dissolution, the other at the time of my resurrection. For my burial, I desire it may be in St Michael's church, near St Alban's; there was my mother buried, and it is the parish church of my mansion house at Gorhambury, and it is the only Christian church within the walls of old Verulam. I would have the charge of my funeral not to exceed three hundred pounds at the most.

"For my name and memory, I leave it to men's charitable speeches, and to foreign nations, and the next ages. . . ."

★   ★   ★

Essay: Of Death

Men fear Death, as Children fear to go in the dark: And as that Natural Fear in Children, is increased with Tales, so is the other. Certainly, the Contemplation of Death, as the wages of sin, and Passage to another world, is Holy, and Religious; but the Fear of it, as a Tribute due unto Nature, is weak. Yet in Religious Meditations, there is sometimes, Mixture of Vanity, and of Superstition. You shall read, in some of the Friars' Books of Mortification, that a man should think with himself, what the Pain is, if he but have his Fingers end Pressed, or Tortured: And thereby imagine, what the Pains of Death are, when the whole Body, is corrupted and dissolved; when many times, Death passeth with less pain, than the Torture of a Limb: For the most vital parts, are not the quickest of Sense. And by him, that spake only as a Philosopher, and Natural Man, it was well said; *Pompa Mortis Magis terret quàm Mors ipsa* (The trappings of Death terrify, rather than Death itself). Groans and convulsions, and a discoloured Face, and Friends weeping, and Blacks and Obsequies, and the like, show Death Terrible. It is worthy the observing, that there is no passion in the mind of man, so weak, but it Mates, and Masters, the Fear of Death: And therefore Death, is no such terrible enemy, when a man hath so many Attendants, about him, that can win the combat of him.

Revenge triumphs over Death; Love slights it; Honour aspireth to it; Grief flyeth to it; Fear pre-occupateth it; Nay we read, after Otto the Emperor had slain himself, Pity, which is the tenderest of Affections, provoked many to die, out of mere compassion to their Sovereign, and as the truest sort of Followers. Nay Seneca adds Niceness and satiety; a man would die, though he were neither valiant, nor miserable, only upon the weariness to do the same thing, so oft over and over. It is no less worthy to observe, how little Alteration, in good Spirits, the Approaches of Death make; For they appear, to be the same Men, till the last Instant.

Augustus Ceasar died in a Compliment; Tiberius in dissimulation; Vespasian in a jest, sitting upon the Stoole; Galba with a sentence "Strike, if it be for the good of Rome," holding forth his neck; Septimus Severus in dispatch; "Make haste, if there be more for me to do." And the like. Certainly, the Stoics bestowed too much cost upon Death, and by their great preparations, made it appear more fearful.

Better, saith he, who accounts the close of life as one of nature's blessings.

It is as natural to die, as to be born; and to a little Infant, perhaps the one, is as gainful as the other. He that dies in an earnest Pursuit, is like one that is wounded in hot Blood; who, for the time, scarce feels the Hurt; and therefore, a Mind fixt, and bent upon somewhat, that is good, doth avert the Dolours of Death. But above all, believe it, the sweetest canticle is, Nunc Dimittis; when a Man hath obtained worthy Ends, and Expectations.

Death hath this also; That it openeth the Gate, to good Fame, and extinguishes Envy.

> *Extinctus amabitur idem*
> He that was envied living, shall be loved when he is gone.

Epilogue

Alice Bacon, Lady Verulam, Viscountess St Alban, remained a widow for eleven days. Presumably she waited until her husband had been buried in St Michael's church. Then she married John Underhill. The wedding took place on April 20th, at St Martin-in-the-Fields, where Francis Bacon had been baptised sixty-five years previously. On July 12th John Underhill was knighted at Oatlands, but for what services to his king and country we are not informed. It also happened to be the anniversary of the occasion when, in 1618, Francis Bacon had been created Baron Verulam *Extinctus amabitur idem.* . . .

The Underhills continued to live at Gorhambury, but litigation began almost immediately, and continued for some years. The executors refused to prove the will, knowing the state of the testator's finances. The debts amounted to £19,658. 4s. 4d. The will remained unexecuted until July 15th 1627, when powers of administration were granted to Sir Thomas Meautys, Viscount St Alban's faithful friend and secretary, and to Sir Thomas Rich, both representing the creditors. These gentlemen at once brought in a bill in Chancery against Sir John and Lady Underhill, and the trustees of the various manors and lands. "Fraudulent conveyances and deeds of gift" were mentioned, jewels, rings, stuffs, great quantities of plate, pictures, hangings; many such were taken by the Underhills, so the creditors claimed, for their own use, all of which should have been given up in payment of his late lordship's debts.

Lady Underhill, as defendant, made counter-claims. Many of the lands she had bought in with her own money, to increase her jointure, and because she had refused to join with her husband in selling land he had left her society. She "did not believe that the debts were as great as had been stated, they were largely claimed by his servants, some of whom by vicious courses did him great prejudice."

The trustees of the lands and manors then handed in their resignation to the Court. Finally, on June 12th 1632, the judge, who had failed up till then to find a purchaser for the lands and estates, sold them to Lord Dunsmore for £6,000, on condition that he should pay Lady Underhill £530 a year for her lifetime, and that she and her husband consented to quit Gorhambury at Michaelmas that same year. Certain fixtures were to be left intact, "tables of stone, an ancient picture hanging at the upper end of the hall, brewing vessels, images of wood and stone in the gardens," etc., etc. On February 17th 1633, Sir Thomas Meautys was granted the manors and the estate of Gorhambury by Lord Dunsmore and his co-trustees, who declared that they had been acting in his interests all the time.

Sir John and Lady Underhill parted after thirteen years. Perhaps the yelping hounds of Scylla were still about her loins. On February 21st 1639, a deed of separation was signed. Lady Underhill remained childless and spent much of her time with her mother at Eyeworth in Bedfordshire. Her mother had herself remarried twice since parting from her "Lusty" Packington, Viscount Kilmorey was her third husband, and the Earl of Kellie her fourth.

Lady Underhill died on June 29th 1650. She was fifty-eight years old. The parish register of burials for 1650 records that, "Alice Viscountess St Alban, widow Dowager to Francis Viscount St Alban, was buried in the Chancell of Eyeworth in the south side thereof on the 9th day of July 1650," and the inscription on the chancel floor reads, "Here lyeth the body of Dame Alice, baroness Verulam, viscountess St Alban, one of the daughters of Benedict Barnham, Alderman of London. She departed this life the 29th June Anno Dni 1650." Her sister Dorothy Constable, who had died the year before, lay beneath the chancel floor beside her. Alice believed in taking of rank over other ladies even in death.

Sir John Underhill lived to be eighty-six or eighty-seven, surviving the Civil War and the Restoration but suffering from "weakness of his eyes and infirmity in his head." He lived in London, in St Giles-in-the-Fields, where he died in April 1679, his executor being his "loving cousin Thomas Underhill of Oxhill," who, as a lad, had been a patient of Dr Hall, son-in-law to Mr William Shakespeare.

Francis Bacon would have been happy to have known that Sir Thomas Meautys succeeded him as owner of Gorhambury. In 1641 Sir Thomas married Anne Bacon, the daughter of Sir Nathaniel Bacon of Culford, Francis's nephew and a well-known portrait painter of his day. Meautys settled upon her Verulam House and the manor of Redbourne. He also erected a fine monument to his former friend and employer in St Michael's church, St Albans. The monument bears a Latin inscription, which translates as follows.

Francis Bacon
Baron of Verulam, Viscount St Alban
or, by more conspicuous titles,
of Science the Light, of Eloquence the Law,
sat thus.

Who after all Natural Wisdom
And Secrets of Civil Life he had unfolded
Nature's Law fulfilled—
Let Compounds be dissolved!
In the year of our Lord 1626, aged 66.

Of such a man, that the memory
might remain,
Thomas Meautys
living his Attendant, dead his Admirer,
places this Monument.

Unfortunately Sir Thomas did not live long to enjoy the property. He died in October 1649, and was buried in St Michael's church near to his patron. The ownership passed to his brother Henry Meautys, while his widow later married Sir Harbottle Grimston, who became Master of the Rolls and Speaker of the House of Commons, and bought the estate from Henry Meautys.

Anne Bacon, Lady Grimston, died in 1680. The estate passed on Sir Harbottle's death to his only surviving son by his first marriage, Samuel Grimston, 3rd Baronet, and so through successive generations to the present descendant of the Grimston family, Earl Verulam.

Sir Harbottle Grimston does not appear to have lived at Verulam House, but sold it in about 1665 or 1666 for £400 to two carpenters, who bought it for the materials. The old mansion of Gorhambury also gradually fell into decay. A new mansion, a short distance away, was built for the 3rd Viscount Grimston between the years 1777 and 1784, which holds today some of the possessions of Francis Bacon, brought from the origional house: the portraits of his father and mother, Sir Nicholas and Lady Bacon, the three busts that once stood in the long gallery, portraits by his nephew Sir Nathaniel Bacon. There were also books from the library, perhaps most interesting of all—bound together in one volume, and now on loan to the Bodleian Library, Oxford—the following: Quarto of *Richard II*, 1614; Quarto of *King Richard III*, 1602; Quarto of *King Henry IV*, 1613; Quarto of *King Lear*, 1608; Quarto of *Hamlet*, 1605; Quarto of *Titus Andronicus*, 1611; Quarto of *Romeo and Juliet*, 1599; *The Tragedy of Caesar & Pompey* (no date); *The Tragedy of Claudius Tiberius* (no date); First and Second Parts of *King John,* 1611; *King Edward IV* by Heywood; *Wonder of Women* by Marston, 1606; *Segaris* by Ben Jonson, 1605; *The Malcontent* by Marston, 1604; *Siege of Troy* by Lydgate; *Volpone* by Ben Jonson, 1607.

Owing to the refusal of executors to handle Francis Bacon's will at his death in 1626, it seems doubtful whether the remaining books, papers and unfinished works ever came into the hands of Sir John Constable, as Francis had wished. Some were indeed handed over to the Mr Bosvile who had been named with Sir John as an executor at the time; this would have been in 1627 after Sir Thomas Meautys had been granted letters of administration. These were mostly Latin works, and Mr Bosvile, or Sir William Boswell as he was later known when an agent for the United Provinces at The Hague, had them published in Amsterdam in 1653.

Other works were entrusted to Viscount St Alban's chaplain William Rawley, and he could not have hoped for a more zealous or faithful editor. A year after his employer's death, in 1627, Rawley published *The New Atlantis* along with *Sylva Sylvarum* (*A Natural History*), a series of scientific experiments. In 1629 appeared *Certain Miscellany Works,* and in 1638 Rawley's own translation into Latin of the famous essays, with a dedication to King Charles. In 1657 came "Resusatatio, or bringing into publick Light severall pieces of his Works hitherto sleeping . . . together with his Lordship's Life," and in the following year the Latin translation of all these.

William Rawley, rector of Lanbeach, died there in 1667. The remaining Bacon letters and papers then came into the possession of Thomas Tenison, later Archbishop of Canterbury, a close friend of William Rawley's son, who had died of the plague in 1666. Bishop Tenison published *Baconia, or Certain Genuine Remains of Lord Bacon,* in 1679. Almost a century passed before the next appearance of the works and letters in 1765.

Sir Edward Coke, Francis Bacon's lifelong rival in the legal and political field—and at one time in an affair of the heart—outlived him for just over eight years. He was still in full vigour when King Charles called his Third Parliament, in 1628, and he introduced the famous Petition of Right, which struck at the royal prerogative, and to which his Majesty was obliged to give a reluctant assent. Four years later Sir Edward fell when riding round his estate at Stoke Poges. He was eigthy-one years old, and never fully recovered his strength afterwards. He died on September 3rd 1634.

His widow, the tireless Lady Hatton, at once laid claim to Stoke

Park, and was living there at the start of the Civil War. Surprisingly, for one who had been a lively and brilliant member of Court society during most of her life, she was a passionate supporter of the Parliamentary cause, and entertained many of the Roundhead leaders under her roof. When London became almost a fortified city in 1643 Parliament allowed her undisputed possession of Hatton House.

In June 1645, ten days before the King's forces were defeated at the battle of Naseby, her unhappy daughter Frances died at Oxford. Lady Hatton, whose arguments and disputes with her daughter had never entirely ceased through the latter's many trials and tribulations, was nevertheless devoted to her, and her death came as a considerable shock. Her time of activity was over; she passed the rest of the year sombrely at Hatton House, and in December, aged sixty-seven, made her will, in which she stated that, "My very being was a burthen to me untill the infinite mercyes of the auth'r of all comforts raysing my thoughts to an higher contemplation And opened myne understanding . . . that I might fly into his arms for refuge. . . ." She died on January 3rd 1646, and was buried in St Andrew's Church, Holborn, after lying in state in her home for nearly six weeks. Her ghost was long said to haunt the gardens of Hatton House before the diamond merchants trampled them into oblivion.

Tobie Matthew survived his patron and friend Viscount St Alban for twenty-nine years. Suspected of being a papal spy in 1640, he retired to Ghent, where he died on October 13th 1655. Five years later his collection of letters was published, including many from Francis Bacon. In his prefatory address to the reader he wrote, "It will go near to pose any other nation of Europe, to muster out in any age, four men, who in so many respects should excel four such as we are able to show them: Cardinal Wolsey, Sir Thomas More, Sir Philip Sidney and Sir Francis Bacon. The fourth was a creature of incomparable abilities of mind, of a sharp and catching apprehension, large and faithful memory, plentiful and sprouting invention, deep and solid judgement, for as such as might concern the understanding part. A man so rare in knowledge, of so many several kinds endued with the facility and felicity of expressing it all in so elegant, significant, so abundant, and yet so choice and ravishing a way of words, of metaphors and allusions as, perhaps, the world hath not seen, since it was a world. I know this may seem a great hyperbole, and strange kind of excess of speech, but the best means of putting me to shame will be, for you to place any other man of yours by this of mine."

Bacon's Essays

The original edition, published in 1597, contained ten essays:

Of Study; Of Discourse; Of Ceremonies and Respects; Of Followers and Friends; Suitors; Of Expense; Of Regiment of Health; Of Honour and Reputation; Of Faction; Of Negotiating.

The second edition, published in 1612, contained thirty-eight essays: the original ten (with the exception of that on *Honour and Reputation*), altered and enlarged, plus twenty-nine new ones:

Of Religion; Of Death; Of Goodness and Goodness of Nature; Of Cunning; Of Marriage and Single Life; Of Parents and Children; Of Nobility; Of Great Place; Of Empire; Of Counsel; Of Despatch; Of Love; Of Friendship; Of Atheism; Of Superstition; Of Wisdom for a Man's Self; Of Regiment; Of Health; Of Expenses; Of Discourse; Of Seeming Wise; Of Riches; Of Ambition; Of Young Men and Age; Of Beauty; Of Deformity; Of Nature in Men; Of Custom and Education; Of Fortune; Of Studies; Of Ceremonies and Respects; Of Suitors; Of Followers; Of Negotiating; Of Faction; Of Praise; Of Indicature; Of Vain Glory; Of Greatness of Kingdoms.

The third and last edition was published in 1625, the year before Bacon's death. This contained fifty-eight essays—twenty new ones, and the earlier ones altered or enlarged.

Of Truth; Of Death; Of Unity in Religion; Of Revenge; Of Adversity; Of Simulation and Dissimulation; Of Parents and Children; Of Marriage and Single Life; Of Envy; Of Love; Of Great Place; Of Boldness; Of Goodness, and Goodness of Nature; Of Nobility; Of Seditions and Troubles; Of Atheism; Of Superstition; Of Travail; Of Empire; Of Counsel; Of Delays; Of Cunning; Of Wisdom for a Man's Self; Of Innovations; Of Despatch; Of Seeming Wise; Of Friendship; Of Expense; Of the true Greatness of Kingdoms and Estates; Of Regiment of Health; Of Suspicion; Of Discourse; Of Plantations; Of Riches; Of Prophecies; Of Ambition; Of Masks and Triumphs; Of Nature in Men; Of Custom and Education; Of Fortune; Of Usury; Of Youth and Age; Of Beauty; Of Deformity; Of Building; Of Gardens; Of Negotiating; Of Followers and Friends; Of Suitors; Of Studies; Of Faction; Of Ceremonies and Respects; Of Praise; Of Vain Glory; Of Honour and Reputation; Of Indicature; Of Anger; Of Vicissitude of Things.

Of Fame, a fragment

The Eighteen Plays of William Shakespeare
First Published in 1623

King John
King Henry VI, Pt I
King Henry VIII
The Tempest
Measure for Measure
A Comedy of Errors
As You Like It
The Taming of the Shrew
All's Well that Ends Well
Twelfth Night
The Winter's Tale
Two Gentlemen of Verona
Coriolanus
Timon of Athens
Julius Caesar
Macbeth
Anthony and Cleopatra
Cymbeline

Selected Bibliography of Printed Sources

AUBREY, JOHN, *Francis Bacon, Viscount St Alban. Brief Lives* (Folio Society, 1975)

BACON, FRANCIS, *Works*, 5 vols (A. Millar, 1765)

——*Works*, 7 vols, edited by Spedding, Ellis & Heath (Longman & Co., 1857)

——*Cogitata et Visa*

——*Redargutio Philosophiarum*

——*Temporis Partus Masculus:* all translated by Benjamin Farrington in *The Philosophy of Francis Bacon* (Liverpool University Press, 1964)

——*The Advancement of Learning* and *New Atlantis*, edited by Arthur Johnson (Clarendon Press, 1974)

——*Moral and Civil Essays* (University Press, 1906)

BEVAN, BRYAN, *The Real Francis Bacon* (Centaur Press, 1960)

BIRCH, THOMAS, *The Court and Times of James the First*, 2 vols (Henry Colburn, 1848)

——*Letters, Speeches, Advices Et Cetera* (Bindley, 1763–64)

BOWEN, CATHERINE DRINKER, *The Lion and the Throne* (Hamish Hamilton, 1957)

BRABAZON, JAMES, 5th Earl Verulam, *The Bacon Family* (St Albans City Council, 1961)

BROWN, IVOR, *London* (Studio Vista, 1965)

CAMPBELL, OSCAR JAMES and QUINN, *A Shakespeare Encyclopaedia* (Methuen, 1967)

CECIL, DAVID, *The Cecils of Hatfield House* (Constable, 1973)

DIXON, W. HEPWORTH, *The Story of the Life of Lord Bacon* (John Murray, 1862)

Encyclopaedia Britannica, 1947 edition

FARRINGTON, BENJAMIN, *The Philosophy of Francis Bacon* (Liverpool University Press, 1964)

FRASER, ANTONIA, *King James VI of Scotland, I of England* (Weidenfeld & Nicolson, 1974)

HAKLUYT, RICHARD, *The Tudor Venturers* (Nonesuch Press, 1972)

HOTSON, JOHN LESLIE, *Shakespeare's Sonnets Dated* (Hart-Davis, 1949)

JOHNSON, PAUL, *Elizabeth I: A Study in Power and Intellect* (Weidenfeld & Nicolson, 1974)

MCCLURE, N. E., *The Letters of John Chamberlain* (Philadelphia, 1939)

MATHEW, DAVID, *Sir Tobie Matthew* (Max Parrish, 1950)

MATTHEW, SIR TOBIE, *A Collection of Letters* (London, 1660)

MOOR, REV. C., *Bacon Deeds at Gorhambury* (Genealogist's Magazine, 1973)

MORRISON, J. A., *The Underhills of Warwickshire* (Cambridge University Press, 1932)

NORSWORTHY, LAURA L., *The Lady of Bleeding Heart Yard* (Murray, 1953)

PARES, MARTIN, *Francis Bacon and the Utopias* (printed privately)

REYNOLDS, GRAHAM, *Nicholas Hilliard and Isaac Oliver* (H.M.S.O., 1971)

ROGERS, JOHN G., *The Manor and Houses of Gorhambury* (St Albans and Herts Architectural and Archaeological Society, 1936)

ROWSE, A. L., *Bisham and the Hobys in the English Past* (Macmillan, 1951)

——*The Tower of London* (Sphere Books, 1974)

——*Shakespeare's Sonnets* (Macmillan, 1964)

SHAKESPEARE, WILLIAM, *Complete Works*. Text of First Folio with Quarto variants, 4 vols (Nonesuch Press, 1953)

SPEDDING, JAMES, *The Letters and the Life of Francis Bacon*, 7 vols (Longmans Green & Ryder, 1861–72)

STRONG, ROY, *Nicholas Hilliard* (Michael Joseph, 1975)

WILLIAMS, ETHEL CARLETON, *Anne of Denmark* (Longmans, 1970)

YATES, FRANCES AMELIA, *The Rosicrucian Enlightenment* (Routledge & Kegan Paul, 1972)

Sources

CHAPTER I

The Letters and the Life of Francis Bacon, Vol. III   Spedding
Bacon Deeds at Gorhambury   The Genealogists' Magazine, September
    1937 (an address to the Society by the Rev. C. Moor)
Elizabeth I   Johnson

CHAPTER II

The Letters and the Life of Francis Bacon, Vol. III   Spedding
The Court and Times of James I   Birch
Medical Remains   Bacon
Anne of Denmark   Williams
The Philosophy of Francis Bacon   Farrington
The Story of the Life of Lord Bacon   Dixon

CHAPTER III

The Court and Times of James the First   Birch
The Letters and the Life of Francis Bacon, Vol. III   Spedding
King James   Fraser
Anne of Denmark   Williams
Valerius Terminus   Bacon

CHAPTER IV

The Advancement of Learning   Bacon
The Court and Times of James the First   Birch
The Letters and the Life of Francis Bacon, Vol. III   Spedding

CHAPTER V

The Letters and the Life of Francis Bacon, Vol. III   Spedding
The Court and Times of James the First   Birch
The Story of the Life of Lord Bacon   Dixon
The Genealogist's Magazine
Essays of Francis Bacon, edition of 1612   Ed. Spedding
Cogitata et Visa   Bacon
Queen Anne   Williams
Bisham and the Hobys in the English Past   Rowse

CHAPTER VI

The Letters and the Life of Francis Bacon, Vol. IV   Spedding
Sir Tobie Matthew   Mathew
Dictionary of National Biography
The Cecils of Hatfield House   Cecil
Cogitata et Visa   Bacon
Redargutio Philosophiarum   Bacon

CHAPTER VII

The Court and Times of James the First   Birch
The Letters and the Life of Francis Bacon, Vol. IV   Spedding
Queen Anne   Williams
Sonnets   Shakespeare
The Underhills of Warwickshire   Morrison
King James   Fraser
De Sapientia Veterum   Bacon

CHAPTER VIII

A Shakespeare Encyclopaedia   Campbell & Quinn
Comedies, First Folio   Shakespeare
The Cecils of Hatfield House   Cecil
Essays of Francis Bacon, edition of 1612
The Court and Times of James the First   Birch
Queen Anne   Williams
Tribute to Henry Prince of Wales   Bacon

CHAPTER IX

The Letters and the Life of Francis Bacon, Vol. V   Spedding
The Court and Times of James the First   Birch
King James   Fraser

CHAPTER X

The Letters and the Life of Francis Bacon, Vol. V   Spedding
The Tower of London   Rowse
The Court and Times of James the First   Birch

CHAPTER XI

King James   Fraser
The Letters and the Life of Francis Bacon, Vols. V and VI   Spedding
Essays of Francis Bacon, edition of 1625
Queen Anne   Williams
The Court and Times of James the First   Birch

CHAPTER XII

The Letters and the Life of Francis Bacon, Vol. VI   Spedding
The Court and Times of James the First   Birch
The Lady of Bleeding Heart Yard   Norsworthy
The Letters and the Life of Francis Bacon, Vol. IV   Spedding
A Winter's Tale   Shakespeare

CHAPTER XIII

Sir Tobie Matthew   Mathew
Dictionary of National Biography
The Letters and the Life of Francis Bacon, Vol. VI   Spedding
The Court and Times of James the First   Birch
The Lady of Bleeding Heart Yard   Norsworthy

CHAPTER XIV

The Letters of John Chamberlain, Vol. II   McClure
The Letters and the Life of Francis Bacon, Vol. VI   Spedding
Queen Anne   Williams
Medical Remains   Bacon
The Story of the Life of Lord Bacon   Dixon
Nicholas Hilliard   Strong
The Manor and Houses of Gorhambury   Rogers
Essays of Francis Bacon, edition of 1625
Novum Organum   Bacon

214

CHAPTER XV

The Letters and the Life of Francis Bacon, Vols. VI and VII   Spedding
The Letters of John Chamberlain, Vol. II   McClure
Anne of Denmark   Williams
Essays of Francis Bacon, edition of 1625

CHAPTER XVI

The Letters and the Life of Francis Bacon, Vol. VII   Spedding
Novum Organum   Bacon
The Letters of John Chamberlain, Vol. II   McClure

CHAPTER XVII

The Letters and the Life of Francis Bacon, Vol. VII   Spedding
The Story of the Life of Lord Bacon   Dixon
De Sapientia Veterum   Bacon
The Letters of John Chamberlain, Vol. II   McClure
King Henry VIII   Shakespeare

CHAPTER XVIII

The Letters and the Life of Francis Bacon, Vol. VII   Spedding
The Reign of Henry the Seventh   Bacon
The Letters of John Chamberlain, Vol. II   McClure
Historia Ventorum and *Historia Vitae et Mortis*   Bacon

CHAPTER XIX

The Letters and the Life of Francis Bacon, Vol. VII   Spedding
The Letters of John Chamberlain, Vol. II   McClure
Letters, Speeches, Advices Et Cetera   Birch
A Shakespeare Encyclopaedia   Campbell & Quinn
Essays of Francis Bacon, edition of 1625

CHAPTER XX

New Atlantis   Bacon
The Tudor Venturers   Hakluyt
The Rosicrucian Enlightenment   Yates

As You Like It   Shakespeare
The Letters of John Chamberlain, Vol. II   McClure

CHAPTER XXI

The Letters and the Life of Francis Bacon, Vol. VII   Spedding
Sir Tobie Matthew   Mathew
The Lady of Bleeding Heart Yard   Norsworthy
The Letters of John Chamberlain, Vol. II   McClure
Medical Remains   Bacon
Essays of Francis Bacon

EPILOGUE

The Genealogist's Magazine, Vol. VII
The Bacon Family   Brabazon
The Underhills of Warwickshire   Morrison
The Lady of Bleeding Heart Yard   Norsworthy
A Collection of Letters   Matthew
Parish Records, All Saints' Church, Eyeworth

Index

217

219

R